Reading Disability

"If reading is so much fun, how come she
assigns three extra chapters for punishment!"
The Wall Street Journal

READING
DISABILITY

A Human Approach to Evaluation and Treatment of Reading and Writing Difficulties

---

FOURTH EDITION, REVISED & EXPANDED

FLORENCE G. ROSWELL
AND
GLADYS NATCHEZ

Foreword by Jeanne S. Chall

Basic Books, Inc., Publishers   *New York*

Frontispiece reprinted from the *Wall Street Journal* with the permission of Cartoon Features Syndicate.

Appendix D reprinted by courtesy of the Educational Testing Service.

Library of Congress Cataloging-in-Publication Data

Roswell, Florence G.
    Reading disability.

    Includes bibliographies and index.
    1. Reading disability.   2. Reading—
Remedial teaching.   I. Natchez, Gladys.
II. Title.
LB1050.5.R6   1989   428.4'2   88–47893
ISBN   0–465–06846–4

Copyright © 1989 by Basic Books, Inc.
Printed in the United States of America
Designed by Vincent Torre
89 90 91 92 HC 9 8 7 6 5 4 3 2 1

To our families

Contents

Part I
Basic Considerations

Part II
Diagnosis

Part III

Treatment

Illustrative Examples

Foreword

THIS BOOK is unique in the area of reading and related learning difficulties. In a discipline that contains so many varied and conflicting views, the authors bring a clear voice, based not on a narrow vision but on their rich clinical experience and wisdom, further rooted in a solid understanding of theory and practice.

Out of the growing knowledge in this field, they have selected those aspects of causation, diagnosis, and treatment that are practical and theoretically sound. These will work for classroom teachers, reading and learning disability specialists, resource teachers, psychologists, and others who do diagnostic assessments and teach children with reading and learning difficulties.

This new edition is highly readable and useful for beginners as well as for those with considerable experience. The added chapters, particularly those on adult and college remedial programs, make it especially timely for treating the full range of people who need help with reading and related skills.

JEANNE S. CHALL
Harvard University
March 14, 1988

Preface to the Fourth Edition

THIS BOOK is a new edition of *Reading Disability: A Human Approach to Learning.* To broaden the scope of our presentation concerning the causation, diagnosis, and treatment of learning difficulty we have invited several specialists to make unique contributions in related areas: "Neurological Aspects of Learning Difficulty" (Ursula Kirk), "Reading Expository Texts Is Different—And Harder" (Florence G. Schoenfeld), "Teaching Reading to Underprepared College Students" (Lila Soll), "Writing as a Tool for Learning" (Steven Tribus), and "Integrating Word Processing into Writing Instruction" (Barbara Sherr Roswell). This book covers instructional procedures for levels one through college.

The book will be useful to classroom teachers facing a wide range of reading problems who need to develop programs for students with reading difficulty. It will also help teachers, guidance counselors, tutors, and school psychologists to make the best use of special treatment centers. The procedures we describe form the basis for individualizing reading programs in the regular classroom, for evaluating students' problems, and for developing appropriate instruction and remedial work. We include varied case studies of individual students and group treatment. The illustrations are typical of the range of problems found in many different classrooms so that teachers can incorporate these instructional techniques in their own work with students.

We have found that grade scores alone provide a limited estimate of a student's functioning. For a fuller understanding we use additional informal procedures in which we try out various methods and materials to determine appropriate approaches and reading levels. The students' reactions in a typical learning situation can then be used in planning effective programs. We also show how to integrate the viewpoints of the teacher, learning specialist, psychologist, guidance counselor, parents, and others with whom students interact.

Throughout this book we emphasize the human approach; we try to accept the students unconditionally, help them to understand their needs, and then attempt to alleviate their difficulty. We encourage mutual interaction and honesty between teachers and students. We accentuate the collaborative relationship between them. We discourage repetitive drill, which can stultify spontaneous learning. We avoid tedious material wherever possible. If a problem becomes too great we encourage the teacher to seek appropriate assistance.

Children, adolescents, and adults want to learn about themselves and the world. When they feel understood and appreciated, they want to expand their knowledge; they are curious and inquisitive; they search for active fulfillment and heightened awareness. When they are deterred from their path for any number of reasons—such as pressure from adults, insistence from parents that they learn, discouragement, and insufficient attention from staff—they become disenchanted and they falter. Then the teacher needs to investigate their difficulty more fully and formulate an appropriate plan. This book addresses these issues in detail and supplements them with illustrative cases.

We acknowledge our gratitude to teachers, parents, colleagues, and students who have increased our understanding and knowledge throughout the years. We give special thanks to Claudia Grose, who spent hours collecting new material for this edition; to Virginia Miller, who contacted specialists in the field to ensure the accuracy of our manuscript and who contributed information and suggestions that proved invaluable; and to Jo Ann Miller, Gordon Kato, Suzanne Wagner, and Nola Lynch at Basic Books. Robert Roswell deserves our gratitude for his help on the subject of computers as a teaching tool. We also wish to acknowledge Ruth Adams, Miriam Balmuth, Joan Raim, and Phyllis Zeigler for their assistance.

Part I

Basic Considerations

Students described in this book are used as examples to illustrate problems that occur frequently in the schools. If readers are reminded of similar individuals, we will consider our examples realistically drawn.

1

An Introduction to Reading Difficulties

READING DIFFICULTY signifies disharmony in the life of a child. The disharmony may arise from a variety of problems related to neurological, psychological, physical, educational, environmental, and other factors, or from the interaction that occurs among them.

It is the purpose of this book to examine the complex causes of reading and other learning difficulties, ranging in nature from mild to severe, and to suggest methods for diagnosis and treatment. Scholars in a number of disciplines—including psychology, neurology, and education—each approach the problem with a particular bias. Here we are attempting to combine pertinent theory and methodology from each area with the goal of assessing the problem from the broadest possible perspective.

An Overview of the Research

As we look back at the historical picture, we can see how each contributing element received primary importance at one time. In the first decade of this century, German and French ophthalmologists and neurologists concerned themselves with eye movements, brain mechanisms, and what are now termed perceptual problems. Studies published between 1910 and 1916 centered on learning in the classroom and on environmental influences. During that period, interest also focused on theories of how people learn to read. Later, between 1935 and 1955, investigators reported for the first time on the relationship between personality traits and reading achievement.

The years from 1937 to 1971 saw the publication of various theories of brain functioning as possible causes of learning disability.[1] These theories expressed different points of view. However, despite many areas of disagreement, a considerable amount of research has led to the understanding of children's difficulties; it is encouraging that blame has not been directed at the children or teachers.[2]

Recent advances in neuropsychology research and the study of brain functioning have been striking.[3] Another area that has received wide attention has been information-processing theory: a considerable amount of research has been produced in the areas of memory, language, and cognitive functioning. Behavioral psychology has made an important contribution. And in another vein, the use of computers for teaching children with learning difficulties has affected the field.

What Is a Reading Disability?

A child has a reading disability when there is a significant discrepancy between his reading level and his intellectual potential as measured by standardized tests. However, quantitative evaluation is always used with caution because test scores alone do not provide accurate appraisal of a process as complex as reading (see chapter 5).

The word *dyslexia* is often used loosely in connection with reading disorders. There are differing opinions among professionals regarding this term. Although it is sometimes used to describe a specific condition involving some degree of neurophysiological dysfunction, it is frequently considered to be synonymous with the term *reading disability.*

Learning disability is another term widely used, but it is also somewhat

1. W. Orton, *Reading, Writing and Speech Problems in Children* (New York: W. W. Norton, 1937); A. A. Strauss and L. E. Lehtinen, *Psychopathology and Education of the Brain Injured Child* (New York: Grune & Stratton, 1947); N. C. Kephart, *The Slow Learner in the Classroom* (Columbus, Ohio: Charles E. Merrill, 1963); S. A. Kirk and W. D. Kirk, *Psycholinguistic Learning Disabilities: Diagnosis and Remediation* (Chicago: University of Chicago Press, 1971).

2. J. K. Torgesen, "Learning Disabilities Theory: Its Current State and Future Prospects," *Journal of Learning Disabilities* (no. 7, 1986).

3. F. Duffy and N. Geschwind, eds., *Dyslexia: A Neuroscientific Approach to Clinical Evaluation* (Boston: Little, Brown, 1985).

Table 1-1

Some Major Definitions of Learning Disabilities *

---

1. Federal

   Individuals with specific learning disabilities are those who have a disorder in one or more of the basic psychological processes involved in understanding or in using language, spoken or written, which may manifest itself in an imperfect ability to listen, think, speak, read, write, spell, or do mathematical calculations. The term includes such conditions as perceptual handicaps, brain injury, minimal brain dysfunction, dyslexia, and developmental aphasia. The term does not include children who have learning problems which are primarily the result of visual, hearing, or motor handicaps, of mental retardation, or of environmental, cultural, or economic disadvantage.

   (As defined in U.S. Public Law 94-142—the Education for All Handicapped Children Act of 1975; see *Federal Register,* 1977, p. 64)

2. National Joint Committee for Learning Disabilities (NJCLD)

   Learning disabilities is a generic term that refers to a heterogeneous group of disorders manifested by significant difficulties in the acquisition and use of listening, speaking, reading, writing, reasoning or mathematical abilities. These disorders are intrinsic to the individual and presumed to be due to central nervous system dysfunction. Even though a learning disability may occur concomitantly with other handicapping conditions (e.g., sensory impairment, mental retardation, social and emotional disturbance) or environmental influences (e.g., cultural differences, insufficient/inappropriate instruction, psychogenic factors), it is not the direct result of those conditions or influences.

3. Association for Children and Adults with Learning Disabilities (ACLD)

   Specific Learning Disabilities is a chronic condition of presumed neurological origin which selectively interferes with the development, integration, and/or demonstration of verbal and/or nonverbal abilities.

   Specific Learning Disabilities exists as a distinct handicapping condition in the presence of average to superior intelligence, adequate sensory and motor systems, and adequate learning opportunities. The condition varies in its manifestations and in degree of severity.

   Throughout life the condition can affect self-esteem, education, vocation, socialization, and/or daily living activities.

---

*The National Task Force analyzed all definitions used by state educational agencies in the United States. The analysis found the following five factors cited in various combinations: a component referring to (a) academic failure, (b) psychological processes, (c) exclusionary factors, (d) etiology, and (e) significant discrepancy between aptitude and achievement. The federal definition had been adopted by twenty-two states and the District of Columbia, fourteen states were using a modified version of this definition, eleven had written their own, one had supplemented the federal definition with that proposed by the National Joint Committee for Learning Disabilities (NJCLD), and two had taken a noncategorical approach and thus were not using the LD label.

SOURCE: *Journal of Learning Disabilities* 19 (November 1986).

ambiguous. Nevertheless, federal law and national groups have tried to clarify its meaning (table 1-1). In this book we do not categorize students with learning difficulties. Instead, we consider the broad range of learning problems representing varying degrees of severity and a number of causal factors. We prefer to use the term *reading difficulty* in connection with the entire spectrum of reading problems.

The Backgrounds of Children with Learning Difficulties

Students with learning difficulties do not fall into set categories. They are found in all age groups, all ranges of intelligence, and all cultural groups, and they have all types of physical and personality traits. Pupils who achieve poorly grow up in diverse environments; they may live with understanding or punitive parents, in happy or broken homes. Some may be affected by these conditions; others remain untouched. In some instances, a child with academic problems shows severe emotional difficulty at the outset; sometimes the maladjustment manifests itself only after the appearance of poor achievement. But all students with learning problems manifest some disequilibrium in their lives.

THE CHILD'S EARLY LEARNING EXPERIENCES

Let us consider briefly how these characteristics may develop. The infant has great potential for healthy growth despite possible minor handicaps but must depend on others for nurture. Parents are likely to allow the youngster more freedom in the early years than later on: rarely will they insist, for instance, that an infant go to sleep or awaken at a given hour. Undoubtedly they also recognize their limitations in imposing an arbitrary timetable on walking and talking. Even if they try to hurry their child along for their own purposes, they soon resign themselves if he or she fails to respond. In the young child they seem willing to accept an innate physiological and psychological pattern. As one youngster put it, "After you are born, you have about five years of relaxation; but once you reach the age of five, your parents decide your life for you." The initial acceptance and indulgence may have a significant influence on the fact that a child's speed of learning in the early years is rarely equaled later on.

Take parents' attitudes toward their child's early speech as one example, and contrast it to their reactions toward the beginning efforts in reading. The first sound that a child makes may be the famous nonsense syllables *da da.* Proud Papa undoubtedly considers himself crowned king and the baby's accomplishment is greeted accordingly. Soon the baby catches on to the language around him. A response to a game of peekaboo sometimes gains the child a virtual standing ovation. The rate at which new words begin to appear is startling to parents. According to various estimates, vocabulary growth progresses from approximately a dozen words at eighteen months to two to six thousand or more for the first-grade child. But vocabulary growth is only one source of wonder; phrases, sentences, gram-

6

matical structure, meaning, and thought are all learned spontaneously in varying degrees by most children during their first few years.

All this time parents usually allow the child to talk in his or her own way and at an individual pace. They are not likely to ask the pediatrician how many words their child should be saying. And with regard to mispronunciation, the toddler can probably repeat the words *wy bwed* for *rye bread* over and over to the accompaniment of delighted giggles from parents and friends.

THE SCHOOLCHILD'S NEW EXPECTATIONS

Although talking tends to proceed according to the child's natural urges, reading, writing, and arithmetic seem to be in the province of adult prescription. When a child is slow in reading, for example, parents and teachers become alarmed. When will he learn? How will he manage at school? What about college? If it happens that the child misreads *where* for *whom* there is no laughter. Instead, adults wonder whether he will have a serious learning problem. If the child continues to progress slowly, their apprehension mounts. No matter how they try to disguise it, this anxiety is communicated to the child. Then the child's own doubts and uneasiness increase.

Perhaps parents become anxious because they feel they must guide the child's learning. Since reading does not come naturally, maybe the adults feel that *their* success or failure is at stake. For instance, in reading, when the child mistakes one word for another, parents often blame themselves. If the child does not learn easily, they begin coaxing. The child senses their uneasiness and becomes bewildered, not wanting to incur the displeasure of parents or the ridicule of classmates. But disapproval over slow progress is in the air—in the community. The child begins to feel desperate.

It is hard for the child under these conditions to feel assured that he or she simply needs more time than others and that he or she will learn to read eventually. Indeed, the child usually feels stupid and wonders, "What is wrong with me?"

On the other hand, school experiences can reverse a child's doubts and shakiness. If the child finds adults who encourage proceeding at an individual pace, risking mistakes, making discoveries, it is possible to overcome some of the mistrust. The child who begins to feel valued as an individual has a chance to grow more confident.

This presupposes that schools are staffed predominantly by cooperative, constructive people. It assumes also that they generally recognize many of the intricacies involved. They do not depend solely on any one theory or methodology. They do not use tests to evaluate only one aspect of the child's functioning. One-sidedness in approach detracts from seeing the child's full array of strengths and limitations.

The Integrated Approach to Reading Difficulty

Unfortunately, investigations that examine each aspect singly have encouraged a limited viewpoint. Due to the exigencies of research, studies are rarely sufficiently extensive to include the interplay of major forces. Reporting findings in only one area, significant though they may be, can distort the picture because in any student some, any, or all components may be acting in concert or conflict.

Thus, in treating students with reading problems, we cannot rely on any one methodology. We cannot depend on any single solution, no matter how fine the research. For example, while authorities differ on the level of intelligence necessary for the acquisition of beginning reading skills, Maria Montessori was able to engender learning even among the mentally retarded. We consider that certain levels of neurophysiological development are required during the initial stages of reading; yet we find many students with deficits in these areas who are able to compensate sufficiently to learn. There is much data that we have accumulated regarding reading difficulties and much that still remains unclear. The more we delve, the more we recognize that we are still trying to clarify the significance of a dynamic interplay that unfolds in unique ways for each individual.

Throughout this book we propound our ideas and experiences with students regarding the diagnosis and treatment of learning difficulties. Part I considers the ramifications of causation; diagnostic techniques are elaborated in parts II and III. We evaluate each student as completely as possible and plan treatment accordingly. Because the aim of instruction is to liberate the child to learn and to grow, practices are based on each individual's requirements and qualities. In cases where we have been specific, we have not meant for the procedures to be duplicated by others; we hope rather to provide a guide.

We recognize that there is still much that is not known in the area of causation and treatment of reading difficulties, and so we continue to question, to investigate, and to try to deepen our understanding.

8

Suggestions for Further Reading

Adelman, H. S., and Taylor, L. *An Introduction to Learning Disabilities.* New York: Scott Foresman, 1986.

Bruner, J. "Models of the Learner." *Educational Researcher* 14 (June/July 1985).

Bryan, T. H., and Bryan, J. *Understanding Learning Disabilities,* 3d ed. Palo Alto: Mayfield, 1986.

Chall, J. S. *Stages of Reading Development.* New York: McGraw-Hill, 1983.

De Hirsch, K. *Language and the Developing Child.* Baltimore: Orton Dyslexia Society, 1984.

Goodman, K. S. "Unity in Reading." In *Becoming Readers in a Complex Society,* edited by A. C. Purves and O. Niles. Chicago: University of Chicago Press, 1984.

Kirk, S. A., and Kirk, W. D. "On Defining Learning Disabilities." *Journal of Learning Disabilities* 16 (January 1983).

Kirk, S. A., and Chalfant, J. C. *Academic and Developmental Learning Disabilities.* Denver: Love, 1984.

Labov, W. "The Logic of Non-Standard English." In *Language, Society and Education: A Profile of Black English,* edited by J. S. De Stefano. Worthington, Ohio: Charles A. Jones, 1973.

Myklebust, H. R. "Toward a Science of Learning Disabilities." *Journal of Learning Disabilities* 16 (January 1983).

Pearson, P. D., ed. *Handbook of Reading Research.* New York: Longman, 1984.

Piaget, J. *The Grasp of Consciousness.* Cambridge, Mass.: Harvard University Press, 1976.

Popp, H. M. "Current Practices in the Teaching of Beginning Reading." In *Toward a Literate Society,* edited by J. B. Carroll and J. S. Chall. New York: McGraw-Hill, 1975.

Smith, C. R. "The Future of the LD Field: Intervention Approaches." *Journal of Learning Disabilities* 19 (October 1986).

Stanovich, K. E. "Explaining the Variance in Reading Ability in Terms of Psychological Processes: What Have We Learned?" *Annals of Dyslexia* 35 (1985).

Stanovich, K. E.; Cunningham, A. E.; and Feeman, D. J. "Intelligence, Cognitive Skills and Early Reading Progress." *Reading Research Quarterly* 19 (Spring 1984).

———. "The Interactive-Compensatory Model of Reading: A Confluence of Developmental, Experimental and Educational Psychology." *Remedial and Special Education* 5 (May/June 1984).

Torgeson, J. K. "Learning Disabilities Theory: Current State and Future Prospects." *Journal of Learning Disabilities* 19 (August/September 1986).

Turnbull, H. R., III. *Free Appropriate Public Education: The Law and Children with Learning Disabilities.* Denver: Love, 1986.

Yaden, D. B., Jr., and Templeton, S., eds. *Metalinguistic Awareness and Beginning Literacy: Conceptualizing What It Means to Read and Write.* Portsmouth, N. H.: Heinemann, 1986.

2

The Causes of Reading
Difficulty

TO INVESTIGATE the causes of reading difficulty is extremely complicated. In most cases, many kinds of factors are found together in various
combinations, including constitutional, neurological, psychological, intellectual, educational, and cultural factors. Although the interaction among
them is difficult to discern, it yields the most reliable data on learning
problems. Even taken alone, the neurological and psychological factors are
so complex and significant that we devote chapters 3 and 4 to them.

Constitutional and Physical Factors

The constitutional factors of learning include all that we are born with. The
idiosyncracies and commonalities of our natures influence the paths we
follow and the way we learn. Physical ailments, for instance, even those
of a minor or temporary nature, affect efficiency and reading performance.
Consider how an adult's powers of concentration are reduced by hay fever,
a cold, or even an irritating rash; yet children are generally less well
equipped to overcome such discomfort. Such problems as lack of sleep or
even inadequate clothing can make it difficult or impossible for a child to
profit from school instruction.

Obviously, some physical factors are of more importance than others in causing learning disabilities, and these need special medical attention. Inadequate nutrition;[1] defects in hearing, speech, or vision; and endocrine or neurological dysfunction are particularly pertinent.

With regard to vision and learning, the ophthalmologist Herman K. Goldberg writes: "A visual defect does not mean that the visual inefficiency is causing the learning problem. Some students with extremely poor vision are excellent readers. For example, there is no conclusive evidence as to the connection of any eye disorder with the ability to read or even with scholastic achievement in all areas."[2]

Some specialists have devised visual training exercises in an effort to improve the reading of children who suffer from various learning difficulties. This practice has been rejected by the American Academy of Ophthalmology:

> Correctable ocular defects should be treated appropriately. However, no known scientific evidence supports claims for improving the academic abilities of dyslexic or learning disabled children with treatment based on visual training, muscle exercises, ocular pursuit, tracking practice, glasses (with or without bifocals or prisms), neurologic organizational training (laterality training, balance board or perceptual training). Furthermore, training may result in a false sense of security, which may delay or prevent proper instruction or remediation.[3]

However, the foregoing statement should not be interpreted to mean that eye difficulties can be ignored. On the contrary, there is general agreement that visual dysfunction may cause a degree of discomfort and fatigue that leads to unevenness and slowness in handling the printed page and to strong resistance to, even a general avoidance of, learning. Therefore, if a student's visual efficiency seems to be impaired in any way, it is essential that he or she be referred to an eye specialist for examination.

1. A. Simopoulos, "Nutrition in Relation to Learning Disabilities," *Learning Disabilities and Prenatal Risk,* ed. M. Lewis (Urbana: University of Illinois Press, 1986).

2. H. K. Goldberg, G. Shiffman, and M. Bender, *Dyslexia* (New York: Grune & Stratton, 1983), p. 71.

3. American Academy of Ophthalmology, "Policy Statement: Learning Disabilities, Dyslexia, and Vision" (February 18, 1984), *Journal of Learning Disabilities* 20 (August-September 1987): 412–13.

Emotional Factors

Emotional and personality factors make up another part of the learning picture. We can point to three ways in which emotional disturbances and learning difficulties interact.

First, a child who suffers emotional upset and conflict while growing up may face the school situation with heightened anxiety or similar psychic disturbances. In many cases, distracting, unconscious conflicts can diminish the child's concentration in class and lead to learning impairment. In contrast, if the child's parents accept his or her uniqueness, if the child feels welcome and trusted, the scene is set for the development of self-respect and confidence. At an early age the child has self-knowledge and an awareness of what to expect within the family circle and beyond.

Second, although the child may at the outset be fairly free from emotional maladjustment, it may evolve as a direct outgrowth of frustration with schoolwork. Consider a girl and a boy who have a similar emotional disturbance and similar learning problems. The girl is placed in a class where there is some provision in the curriculum to meet her needs and she is given individual attention; the class is composed of pupils not too far ahead of her in achievement, and she is able to make progress. The boy is placed in a class where the pupils are beyond his achievement range; the teacher resents being expected to cope with such deviant functioning, and has no time to give the child special treatment. Although neither of these situations arose in response to the basic problem, it is likely that the first child will become better able to cope with schoolwork and may even develop a stronger ego through academic accomplishment, while the other is likely to recede more and more into negative patterns of defense.

Third, both conditions can be present and reinforce each other. That is, a pupil's negative reactions from poor schoolwork can cause emotional difficulties or increase any that were already present. The personality disturbance then heightens the learning problem and creates a vicious circle. It is this cyclical nature that makes it so difficult to determine whether emotional disturbance is at the root of the learning trouble. Yet for treatment, it is important to attempt a distinction. According to Larry B. Silver, observation and data need to be collected on the child's intrapsychic, interpersonal, family, and environmental systems to make a full attempt to understand the problem.[4] Thus the basis of the personality maladjust-

4. L. Silver, "Acceptable and Controversial Approaches to Treating the Child with Learning Disabilities," *Pediatrics* 55 (March 1975).

ment and its relation to the learning disability need to be explored as far as possible.

Neurological-Developmental Factors

Here we discuss briefly the neurological and developmental factors that are elaborated in chapters 3 and 4. These maturational, intellectual, educational, and cultural factors are essential to our understanding of reading difficulty.

MATURATIONAL FACTORS

In general, *maturation* refers to the multifarious facets of a child's growth in such areas as height, weight, responsiveness, control of behavioral reactions, intelligence, perception, and integrative capacity (that is, the ability to organize stimuli into an ordered pattern). The development of certain of these factors is crucial to learning and is described at length in chapters 3 and 4.

It is important at this point to clear up a common misconception. Because deviant growth is frequently intertwined with emotional disturbance, one factor can easily be mistaken for the other. For example, a slowly developing child may incorrectly be considered emotionally immature if no account is taken of the child's rate of physiological development. Or a child who has not yet attained the neurophysiological development necessary for learning to read may be mislabeled emotionally disturbed. Clearly, such mislabeling may damage the child's self-esteem and hinder remediation of the child's true problems.

INTELLECTUAL FACTORS

Obviously, intellect ultimately determines learning ability. As a result, level of intelligence is used as a criterion for determining a student's level of reading achievement. Thus, a third grader who is above average in intelligence should be reading above third-grade level, while a child of the same age who is below average in ability might be achieving adequately to read at the second-grade level. However, estimates of intelligence or achievement can never be completely valid or reliable; the testing instruments themselves are always subject to a degree of error. Also, such factors as the child's physical, environmental, emotional, and cultural condition affect test results. Therefore, any quantitative scores are useful as rough measures only; they merely suggest the level at which a child may be expected to read. Intelligence is a determinant of reading achievement, but intelligence test scores are not yet solid predictors of reading achievement.

EDUCATIONAL FACTORS

Children show unique learning patterns and differ in their competencies in areas related to learning. In reading, auditory and visual discrimination, auditory blending, visual-motor functioning, understanding of concepts, and ability to give sustained attention need to be developed. Thus teachers need to be alert to the factors underlying the acquisition of reading skills, and they must also be knowledgeable enough to deal with hindrances to learning.

With regard to the disadvantaged child, the extent to which a teacher adapts educational procedures to sociological factors has an important bearing on the child's initial learning. Most often work has to be done in broadening the child's background of information, in fostering verbal skills, and in enhancing abstract ability in relation to academic procedures. Developing these processes facilitates learning and helps prevent early failure.

All children need to acquire a feeling that they *can* learn. The teacher needs to exhibit sufficient confidence in children for successful achievement to be within reach. A constructive attitude on the part of the teacher, along with sound professional training, is indispensable for students' optimal learning.

CULTURAL FACTORS

It is well known that the setting in which children live is an important influence on their learning. Some home environments stimulate children's intellectual curiosity and promote their general knowledge of people and the world around them. Provided there are no interfering factors, this type of background is conducive to learning. On the other hand, some children come from homes where they are exposed to a limited range of experience, where educational materials are scarce, and where language is restricted. Such an atmosphere does not prepare a child adequately for school learning. In addition, many such children are not native English speakers, which increases their difficulty in school.

Teaching methods can be adjusted to the needs of children who have impoverished backgrounds. If instructional materials are unsuitable, the children get off to a poor start and are likely to experience difficulty in

14

learning to read from the outset. Hence, it is well to consider background and environmental elements to gain insight into a student's problem.

The Interaction of Causative Factors

Although we have attempted for purposes of discussion to isolate the separate causes of learning disability, we believe that these factors rarely act independently. Furthermore, the interrelationships are far greater in complexity than are any of the factors taken individually.[5] And no matter what the significant causal factors—intellectual, physical, neurological, environmental, or emotional—failure in school will elicit negative reactions from the student and others. These reactions will heighten or produce emotional disturbance.

Thus we can see the interplay of both obvious and subtle forces in the development of a child's reading ability. The complicated patterns and far-reaching consequences of all the varying possibilities affect the life of the child, the teacher, and the parent. We believe that there is never a separate school problem or an exclusively emotional, neurological, or developmental one. The continued search for causes of learning difficulty by those who are trying to help will throw light on the student's problem and may help to avoid certain pitfalls in remediation. New dimensions will repeatedly arise during the search, and constant rethinking and reformulation will take place in the pursuit of a broader understanding.

Suggestions for Further Reading

Baker, S. M. "A Biochemical Approach to the Problem of Dyslexia." *Journal of Learning Disabilities* 18 (December 1985).

Barrett, D. E.; Radke-Yarrow, M.; and Klein, R. E. "Chronic Malnutrition and Child Behavior: Effects of Early Caloric Supplementation on Social and Emotional Functioning at School Age." *Developmental Psychology* 18 (July 1982).

Benton, A. *Left Side, Right Side: A Review of Laterality Research.* New Haven: Yale University Press, 1986.

Connors, C. K. *Food Additives and the Hyperactive Child.* New York: Plenum Press, 1980.

Duffy, F. H., and Geschwind, N. eds. *Dyslexia: A Neuroscientific Approach to Clinical Evaluation.* Boston: Little, Brown, 1985.

Gaddes, W. H. *Learning Disabilities and Brain Function: A Neurological Approach,* 2d ed., New York: Springer-Verlag, 1985.

Holwerda-Kuipers, J. "The Cognitive Development of Low Birthweight Children." *Journal of Child Psychology and Psychiatry* 28 (March 1987).

5. J. Abrams, "An Interdisciplinary Approach to Learning Disabilities," *Journal of Learning Disabilities* 2 (1969): 575–78.

Johnson, D. "Language Problems of Learning Disabled Children." *Topics in Early Childhood Special Education* 4 (Summer 1984).

Kamhi, A. G., and Catts, H. W. "Toward an Understanding of Developmental Language and Reading Disorders." *Journal of Speech and Hearing Disorders* 51 (November 1986).

Kirk, U., ed. *Neuropsychology of Language, Reading and Spelling.* New York: Academic Press, 1983.

Lerner, J. *Learning Disabilities,* 4th ed. Boston: Houghton Mifflin, 1985.

Lewis, M., ed. *Learning Disabilities and Prenatal Risk.* Urbana: University of Illinois Press, 1986.

Liberman, I. Y. "A Language-Oriented View of Reading and Its Disabilities." In *Progress in Learning Disabilities,* vol. 5, edited by H. Myklebust. New York: Grune & Stratton, 1983.

Lipson, M., and Wixson, K. K. "Reading Disability Research: An Interactionist Perspective." *Review of Educational Research* 56 (Spring 1986).

McGuiness, D. *When Children Don't Learn.* New York: Basic Books, 1985.

Simopoulos, A. P. "Nutrition in Relation to Learning Disabilities." In *Learning Disabilities and Prenatal Risk,* edited by M. Lewis. Urbana: University of Illinois Press, 1986.

Stanovich, K. E.; Nathan, R. G.; and Vala-Rossi, M. "Developmental Changes in the Cognitive Correlates of Reading Ability and the Developmental Lag Hypothesis." *Reading Research Quarterly* 21 (Summer 1986).

Stevenson, J.; Graham, P.; Fredman, G.; McLoughlin, V. "A Twin Study of Genetic Influences on Reading and Spelling Ability and Disability." *Journal of Child Psychology and Psychiatry* 28 (March 1987).

Thatcher, R. W., and Lester, M. L. "Nutrition, Environmental Toxins and Computerized EEG: A Mini-Maxi Approach to Learning Disabilities." *Journal of Learning Disabilities* 18 (May 1985).

Wagner, R. K. "Phonological Processing Abilities and Reading: Implications for Disabled Readers." *Journal of Learning Disabilities* 19 (December 1986).

3

Neurological Aspects of Learning Difficulty

by Ursula Kirk*

MANY CHILDREN of average to above average intelligence and without obvious physical handicaps fail, nevertheless, to learn adequately in ordinary classroom settings. A number of terms have come into common use as a result of efforts to identify these children and to provide them with special instruction. Among the most frequently used terms are dyslexia, minimal brain dysfunction, learning disability, specific reading disability, hyperactivity, attention deficit disorder, social incompetence, and perceptual or linguistic impairment. Although each term describes one or more salient characteristic of children who have difficulty learning, none is diagnostic in the sense of delineating a clearly identifiable syndrome that distinguishes a particular group of children from all others. None has inherent within it a specific prescription for instruction and treatment.

A review of the literature reveals, moreover, a pervasive inconsistency in the use of terminology.[1] In some studies the same label refers to dissimilar groups of children, and in others different labels are applied to groups of children whose problems appear to be similar. As a result, the labels often complicate rather than clarify the problems confronting teachers and children in the classroom. For the purposes of this chapter, the term *learning*

*Associate Professor, Neurosciences and Education, Teachers College, Columbia University.

1. R. M. Knights and D. J. Bakker, eds., *The Neuropsychology of Learning Disabilities* (Baltimore: University Park Press, 1976); P. Satz and R. Morris, "Learning Disability Subtypes: A Review," in *Neuropsychological and Cognitive Processes in Reading,* ed. F. J. Pirozzolo and M. C. Wittrock (New York: Academic Press, 1981).

17

difficulty is used to describe a general condition that may be due to a variety of sources and for which individualized diagnosis and intervention are necessary.

Brain Function and Learning*

Discussions of learning difficulties frequently turn to the questions: Is there a relationship between learning or learning difficulties and brain function or dysfunction? If so, what is it? Inevitably, these questions produce a variety of responses, ranging from the claim that there is a direct and demonstrable link between brain function and learning to the dismissal of brain function as a factor in learning and learning difficulties. The intent of this chapter is to provide a framework for educators and clinicians within which these questions can be addressed. To this end, consideration will be given first to brain–behavior relationships in general and then to the role played by neurodevelopmental and environmental factors in behavior.

BRAIN–BEHAVIOR RELATIONSHIPS IN ADULTS

Knowledge about brain–behavior relationships derives from studies of adults who suffered brain damage as a consequence of war-related injuries or naturally occurring events such as accidents, disease, strokes, and tumors. With time, experience, technological advances, and increased precision of behavioral assessment, researchers have identified specific brain structures that make unique and critical contributions to behavior. How these brain structures mediate behavior is not well understood and is, therefore, the subject of continuous investigation by researchers of neuroanatomical, neurophysiological, and behavioral phenomena.

Among the many factors that have emerged from recent brain research, one general principle appears to be particularly relevant to the concerns of this chapter: brain function is systemic when complex behaviors are involved.[2] Like a computer, the brain functions as a system of tightly coupled subsystems that make specific contributions to the achievement of a desired outcome. Unlike a computer, however, brain subsystems do not turn on and off in the production of an outcome. Rather, each subsystem influences complex behavior in some way. Some subsystems play a major role and others a supporting role. However crucial the role of a particular

---

*Technical terms have been defined in the glossary at the end of the chapter.
2. A. R. Luria, *Higher Cortical Functions in Man,* 2d ed. (New York: Basic Books, 1966).

region may be to particular complex behaviors, the contributions of other structures must also be taken into account.

The adult capacity to understand and produce language is an apt illustration of this principle. Specific structures in the left hemisphere contribute to the proficient understanding and use of the phonology, syntax, and semantics of spoken and written language (figure 3-1). Because each structure makes a different contribution, damage to any structure affects linguistic competence in a different way. The capacity to understand and use complex language is not, however, the sole prerogative of the left hemisphere. Recent studies reveal that right hemisphere structures also make a different but equally important contribution to language: the understanding and use of intonation, context, humor, and metaphor. Thus there is a qualitative difference in the language disturbances that occur following damage to different structures in the adult brain.

Studies of the effects of brain damage in adults provide useful but limited information for understanding learning difficulties in children because the psychological and neurological components that contribute to the *acquisition* of language in children differ from those that mediate the skilled *use* of language in adults. Despite the important evidence derived

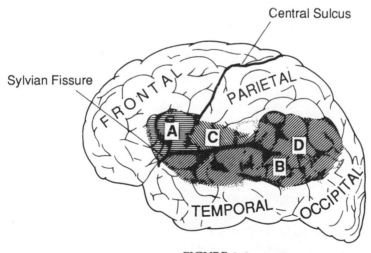

FIGURE 3-1

Cortical structures of the left hemisphere that contribute to proficient understanding and use of oral and written language. Comparable right hemisphere structures contribute to the understanding and use of intonation, context, humor, and metaphorical language.

A: Phonological and syntactic understanding and production of language.
B: Semantic understanding and production of language.
C: Interconnecting fiber tracts.
D: Understanding and use of complex oral and written language.

from the study of adults that many subsystems underlie and contribute to the skilled use of language, such studies cannot provide direct knowledge of the neural and psychological components that contribute to the emergence of this complex cognitive capacity.

Neurodevelopmental Factors

Development of the brain proceeds on a well-regulated timetable. Because almost all neurons (nerve cells) are generated and the basic patterns of neural connections are established before birth, most of the known structural brain abnormalities that are not due to genetic transmission or chromosomal defects have their source in events that occur during pregnancy. The structures that are emerging during each trimester are particularly vulnerable to noxious chemical, metabolic, and mechanical influences (teratogens). During each trimester particular neural events occur that are critical to the development of the brain. Disruption of these processes results in a variety of structural and functional anomalies.[3]

Prenatal Brain Development   Several events of the first trimester of pregnancy are particularly important for brain development: (1) the emergence of a fluid-filled central canal (neural tube) from which the central nervous system arises; (2) the multiplication and migration of neurons to form cortical and subcortical structures; (3) the differentiation of neurons—an increase in size and the appearance of input and output nerve fibers (dendrites and axons), which transmit information between neurons; and (4) the laying down of fiber tracts that interconnect related structures.

Disruption at this early stage of neural development has some predictable, profound, and long-lasting effects on brain development. Among these are, for example, the incomplete closure of the neural tube in the region of the head; the absence of a cortex (anencephaly) or the incomplete development of the cortex (microcephaly) when neurons do not multiply on schedule; the misplacement and misalignment of neurons (ectopic neurons) and the complete or partial absence of the fibers that interconnect the hemispheres (corpus callosum) when neuronal migration fails or is arrested. The precise cause of these abnormalities is not known, but environmental influences such as irradiation, drugs, maternal malnutrition, and infections have been implicated in affecting development during this particularly vulnerable period.

The critical neural events of the second trimester of pregnancy carry forward the processes begun during the first trimester. The growth of the cerebral hemispheres and the establishment of the basic patterns of neural

3. O. Spreen et al., *Human Developmental Neuropsychology* (New York: Oxford University Press, 1984).

connectivity are the primary developmental targets. These events include: (1) the continued migration and maturation of neurons; (2) the multiplication of glial cells, which support and nourish the neurons; (3) the formation of the six cortical layers and their columnar organization; (4) the production of myelin, a fatty substance that coats axons and speeds up the transmission of information; (5) the initial folding in of the cortex to produce the convolutions (gyri) and fissures (sulci) associated with the reception and processing of sensory information from the external environment; and (6) the establishment of the first cortical connections between the hemispheres. Incomplete or arrested development during this trimester produces agyria (a smooth rather than folded brain surface), microgyria (many small gyri), or a few broad gyri. These conditions are associated with both an abnormal arrangement of cells within the cortical layers and abnormal patterns of neuronal connections.

Development of the cerebral hemispheres remains the focus of neural development in the third trimester of pregnancy. The main events include: (1) the formation of gyri associated with the integration and use of information from multiple internal and external environmental sources, and (2) the growth of the corpus callosum. Although these structures continue to evolve long after birth, arrested neural development at this stage affects their maturational course.

Postnatal Brain Development   The brain continues to grow in size and complexity from the time of birth, when it weighs between 300 and 350 grams, through adulthood, when it will weigh between 1,250 and 1,500 grams. Recent research reveals that experience has a crucial role to play in this development. Neither genetic nor environmental factors alone can explain the fact that, despite overall structural similarities, individual brains differ from one another. The differences are most marked in the areas of the brain that integrate complex multimodal information; subserve the capacity to plan, regulate, and adapt activity to situational changes; and modulate emotional and motivational contributions to behavior. These brain regions, which begin to mature during the third trimester, are the most susceptible to the complex interplay between genetic and environmental influences on subsequent brain development.[4]

The electroencephalogram (EEG) is a record of the electrical activity of the brain. When adults are at rest with their eyes closed, large numbers of neurons are synchronously active. A characteristic pattern of high-voltage, low-frequency wave forms (alpha) can be observed in the record. The pattern of rhythmic activity changes when adults are alert and performing

4. J. Conel, *The Postnatal Development of the Human Cerebral Cortex,* 8 vols. (Cambridge, Mass.: Harvard University Press, 1939–1967); W. T. Greenough, J. E. Black, and C. S. Wallace, "Experience and Brain Development," *Child Development* 58 (1987): 539–59.

some type of task. Under these conditions, a less rhythmic, low-voltage, high-frequency pattern of wave forms (beta) appears in the record reflecting the asynchronous activity of neurons.

EEG studies have revealed that different patterns of spontaneous electrical activity occur in infants and young children when the brain is at rest than in older children and adults. A pattern of slow wave activity prevails during the first year of life; alpha activity begins to predominate after age six and becomes progressively more predominant over the course of development. These age-related changes have been interpreted as reflecting progressive cortical organization and maturation.

Early EEG studies revealed that significant regional increments in alpha activity occurs at ages that Jean Piaget described as periods of changing cognitive competence.[5] Because between-hemisphere differences were not examined, the relative development of the left and right hemisphere could not be estimated. A recent study reveals differential rates of development both between and within the hemispheres, as well as indications of age-related growth spurts, which are independent of head circumference and IQ (figure 3-2).[6] Analyses of these results indicated (1) an overall pattern of continuous growth in both hemispheres from birth to age three; (2) a left hemisphere growth spurt, most evident in the left temporal cortex, between ages three and six, succeeded by a period of continuous growth; (3) a pattern of continuous development in the right hemisphere, with a small growth spurt in the right frontal cortex between ages eight and ten; and (4) smaller bilateral growth spurts, which are most prominent in the frontal cortex, between the ages of eleven and fourteen and between age fifteen and adulthood.

This study provides a neurophysiological measure of complex cortical maturational processes that is consistent with neuroanatomical measures of hemispheric development.[7] Neither type of study supports the view that a simple left-to-right gradient prevails in terms of hemispheric maturation.[8] These studies suggest, rather, the presence of a more complex developmental course with different regions of each hemisphere maturing at different times and at different rates. Because the timing associated with specific growth spurts coincides with the timing of changing cognitive competencies, this more complicated view of hemispheric development

5. M. Matousek and S. Peterson, "Frequency Analysis of the EEG in Normal Children and Adolescents," in *Automation of Clinical Electroencephalography,* ed. P. Kellaway and J. Peterson (New York: Ravens Press, 1973).

6. R. W. Thatcher, R. A. Walker, and S. Giudice, "Human Cerebral Hemisphere Development at Different Rates and Ages," *Science* 236 (1987): 1110–13.

7. Conel, *Postnatal Development of the Human Cerebral Cortex.*

8. M. C. Corballis and M. J. Morgan, "On the Biological Basis of Human Laterality: 1. Evidence for a Maturational Left-Right Gradient," *Behavioral and Brain Sciences* 2 (1978): 261–336.

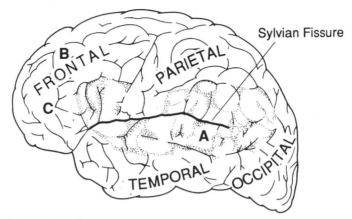

Left Hemisphere

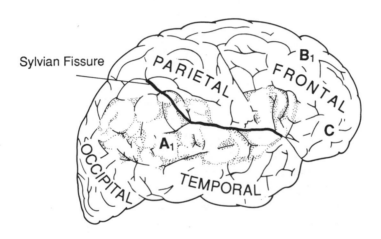

Right Hemisphere

FIGURE 3-2

Regional development of the left and right hemispheres.

A: Left hemisphere growth spurt age 3–6.
A_1: Right hemisphere continuous growth.
B: Left hemisphere continuous growth.
B_1: Right hemisphere growth spurt age 8–10.
C: Bilateral growth spurt at ages 11–14 and 15–adulthood.

may provide a closer approximation of reality than the simpler view. At the very least, it offers another framework for investigating brain behavior relationships in children.

Behavioral Implications of Brain Abnormalities Gross structural anomalies have not been associated with learning difficulties. Nevertheless, recent autopsy examinations of the brains of severe dyslexics revealed the presence of ectopic neurons in cortical regions of the left hemisphere known to be important to reading and in cortical regions of the right hemisphere.[9] These data indicate that microscopic structural abnormalities due to arrested neuronal migration in the early stages of pregnancy produce an unusual pattern of neural circuitry, which may prove to be the neural basis for an inability to learn to read. Because underdevelopment or altered development in one brain area often accompanies overdevelopment in another area, it has been suggested that these structural changes might underlie the patterns of strengths and deficits that have been observed in some children with learning difficulties.[10]

It is of interest to note in this context that unusual patterns have been observed in the EEG recordings of ten-year-old dyslexic boys while they were performing cognitive tasks. Typically, alpha waves occur when the brain is at rest, and marked changes, known as alpha blocking, occur when cognitive activity is undertaken. These changes are thought to reflect the working state of the brain. While the dyslexic boys were carrying out a variety of linguistic tasks, Duffy et al. observed the presence of unexpected alpha in frontal regions of the brain instead of the anticipated shift to an activated state (alpha blocking). The lack of appropriate cortical arousal, which can coexist with behavioral signs of active engagement in cognitive activities, may signal problems in the capacity for selective, focused attention.[11]

It could also be that other subtle cognitive deficits that are associated with learning difficulties involve other microscopic structural anomalies. A change in the rate of dendritic growth would lead to altered patterns of neural connectivity, and defective myelination would affect the speed with which information can be transmitted. Either event would affect the efficiency with which the brain can process information.

ENVIRONMENTAL FACTORS

Plasticity, the capacity for neural and behavioral organization and reorganization, characterizes neural and cognitive development. As the brain develops, neural plasticity is expressed in terms of developmental pro-

9. A. M. Galaburda and T. L. Kemper, "Cytoarchitectonic Abnormalities in Developmental Dyslexia: A Case Study," *Annals of Neurology* 6 (1979): 94; A. M. Galaburda, "Developmental Dyslexia: Current Anatomical Research," *Annals of Dyslexia* 13 (1983): 41–53; A. M. Galaburda et al., "Developmental Dyslexia: Four Consecutive Patients with Congenital Anomalies," *Annals of Neurology* 13 (1985): 222–33.

10. N. Geschwind and A. M. Galaburda, "Cerebral Lateralization: Biological Mechanisms, Associations, and Pathology: 1. A Hypothesis and a Program for Research," *Archives of Neurology* 42 (1985): 428–59.

11. F. H. Duffy et al., "Dyslexia: Automated Diagnosis by Computerized Classification of Brain Electrical Activity," *Annals of Neurology* 7 (1980): 421–28.

cesses: multiplication and migration of neurons, differentiation of neurons, and increased complexity of connections between neurons. As the brain matures, plasticity is reflected in changes associated with dendrites—in the number and in the patterning of synaptic connections (points of contact between neurons).[12] With the failure of one or more of these processes or with damage to the brain, *plasticity* refers to the process of neural reorganization that is set in motion.[13]

At the behavioral level, *plasticity* refers to the capacity to use alternative strategies to attain a desired outcome. In the course of normal development, young children are limited in the strategies they can use to attain an outcome, whereas older children and adults can select from a repertoire of strategies. Memorization studies reveal some strategies that children use at different ages. When asked to memorize a list of words, young children simply listen or look as the information is presented. Older children tend to use verbal or written rehearsal to facilitate the learning process. Still older children may rely on rehearsal, but they may also organize the words categorically or make use of some mnemonic device. Because brain damage may preclude the use of a once preferred strategy to accomplish a task, recourse to a different strategy may underlie the observed behavioral recovery or restitution of function.

Experience Expectant and Experience Dependent Plasticity   Greenough, Black, and Wallace distinguish two kinds of neural plasticity or ways in which the environment influences brain development: experience expectant and experience dependent. Experience expectant plasticity reflects the process of competition for synaptic connections and the subsequent fine tuning of sensory and motor cortical regions in response to the type of environmental stimulation that is expected to be available to all members of the species. Some synapses (connections) are selectively retained and others are selectively eliminated to produce a highly ordered pattern of neural connections that is age dependent and stable. Experience dependent plasticity, on the other hand, occurs across the life span as a consequence of differential life experience. New synaptic connections are generated in response to the complex information-processing demands of the environment. Because environmental demands are different for different individuals, the cumulative effect of experience is that the brain differs from individual to individual.[14]

This concept of plasticity, as both experience expectant and experience dependent, is consistent with Conel's earlier neuroanatomical studies and

12. Greenough, Black, and Wallace, "Experience and Brain Development."
13. S. F. Witelson, "Early Hemispheric Specialization and Interhemispheric Plasticity: An Empirical and Theoretical Review," in *Language Development and Neurological Theory*, ed. S. Segalowitz and F. Gruber (New York: Academic Press, 1977).
14. Greenough, Black, and Wallace, "Experience and Brain Development."

with the more recent neurophysiological research of Thatcher, Walker, and Giudice. Both kinds of investigations revealed the presence of regional growth patterns in the course of development as opposed to growth of the brain as a whole. Conel's studies demonstrated that the maturation of sensory and motor cortical regions occurred at a relatively even pace, which was replicable across individual brains. This regularity did not characterize the maturational course of the cortical regions that process complex, multimodal information. In these regions, variability was the rule both within and across brains. Greenough, Black, and Wallace's distinction between the mechanisms of experience expectant and experience dependent plasticity could account for both the regularity and the variability of brain maturation first observed by Conel.[15]

A Cautionary Note on the Implications of Plasticity   Much has been made of the research findings that enriched environments promote postnatal cortical development in animals.[16] A word of caution is in order here lest this research be misunderstood. Most of this research involves the study of the effects of environments that are still impoverished as compared to the normal environments of the animals in question. Typically, several rats are placed together in an enriched environment consisting of a large cage with a variety of objects to walk on, to play with, and to climb. Although exposure time varies from study to study, laboratory rats are given minimal exposure to minimal enrichment compared with rats that develop in natural surroundings. An enriched environment for a laboratory rat is an impoverished environment for a wild rat. Less well-known research findings show that overstimulation also alters structures at cortical and subcortical levels;[17] that similar experience has differential effects on dendritic branching in male and female rats;[18] and that enrichment may not always have beneficial behavioral effects.[19]

Animal research demonstrates clearly that cortical development is affected by the interplay between genetic endowment and experiential factors. To conclude from this research, as some have done, that the ordinary environment of human infants and toddlers requires enrichment or that the provision of an enriched environment will lead to enhanced cognitive

15. Conel, *Postnatal Development of the Human Cerebral Cortex*; Thatcher, Walker, and Giudice, "Human Cerebral Hemisphere Development"; Greenough, Black, and Wallace, "Experience and Brain Development."

16. Greenough, Black, and Wallace, "Experience and Brain Development"; M. R. Rosenzweig and E. L. Bennett, "Enriched Environments: Facts, Factors, and Fantasies," in *Knowing, Thinking and Believing*, ed. L. Petrinovitch and J. L. McGaugh (New York: Plenum Press, 1976).

17. Greenough, Black, and Wallace, "Experience and Brain Development."

18. M. C. Floeter and W. T. Greenough, "Cerebellar Plasticity: Modification of Purjinke Cell Structure by Differential Rearing in Monkeys," *Science* 206 (1987) 227–29.

19. P. J. Parsons and N. E. Spear, "Long-term Retention of Avoidance Learning by Immature and Adult Rats as a Function of Environmental Enrichment," *Journal of Comparative and Physiological Psychology* 80 (1972): 297–303.

development is to misconstrue and overgeneralize the findings. The animal research does not address issues that are important to understanding human brain development: the nature of an enriched or an impoverished human environment; the possible deleterious effects of either an over-stimulating or an understimulating environment for normal brain development;[20] and the role of readiness in the capacity to benefit from enrichment.[21] Research that addresses these issues is needed before applications to human development can be made.

Plasticity and Brain Dysfunction From what has been said about neurodevelopmental and environmental factors, it should be evident that many factors contribute to the effects of brain damage in children. Consideration has to be given to what was damaged, when the damage was incurred, and the source of damage, as well as to the interplay between genetic and environmental influences. All of these factors play a part in the range of deficits and behavioral recovery that can be observed in children.

The interplay among factors makes children's behavior an unreliable index of the presence or absence of structural abnormalities. There are many examples in which competent performance at the behavioral level has masked the presence of gross structural abnormalities. For example, adequate behavioral performance has obscured the presence of callosal agenesis[22] and cerebellar agenesis.[23] Giftedness has coexisted with agenesis of the left temporal lobe.[24] On the other hand, gross structural abnormalities have not been observed in children with learning difficulties. Galaburda's recent evidence that ectopic neurons are present in the brains of dyslexics suggests that microscopic structural abnormalities might be related to an inability to learn to read.[25] These very different behavioral outcomes suggest that the brain may reorganize more effectively in the absence of certain structures than in the presence of fine structural alterations.

Recent research has shown that the developing brain has a remarkable but limited capacity for plasticity. A study of aphasic (language) deficits in brain-damaged children between the ages of two and fourteen revealed

20. P. J. Donovick and R. G. Burright, "Roots in the Future: Gene-Environment Coaction and Individual Vulnerability to Neural Insult," in *Early Brain Damage,* vol. 2, *Neurobiology and Behavior,* ed. S. Finger and C. R. Almi (New York: Academic Press, 1984).

21. H. Als, "Patterns of Infant Behavior: Analogues of Later Motor Difficulties," in *Dyslexia: A Neuroscientific Approach to Clinical Evaluation,* ed. F. H. Duffy and N. Geschwind (Boston: Little, Brown, 1986).

22. R. Saul and R. W. Sperry, "Absence of Commissurotomy Symptoms with Agenesis of the Corpus Callosum," *Neurology* 18 (1968): 307.

23. F. J. Pirozzolo, P. H. Pirozzolo, and R. Ziman, "Neuropsychological Assessment of Callosal Agenesis," *Clinical Neuropsychology* 1 (1979): 15–21.

24. F. J. Pirozzolo et al., "Left Temporal Lobe Agenesis," *Neuroscience Abstracts* 1 (1979): 273.

25. Galaburda and Kemper, "Cytoarchitectonic Abnormalities in Developmental Dyslexia"; Galaburda, "Developmental Dyslexia."

an incidence that is comparable to what is observed in the adult population: 70 percent of the children with lesions in the language zones of the left hemisphere suffered speech loss; but language was affected in only 7 percent of the children with right hemisphere lesions.[26] The immediate effects of damage to the left hemisphere of young children are on expressive language, independent of the site of the lesion within the hemisphere. Older children are similar to adults in showing expressive deficits with left frontal damage and comprehension deficits with left temporo-parietal damage.[27] Delayed assessment of children with acquired aphasia (language disturbance with left hemisphere damage subsequent to language development) revealed relatively good recovery of language coupled with residual linguistic deficits that persisted over time.[28]

Although much less research has been directed toward the evaluation of skills requiring the special competence of the right hemisphere, similar results have been obtained.[29] Moreover, the level of general cognitive functioning tends to be lowered after brain damage regardless of age or the side of damage.[30] These results suggest that despite the marked plasticity of the maturing brain, recovery processes operate within limitations.

Plasticity and Developmental Delay The possibility that developmental delay or lag is responsible for some early learning difficulties—and, therefore, the inference that developmental catching up is a possibility—needs to be reconsidered in relation to a number of factors that are associated with the interplay of neurodevelopmental and environmental factors in the course of normal development. First, retardation of any of the neural processes associated with the emergence of the brain affects brain development at later stages by producing either gross or fine structural anomalies. Whereas gross structural alterations have been observed upon occasion to support apparently normal behavioral functioning, fine structural alterations have been associated with dyslexia, a persistent cognitive deficit that

26. B. T. Woods and H. L. Teuber, "Changing Patterns of Childhood Aphasia," *Annals of Neurology* 3 (1978): 273–80.

27. U. Brown and J. Jaffe, "Hypotheses in Cerebral Dominance," *Neuropsychologia* 13 (1975): 107–10.

28. D. M. Aram, B. L. Ekelman, and H. A. Whitaker, "Spoken Syntax in Children with Acquired Unilateral Hemisphere Lesions," *Brain and Language* 27 (1986): 75–100; F. Vargha-Khadem, A. M. O'Gorman, and G. V. Waters, "Aphasia and Handedness in Relation to Hemispheric Side, Age at Injury and Severity of Cerebral Lesion during Childhood," *Brain* 108 (1985): 677–96; S. F. Witelson, "On Hemispheric Specialization and Cerebral Plasticity from Birth: Mark II," in *Hemispheric Function and Collaboration in the Child,* ed. C. Best (New York: Academic Press, 1985).

29. B. Kohn and M. Dennis, "Selective Impairments of Visuo-spatial Abilities in Infantile Hemiplegics after Right Hemidecortication," *Neuropsychologia* 12 (1974): 505–12; S. F. Witelson, "Early Hemispheric Specialization."

30. S. Finger and D. F. Stein, *Brain Damage and Recovery: Research and Clinical Perspectives* (New York: Academic Press, 1982); S. F. Witelson, "Neurobiological Aspects of Language in Children," *Child Development* 58 (1987): 653–88.

does not catch up despite compensation through the use of study skills. Second, the range of variability in cognitive abilities is so great that it is difficult to distinguish initially between early indications of delay and normal variability in performance. Once the distinction between delayed and normal development of some cognitive capacity becomes clear, the lack of catching up also becomes evident. Finally, although apparent signs of catching up have been observed in sensorimotor abilities, age-related changes in patterns of cognitive deficits are more common in children with learning difficulties than is growing out of deficits over time.[31] Thus, research does not support the benign view that children with developmentally delayed cognitive capacities will eventually show the full repertoire of cognitive competence.[32]

BRAIN DIFFERENCES AND SPECIALIZED COGNITIVE FUNCTIONS

Throughout this chapter, the word *difference* has been used to refer to the specialized contributions made by specific neural systems and subsystems to cognitive functions. All too often, however, when the word *difference* is used, dysfunction is inferred. This leap occurs because *different* is also used to describe altered patterns of brain organization that occur as a consequence of damage. When the distinction between difference and dysfunction is blurred, the understanding of differences in sex, cognitive style, and lateralized functions within the normal population also becomes blurred. Similar problems arise when the term *dominant* is used to describe specialized functions. To interpret dominant as superior and, by default, nondominant as inferior confuses efforts to understand the neural bases of cognitive functioning.

The Asymmetric Brain and Complex Cognitive Functions Research has shown that left hemisphere cortical regions, which are essential to language comprehension in most of the population, are larger than comparable right hemisphere cortical regions.[33] These regions include the length of the Sylvian fissure, the parietal lobe region that abuts this fissure (operculum), and the superior surface of the left temporal lobe. These anatomic differences are reliably present in neonates.[34]

31. B. P. Rourke, "Reading and Spelling Disabilities: A Developmental Neuropsychological Perspective," in *Neuropsychology of Language, Reading and Spelling,* ed. U. Kirk (New York: Academic Press, 1983).

32. M. B. Denckla, "Motor Coordination in Dyslexic Children: Theoretical and Clinical Implications," in *Dyslexia,* ed. Duffy and Geschwind.

33. A. M. Galaburda et al., "Right-Left Asymmetries in the Brain," *Science* 199 (1978): 852–56.

34. J. Wada, R. Clarke, and A. Hamn, "Cerebral Hemispheric Asymmetry in Humans," *Archives of Neurology* 32 (1975): 239–46; S. F. Witelson and W. Pallie, "Left Hemisphere Specialization for Language in the Newborn: Neuroanatomical Evidence of Asymmetry," *Brain* 96 (1973): 641–47.

Similarly, the frontal cortical regions essential to language production are more extensive in the left hemisphere than in the right. In contrast, cortical regions that lie behind the Sylvian fissure are larger in the right hemisphere than in the left, and the left hemisphere frontal cortex adjacent to the language zone is smaller than the comparable right hemisphere frontal cortex.[35]

The presence of anatomic asymmetries in regions that are essential to language suggests (1) that functional differences may also exist between the hemispheres, and (2) that lateralization for language is biologically predetermined and not the outcome of progressive development during and after the onset of language. Recent research supports this view.[36]

Witelson takes this possibility one step further by suggesting that left hemisphere lateralization involves a "unique mode of processing stimuli as discrete items with reference to their temporal framework."[37] It is necessary, for example, to translate rapidly changing acoustic information into temporally ordered linguistic units in order to understand the spoken word. Cognitive capacities that depend on this specialized type of information processing, such as language comprehension, language production, and sequential motor activity, are lateralized to the left. According to Witelson, the right hemisphere also processes information in a unique and specialized way "by collapsing stimuli into a unit or configuration without sustaining the temporal information of the order of stimulus input."[38] Functions that require this type of information processing are lateralized to the right.

These unique processing characteristics of the left and right hemispheres are present at birth and do not change or grow with development. What develops over time is the repertoire of cognitive abilities that require a particular type of processing. As language develops, therefore, the left hemisphere mediates the skills that entail the use of rapid, sequential, time-referenced information.

The merit of this hypothesis lies in its capacity to account for both cognitive development and the asymmetric mediation of skill. Neverthe-

35. Galaburda et al., "Right-Left Asymmetries in the Brain."
36. M. Hiscock and M. Kinsbourne, "Selective Listening Symmetry in Preschool Children," *Developmental Psychology* 13 (1977): 217–24; M. Hiscock and M. Kinsbourne, "Selective Listening and Attention Switching in Children," *Developmental Psychology* 16 (1980): 70–82; D. L. Molfese and V. J. Molfese, "Cortical Responses of Preterm Infants to Phonetic and Nonphonetic Speech Stimuli," *Developmental Psychology* 16 (1980): 574–81; V. J. Molfese and D. L. Molfese, "Predicting a Child's Preschool Language Performance from Perinatal Variables," in *Individual Differences in Cognition,* vol. 2, ed. R. Dillon (New York: Academic Press, 1985); N. White and M. Kinsbourne, "Does Speech Output Control Lateralize over Time? Evidence from Verbal-Manual Time Sharing Tasks," *Brain and Language* 10 (1980): 215–23.
37. Witelson, "Neurobiological Aspects of Language in Children," p. 678.
38. Ibid.

less, it does not address two important issues: (1) complementary mediation of complex skills and (2) the possibility of within-hemisphere differences in the mode of information processing. Because complex cognitive, motor, and sensory skills are executed in space and time and require both time-referenced and context-based information, neither hemisphere is competent when acting alone. The adequate mediation of complex skills entails the integration of the specialized contribution of both hemispheres and, perhaps, special regional contributions from within each hemisphere.[39]

Witelson's hypothesis does not contradict the view that complementary mediation of skill is essential for competence. Nevertheless, the argument advanced for lateralization of specialized hemispheric processing capacities can be misleading. The emphasis placed on the characteristic modes of information processing proper to each hemisphere creates the erroneous impression of one-sided mediation of complex skills—a view that is not supported by research. Complementary contribution to function is consistent with the findings of research on the neuroanatomy, neurophysiology, and neurochemistry of the brain. Psychological and neuropsychological theories that attempt to explain brain–behavior relationships must take these structural and functional neural properties into account. A theory that does not address complementary function is limited and falls short of explaining how the brain mediates complex human functions and dysfunctions.

An Approach to Understanding Reading Difficulty

RIGHT-BRAINED/LEFT-BRAINED CHILDREN: FACT OR FICTION?

One of the most unfortunate consequences of recent neuropsychological research comes from applying to children information derived from the study of split-brain patients. These patients are adults whose corpus callosum has been surgically separated in order to control the spread of longstanding and intractable seizures.[40] As a result of these laboratory studies, it became clear that some cognitive competencies and some language abilities are mediated by right hemisphere systems. The enthusiasm with which these findings were greeted led to oversimplification and to the

39. Luria, *Higher Cortical Functions in Man.*

40. R. W. Sperry, "Hemisphere Deconnection and Unity in Conscious Awareness," *American Psychologist* 23 (1968): 723–33.

uncritical application of the findings to normal brain function. As a result, the popular notion arose that some adults and some children are fundamentally left-brained while others are right-brained. This misconception was translated into educational terms and, regrettably, continues to some degree to pervade current diagnostic and educational practice.

Several critical factors were overlooked in the popularization of the split-brain studies. First, the subjects of these studies over the course of development had suffered unremitting seizures that did not respond to medication. The degree of damage caused by the seizures and the accompanying neural reorganization must be taken into account when applications to normal brain function are considered. Second, many of the phenomena associated with split-brain patients are demonstrable only in the restricted laboratory setting. They do not occur in everyday life when, in fact, the patients compensate for the absence of the corpus callosum by active information-seeking behavior. Moreover, individuals with agenesis of the corpus callosum and no other damage do not show any behavioral sign of a lack of integration of information.[41] Finally, in its normal state the brain consists of interconnected hemispheres that function in conjunction, not in isolation. Because information enters the system and reaches both hemispheres in many different ways it is anatomically impossible to restrict information, and therefore its processing, to a single hemisphere.

The situation is further complicated by the confusion that surrounds issues related to cognitive information-processing strategies and lateralized hemispheric functioning. The advocacy of classes to educate the hitherto neglected right brain is based on this confusion. Clarification of the subtle distinction between preferred cognitive style and hemispheric lateralization of information processing is necessary to avoid this confusion.

Cognitive style refers to an individual's preferential use of particular problem-solving strategies. It has been described variously as analytic versus holistic, sequential versus concurrent, and field dependent versus field independent. For adults and older children, the use of a cognitive style reflects an initial approach to solving a problem, which is complemented by the simultaneous contribution of the alternative approach. For example, reproducing a complex figure requires both an analysis of elements and a grasp of the relationships among the elements. One individual may proceed from taking in the whole to an analysis of its component parts, while another may proceed from an analysis of the elements to an appreciation of the whole. Use of a preferred style can be discerned in both approaches. In neither approach is preference an indication of either sole or separate

41. Witelson, "Neurobiological Aspects of Language in Children."

reliance on an information-processing style. The accurate reproduction of a complex figure requires the complementary contribution of both cognitive styles.[42]

The situation with young children is not as clear cut as it is with adults and older children. As has been pointed out, the hemispheres—and regions within each hemisphere—mature at different rates, and the corpus callosum keeps pace with regional hemispheric maturation. Under normal developmental conditions, the use of a preferred strategy is evident in the performance of five- and six-year-olds when they are asked to reproduce a complex figure. At these ages, use of an alternate information-processing strategy appears to follow rather than to complement the initial approach. Some children will outline the figure first and then proceed to complete the figure detail by detail, while other children will work detail by detail from the outset. Simultaneous and complementary use of strategies appears around the age when the corpus callosum has reached functional maturity.[43] It should be noted, however, that even when young children use a preferred strategy, they also make use of an alternative strategy rather than rely solely on a single mode of processing information.

What is lateralized, then, is a particular mode of information processing.[44] Independent of modality, the left hemisphere is specialized to extract from the environment sequential and time-referenced information and to interface this type of information with information being received and processed by other subsystems. Likewise, the right hemisphere is specialized to extract information from the environment without reference to timing and order, to act on it so as to synthesize the various elements into a whole, and to integrate this information with what is being received and processed by other subsystems. Use of a preferred strategy does not reflect either separate or sole reliance on one hemisphere or another; carrying out complex cognitive activities requires the concerted and specialized contribution of each hemisphere. It is time to discard the left brain/right brain fiction in favor of integrated and complementary contributions to cognitive functioning.

INFORMATION PROCESSING AND LEARNING

The concept of brain that has been developed in this chapter is that of an active information-processing system composed of tightly coupled,

42. U. Kirk, "Hemispheric Contribution to the Development of Graphic Skill," in *Hemispheric Function and Integration in the Child*, ed. C. T. Best (New York: Academic Press, 1985).
43. Ibid.
44. Witelson, "Neurobiological Aspects of Language in Children."

specialized subsystems each of which makes its unique and essential contribution to complex cognitive activity. Because it both acts on and is acted on by the environment, insight into how the brain extracts, processes, and uses information from the environment may clarify the bases for many of the learning difficulties that have been observed in children. The steps involved at each level of processing are summarized in the following discussion and implications for understanding reading difficulties are explored.

Task Analysis and Initial Problem-Solving Activity Solving a problem or acquiring new information involves the analysis of task requirements and the adoption of effective strategies. Information is coded for neural processing as it enters the system through a variety of sensory channels: sight, hearing, touch, movement. The manner in which relevant information is extracted from the environment depends both on the strategy that is used to guide the search and on the environmental event itself. For example, watching a jet's vapor trail form in the sky is registered through the visual system as a series of successive events. Observing the formed jet trail is registered as a single or simultaneous event. Thus, visual information can be extracted from the environment either successively or simultaneously.[45] Each strategy provides somewhat different information about the actual event. Implicit in the information acquired by watching the jet's trail unfold is knowledge of the formed trail. So too, information about the formed vapor trail contains within it knowledge of how it comes into being. Although use of either strategy can yield adequate information about an environmental event, one strategy may be more efficient than the other to accomplish the purpose for which the information is sought.

Independent of how information enters and is coded by specific sensory systems, it is transmitted serially for central processing. Not all information that is available to the sensory systems undergoes further central processing. Information is selected for transmission and further processing as a result of complex interactions among neural subsystems that mediate arousal levels, attentional factors, motivation, and planning as well as the purpose for which the information was sought.[46]

Information that undergoes central processing is acted upon in different ways by each hemisphere regardless of the sensory channel through which it was first received or the manner of its reception. The left hemisphere processes rapidly changing information as discrete bits with reference to the time of their occurrence. The right hemisphere processes the same

45. J. P. Das and C. K. Varnhagen, "Neuropsychological Functioning and Cognitive Processing," in *Child Neuropsychology*, vol. 1, *Theory and Research*, ed. J. E. Obrzut and G. W. Hynd (New York: Academic Press, 1986).
46. Ibid.

information but restructures it to create a unit without reference to time. For example, although a musical chord constitutes a single unit of information, it is acted upon centrally both as a whole—a set of notes (right hemisphere)—and as a series of separate tones (left hemisphere). Both modes of central processing take place simultaneously; both contribute to understanding different aspects of the information extracted from the environment.

Although one or the other mode of processing may predominate as a function of a person's preferred cognitive style, the nature of the task itself must be considered. Different combinations of strategies may be more or less efficient depending on what a particular task requires. To return to an example from music, the detection of recurring themes requires analysis of sequential bits of information, but this must be done in relation to the framework of the overall composition. Serial analysis alone is not adequate for the task. Under normal conditions, flexible and complementary use of information-processing strategies is the rule.

A further step in the process needs consideration here. This step involves the way that complex cognitive processes are expressed in action. Just as information can be extracted from the environment and processed both simultaneously and successively, so, too, action strategies can be organized in either manner. Again the use of an effective strategy is related to the nature of the task. For example, a list of serially presented words can be recalled either by grouping them according to semantic categories (simultaneous processing) or by using a sequential strategy and reporting the words in the order of their presentation.[47] Although either strategy is effective for short lists, long lists are remembered better when words are organized categorically. Flexible use of action strategies is necessary for proficient performance.

Age and level of maturation influence the speed and efficiency with which the brain extracts and processes, integrates, and organizes information. These factors also influence the degree to which different subsystems contribute to behavior at different times. Because, for example, anterior cortical regions mature gradually over time, as do the capacities that they will eventually mediate, some aspects of cognitive functioning will be less available to the child of six than to the twelve-year-old or to the adult. It is to be expected that children of different ages will differ in the degree to which they can plan ahead; monitor and adjust behavior to changing circumstances; develop, maintain, then shift a learning set; and screen out interference. Posterior cortical regions, which integrate converging information from many sources, also mature gradually. These regions are criti-

47. Ibid.

cal to the mediation of complex symbolic skills such as reading and math, and different degrees of proficiency are expected of children at different ages.

Implications for Understanding Reading Difficulties Some reading difficulties may be due to inefficiency at one or other level of information processing: extraction of information, transmission of information for central processing, and selection of an appropriate action strategy. Problems can arise at any stage of processing, and the nature of the reading difficulty will differ in relation to where the process breaks down.

EXTRACTION OF INFORMATION FROM THE ENVIRONMENT. At least two components are involved in the process of extracting information from the environment: the use of an effective search strategy and the initial encoding of incoming information. Research has shown that reading is more a language-based skill than a vision-based skill. Learning to read requires that visually presented words be processed in a distinctly linguistic way. Inefficiency in extracting visual information rarely interferes with learning to read or with understanding what is read. Poor readers often do well on tasks that require nonverbal visual discrimination or memory abilities, but they have considerable difficulty with visual tasks that require specific linguistic analysis.[48]

Tallal has demonstrated that some language-delayed children are unable to process rapidly changing acoustic information effectively—a capacity that is essential for breaking the language code.[49] Inefficiency at this input level underlies both delayed or deficient language development and subsequent problems in learning to read. These findings suggest that learning to read is related more to efficient encoding of acoustic information in terms of its phonetic and phonological properties, "an abstract linguistic scheme that provides a structure for the language processes,"[50] than to auditory discrimination or to search strategies per se.

TRANSMISSION OF INFORMATION FOR CENTRAL PROCESSING. According to Luria, there is an appropriate level of cortical arousal for carrying out complex cognitive activities.[51] Either too much or too little arousal will impair the capacity for selectivity. The seemingly paradoxical effect of stimulants on some children with an attention deficit disorder (ADD) may not be paradoxical after all. The effect of the commonly used stimulant Ritalin may be to regulate cortical activation which, in turn, can facilitate selective attention, sustained concentration, and goal-directed activity.

48. I. Y. Liberman, "Should So-Called Modality Preference Determine the Nature of Instruction for Children with Reading Disabilities?" in *Dyslexia,* ed. Duffy and Geschwind.

49. P. Tallal, "Auditory Temporal Perception, Phonics, and Reading Disabilities in Children," *Brain and Language* 9 (1980): 182.

50. Liberman, "Modality Preference," p. 98.

51. Luria, *Higher Cortical Functions in Man.*

Motivation is an important factor that appears capable of affecting the level of cortical arousal. Geschwind reported that language learning is most rapid under the pressure of needing it to communicate with peers. He speculated that although most dyslexic children master their native language readily, second-language learning would proceed slowly if the second language were not absolutely necessary for peer communication.[52] Implicit in this suggestion is the idea that motivation is a powerful force that can facilitate learning even in a somewhat inefficient system.

CENTRAL PROCESSING OF INFORMATION. A number of factors influence the way information is processed centrally. The integrity or lack of integrity of the information that is available affects the way it is processed in the left and right hemispheres. For children similar to those described by Tallal, who cannot extract linguistic information from a rapidly changing acoustic stream, incomplete information is available for further elaboration.[53] Slowing down the rate of presentation can help such children to break the basic linguistic code and to develop additional language skills.

Other children with reading difficulties have proven to have adequate auditory discrimination for speech and nonspeech sounds under quiet conditions, but to have a specific deficit in discriminating speech sounds in the presence of background noise.[54] For such children, inconsistent information is available for central processing and, consequently, the efficiency of central processing is compromised. Because most early classroom instruction in reading is done in groups and background noise is unavoidable, children with this kind of processing problem frequently have difficulty in learning to read.

Under normal conditions, reliable information is available for central processing. In the early stages of learning to read, left hemisphere analyses contribute to the establishment of sound-symbol correspondence, the segmentation of words into their component sounds, the correct sequencing of phonemes, and the retrieval of words on demand. Meaning is derived first from the word and then from phrases and sentences by means of phonological and syntactic analyses for which the left hemisphere is uniquely specialized. At later stages, when the task involves reading to learn, these linguistic analyses facilitate rapid reading and the understanding of syntactic constructions on which the meaning of complex written text frequently depends.

Some children with an inefficient or compromised capacity for linguistic analysis may succeed during the beginning stages of reading by relying on

52. N. Geschwind, "Biological Foundations of Reading," in *Dyslexia,* ed. Duffy and Geschwind.
53. Tallal, "Auditory Temporal Perception, Phonics, and Reading Disabilities."
54. S. Brady, D. Shankweiler, and V. Mann, "Speech Perception and Memory Coding in Relation to Reading Ability," *Journal of Experimental Child Psychology* 35 (1983): 345.

visual memory for whole words. Other children, who cannot break the linguistic code, may require specific intervention to develop automatic recognition of sight words during these early stages of learning to read. All of these children are at risk during the later stages of learning to read due to their slow reading rate and their difficulty in deriving the meaning embedded in syntactic elements.

Similarly, right hemisphere analyses facilitate letter discrimination and the learning of sight words during the early stages of learning to read. Contextual and inferential meaning can be derived from words, phrases, and sentences as tone and inflection are understood, as information is restructured, and as new relationships are established. What is understood goes beyond what is explicitly stated. Such children, whose difficulties stem from inadequate reconstructive capacities rather than from deficient linguistic skills, are successful in learning to read and in understanding what they have read as long as comprehension is measured by memory for factual information. Problems arise, however, when reading requires drawing inferences and identifying the theme or main idea.

EFFECTS OF AGE AND MATURATION. Proficient reading requires the concerted working of both hemispheres, with each making its proper contribution. Over time, experience and maturation contribute to the integration of the neural systems that make this concerted working possible. The reading process becomes more and more automatic; the capacity to anticipate, plan ahead, and monitor progress enhances the comprehension of complex written text; and details of what is read are understood in relation to the overall context. As children gradually extend the repertoire of skills that can be brought to bear on reading for meaning, reading becomes a way of thinking.[55] It is at this stage that some children have difficulties that may reflect inadequate interhemispheric integration. Such children learn verbal and nonverbal information slowly. They do not discover and use mnemonic or organizational strategies automatically and have difficulty matching sequentially presented information to a spatial array. Intensive training in study skills may help these children to compensate and become effective readers.

CONCLUSION

This chapter has provided a framework within which to explore relationships between brain function and learning and to draw implications for learning and learning difficulties. Although reading difficulties have been

55. Kirk, "Hemispheric Contribution to the Development of Graphic Skill."

made the primary focus, similar analyses could be made with regard to other learning difficulties. The value of this approach lies in its ability to account for the multiple neurological factors that may contribute to learning and to difficulties in learning. Caution must be exercised, however, when this kind of thinking through of implications is undertaken. Precise understanding of brain–behavior relationships in children lies in the future. To the extent that a process approach to understanding learning difficulties suggests ways of enhancing instruction and learning, the approach is of value. It is too soon, however, to conclude that such an analysis is an accurate description of how the brain mediates learning.

Glossary

Agenesis   Failure of tissue or an organ to grow or develop normally.

Agyria   Absence of infolding or cortical convolutions.

Alpha   The pattern of synchronous, high-voltage, low-frequency electrical activity characteristic of the adult brain at rest.

Anencephaly   Failure of normal development of the cortex.

Aphasia   Partial or total inability to understand or produce language as a result of brain damage.

Asymmetric (hemispheric)   Used with reference to structural and functional differences between the left and right cerebral hemispheres.

Axon   A nerve fiber that serves as the major communication link from one neuron to another. Shorter axons connect (project to) adjacent neurons; longer axons connect (project to) neurons in distant parts of the brain and spinal column. Longer axons group together to form large fiber bundles or tracts.

Beta   Asynchronous pattern of low-voltage, high-frequency electrical activity characteristic of the adult brain during the performance of a task.

Corpus Callosum   The large bundle of axons that interconnect the left and right hemispheres.

Cortex   The multilayered brain tissue that forms the outer surface of the left and right hemispheres.

Dendrite   A branched nerve fiber projecting from a neuron that receives information from the axons of other neurons.

Differentiation (neuronal)   Refers to the process of neuronal maturation that is characterized by an increase in size, complexity of dendritic branching and axonal connections, and degree of myelination.

Ectopic   Used to describe displaced and misaligned neurons.

Electroencephalogram (EEG)   A record of the pattern of electrical activity in various parts of the brain as measured by electrodes placed on the surface of the scalp.

Fissure   Prominent groove or infolding in the surface of the cortex. Less prominent grooves are referred to as sulci.

Glial cell   A type of cortical cell that nourishes and supports neurons in the cortex.

Gradient   Refers to the rate at which the left and right hemispheres mature over the course of development.

Gyrus   A convolution or convex outfolding between sulci that characterizes the human cortex. The pattern is variable from person to person.

Hemisphere   The upper part of the brain composed of interconnected cortical and subcortical structures. The left and right hemispheres are separated by a fissure and connected by the corpus callosum.

Migration (neuronal)   The developmental process by which neurons move to their appropriate locations in the cortex.

Multiplication (neuronal)   The process by which neurons that will form the cortex are generated.

Myelin   The fatty substance covering axons that increases the speed and precision with which information is communicated from one neuron to another.

Myelination   The process by which myelin forms around an axon or collection of axons.

Plasticity (behavioral)   The capacity to change strategies to attain a goal.

Plasticity (neural)   Modification of connections between neurons in response to environmental experience.

Sulcus (pl., sulci)   A distinct groove or infolding in the surface of the cortex. The human cortex is characterized by a large and complicated pattern of sulci.

Synapse   The region of communication between the axon of one neuron and the dendrite or cell body of another neuron.

Teratogen   Any toxic substance or damaging event that results in developmental abnormality. It may be chemical, metabolic, or mechanical, or caused by irradiation or malnutrition.

Suggestions for Further Reading

Levine, M. D. *Developmental Variation and Learning Disorders.* Cambridge, Mass., and Toronto: Educators Publishing Service, 1987.

Obrzut, J. E., and Hynd, G. W. *Child Neuropsychology: Theory and Research.* Orlando: Academic Press, 1986.

———. *Child Neuropsychology: Clinical Practice.* Orlando: Academic Press, 1986.

Rudel, R. G., Holmes, J. M., and Pardes, J. R. *Assessment of Developmental Learning Disorders: A Neuropsychological Approach.* New York: Basic Books, 1988.

4

Psychological Aspects
of Learning

MAJOR FACTORS in learning include the psychological, physical, neurological, emotional, intellectual, and cultural patterns. Each modality affects the other in a complex aggregate. We will look briefly at three major theoretical areas: Freud's psychoanalytic system, Sullivan's interpersonal formulation, and Kohut's self system.[1] These theories are too complicated to discuss extensively here, but each one attempts an understanding of human behavior, motivation, and crucial aspects of learning.

The Major Theories

Problems are likely to result when social and cultural forces conflict with the fulfillment of biological and social needs. Consider how children might develop learning difficulty. If all goes smoothly and there is enough encouragement, they will want to learn through their biological and social development. Just as children learn to eat and dress themselves, they learn to master academic subjects in due time. If there is approval along the way, the child is likely to be confident and competent.

Many children are not so fortunate. The structure of personality devel-

1. S. Freud, *An Introduction to Psychoanalysis* (New York: Perma Giants, 1949), pt. 2; H. S. Sullivan, *The Interpersonal Theory of Psychiatry* (New York: W. W. Norton, 1953), pt. 2; H. Kohut, *The Analysis of the Self* (Madison, Conn.: International University Press, 1987), pp. 203–21.

ops through the interaction of what we want, what we can get, and what we come to consider appropriate. Freud labeled these personality parts the id, ego, and superego. He reminds us that the child is totally dependent on mother or a significant person to care for the elemental needs of hunger, protection, warmth, and so on. The dependency period extends for several years, and the way the child is cared for determines an initial outlook on life. A person welcomes or shuns people and ideas in direct relation to early experiences. As parents care for their children, they identify with them and wish to maintain their love and approval. If experiences are unpleasant, a child may wish to rebel even though it is difficult to risk parents' antipathy. After all, they are dependent on their family. Conflict, if it persists, leaves them with a high degree of intrapsychic disturbance. Learning can become part of this inner conflict. For example, a child may feel his or her parents' deep resentment (maybe they never wanted a child or perhaps they are frightened of the responsibility, and so on). The child cannot understand their lack of affection but dares not show anger and terror directly; so the child may withdraw or get "sick" or disobey in order to gain attention. These characteristics can carry over to school. Heinz Kohut further indicates that we learn to mistrust our inner promptings because we so desperately need the approbation of those around us.[2] Thus children often learn to disregard their inner experiences when they conflict with those on whom they depend. In this way they cut themselves off from their own desires. Consider the possible confusion in the child who hears his mother say, "You can't be hungry; you just ate!" Or imagine a child who says that she's afraid to stay alone. If her parents tell her, "Don't be silly; you're not going to be afraid," she may feel ashamed and bewildered. She is told that her fear is unacceptable, yet she still feels frightened.

Personality difficulty arises not only when the instinctual needs are frustrated but also when they are overindulged. For instance, when parents do not wish their daughter to experience anything painful or disappointing, they may overprotect her so that she will never be "unhappy." As a consequence, the development of her ego is greatly retarded. She does not put forth the effort to overcome obstacles. She wishes to remain a baby, perhaps, to retain her blissful state. Her inability and refusal to cope can include difficulty in learning.

Harry Stack Sullivan considers that psychological difficulty occurs when forces are antithetical to human needs, but the reactions to this dilemma are somewhat unique. According to Sullivan, the individual who cannot bear dissonance will react with "selective inattention."[3] In other words, the person listens only to what is tolerable. This restriction can even extend

2. Kohut, *The Analysis of the Self,* pp. 300–24.
3. Sullivan, *The Interpersonal Theory of Psychiatry,* chap. 1.

to perceptual-cognitive processes and can eventuate in "dissociative security operations." In other words, the student may not attend to learning because learning represents the unbearable. Again, the child who is not ready to learn for whatever reasons may blot out reading instruction (and we rarely know whether such factors as brain damage or autism are interfering). These factors can restrict the child's energy in learning. Furthermore, the individual may not have the foggiest idea of what is the matter. (Nor, perhaps, will parents or teachers.) Have we not all had such experiences? For instance, if we are unsure of our acceptance by someone important to us but the person seems preoccupied in our presence, are we not likely to interpret this inattention as personal rejection? Or if we know that we are fearful of mathematics, are we not likely to draw a blank when we are asked to estimate even the simplest sum?

Motivation

A common factor in these theories is motivation.[4] We assume that children want to learn about themselves and the world. Barring obvious impairment of physical, neurological, or psychological elements, we believe they can learn. How is it then that sometimes they do not?

All children are born with certain constitutional components, with certain family constellations, into a particular culture. This uniqueness allows for endless combinations and permutations in what we are, how we learn, and what paths we follow. An infant may have been born with learning deficits that are never detected because the growing child has come to compensate and master them through high motivation and dogged determination. Yet another child with parallel deficits may suffer years of academic failure. People like Helen Keller or Franklin Roosevelt were able to compensate for their handicaps despite the odds against them. We also know of those who seem limited in their talents but who become stalwart, contributing members to their families, their vocations, and their communities. Perhaps it is not so much what we are born with or into, but how we use what we have.

Curiosity and Anxiety in Learning

We will now discuss briefly two important elements connected with motivation: curiosity and anxiety. Curiosity tends to accelerate learning; anxiety tends to disrupt it. The extent to which curiosity is fostered or hampered influences the way we pursue learning about the world both

4. C. Maslow, *Psychology of Being* (New York: Van Nostrand, 1962).

43

informally and academically.[5] Think of how the infant begins exploring. Perhaps a finger is found to satisfy sucking urges. Then the search broadens to body, certain objects, and so on. The "whys" begin at around two years of age, accompanied by extended exploration—of plugs, cupboards, supermarket shelves, whatever. Although this is wonderful for the child, it is often trying for the adults. We find parents saying "No! No! No!" interminably. Too much restriction can kill curiosity; too much protection can make it hard to find meaning and the joy of mastery.[6] These restrictions or indulgences may or may not be carried over to schoolwork.

A major disruptive force with regard to motivation is anxiety. Anxiety is the central problem in neurosis. Karen Horney made basic anxiety a pivotal concern in her theories and suggested that any feared social situation can cause it.[7] When anxiety is attached to family or school situations in which the child fails every day, the child can develop a learning problem. Anxiety fosters the need to use defenses such as denial, rationalization, repression, and regression. These defenses tend to intrude upon intellectual functioning and may account for some of the distorted ideas among individuals with anxiety disorders.

However, acute anxiety, in some instances, can *increase* learning by raising motivation to the level of a challenge. During high anxiety, many people overcome tasks that afterward seem impossible to accomplish. On the other hand, anxiety often results in disaster. If the child experiences repeated fear—fear of failure, fear of ridicule, or fear of humiliation—the result may be generalized anxiety. If this anxiety is experienced in schoolwork, it can cause serious learning difficulty.

Factors That Contribute to Learning

Most of our theoretical knowledge indicates that learning depends on a constellation of growth factors, primarily the maturing personality in a context of family and society, the integrity of the central nervous system, and through the interplay of these and other contributing factors.

Personality matures through the child's relationship with the significant people in his or her life. When a person enters school, teachers and classmates assume similar importance. Disturbance occurs or accelerates when the child experiences heavy doses of disregard, ostracism, or other negative

5. Sullivan, *The Interpersonal Theory of Psychiatry,* p. 312.

6. O. Kernberg, *Object Relations Theory and Clinical Psychoanalysis* (Northvale, N.J.: Jason Aronson, 1984), pp. 28, 29.

7. K. Horney, *Neurosis and Human Growth* (New York: W. W. Norton, 1950).

attitudes that lower feelings of worth. When these feelings arouse anxiety and frustration and interfere with curiosity, the child frequently loses motivation to learn. When these feelings cloud self-understanding, meaning becomes murky. For instance, Jimmy's teacher comments, "But, Jimmy, we just finished practicing that word. You *must* know it!! You're in second grade now. You're a big boy." Of course he recognizes that he does not know the word and becomes confused; but it takes courage to challenge powerful grown-ups. Knowing his own feelings while others impose their notions of how he is supposed to feel reinforces his perplexity.

We are reminded of a vignette with Dennis the Menace, whose mother has just insisted that he hold her hand while crossing the street because he is so young. He blurts out, "How come I'm such a big boy when you take me to the dentist, and I'm too little to cross the street by myself?" If a child's feelings are repeatedly given little credence, perceptions become more and more distorted. Obviously, such transactions cause little trouble if they are infrequent. It is repeated disrespect, denigration, and discomfort that can cause varying degrees of emotional upset. Depending on the circumstances, a wide variety of psychological disturbances can occur, ranging from the extreme childhood psychoses—including autism and childhood schizophrenia—to the less severe neurotic involvements.

Factors That Hinder Learning

SOCIAL FACTORS

The major factors that hinder learning are psychological, neurological, and constitutional. Some children have severe problems that are beyond the scope of this discussion. But many students who have academic and social problems can be helped with special assistance when necessary.

Teachers and parents who have negative attitudes hinder students with learning difficulty. These adults may be uneasy with students who have disturbing qualities such as uncommunicativeness, insensitivity, inflexibility, unresponsiveness, or inattentiveness. For example, some students have a problem concentrating on what another person is saying; they seem egocentric and uninterested, when actually they are confused. Their lack of self-control often disguises their ability to use desirable behavior even in less stressful situations. Sometimes these students feel like outcasts, and their poor self-image can cause them to slouch, neglect their grooming, or withdraw into themselves. It is not unusual for school personnel and even parents to find them unappealing.

Basic Considerations

We cannot always distinguish whether students' difficulties in learning lie in psychological or neurological processes, social perception, social cognition, or other factors. Despite the substantial number of students who lack social ease, teachers rarely consider emphasizing such skills. Perhaps they consider it a family affair and beyond the scope of the classroom. Or perhaps they feel that students will learn these attributes as they get older. The need for such skills is obvious, but the salient question is how to find a way to teach them. There are several published programs for training in social skills, but they need to be carefully evaluated.[8] Although the programs have certain advantages, the teacher needs to ensure that communication between student and teacher remains meaningful.

Informal procedures that the classroom teacher can use for students with learning difficulties include initiating cooperative play and study, making transitions from one activity to another at home and at school, and encouraging a cooperative classroom climate. Perhaps the most useful procedure for the teacher is finding suitable jokes, anecdotes, and stories to be read aloud or acted out. For example, the tale of Daniel in the lion's den shows how Daniel's kindness was repaid when the lion saved his life; *The Emperor's New Clothes* illustrates how a little boy is the only one willing to say the truth at all costs. Folktales, fables, and stories can be relevant as examples for these children.[9]

Parents may not be able to follow a formal program while raising their children in the amenities of living. But that is not the only way to teach such skills. The parent, like the teacher, needs to be a model. Wise teachers and parents try to show children as much decency, fairness, understanding, respect, forgiveness, affection, and wisdom as they can. They also need to show their disapproval, irritation, frustration, mistakes, and humanness. Adults need to emphasize interpersonal communication to promote interpersonal ease. The home and the school need to facilitate cooperation, promote friendships, and encourage enjoyment in learning.

Since students with learning difficulties are at risk for becoming social rejects, they frequently become uninvolved and solitary as a defense. Their frustration reduces their self-esteem; their lower status reminds them that they are second-class citizens. The end result is loneliness, or even despair.

8. A. Bandura, "Influences of Model's Reinforcement Contingencies on the Acquisition of Imitative Responses," in *The Reinforcement of Social Behaviors,* ed. E. McGinnies and C.B. Ferster (Boston: Houghton Mifflin, 1971); S. R. Vaughn, C. A. Ridley, and D. D. Bullock, "Interpersonal Problem Solving Skills Training with Aggressive Young Children," *Journal of Applied Developmental Psychology* 5 (1984): 213–23; J. M. McCarthy et al., "The Arizona Basic Assessment and Curriculum Utilization System for Young Handicapped Children," *Socialization* (Denver: Love, 1984).

9. E. Landau, S. Epstein, and A. Stone, *The Exceptional Child through Literature,* 4 vols. (Englewood Cliffs, N.J.: Prentice-Hall, 1978), has many stories especially compiled for students who have learning difficulties and serves as an excellent resource.

When students' social skills are inadequate, not only do they suffer socially but their academic learning may be hindered as well.

CONSTITUTIONAL FACTORS

Although it is difficult to determine pure, innate capacities, nevertheless they influence our personality development. For instance, some of us are more susceptible to respiratory ailments than others, just as some of us are more musical. This does not mean that these proclivities are stereotyped and inflexible or that there is no chance for change. It does mean that our physical makeup facilitates or impairs our reactions, including those connected with learning.

Related to constitutional problems are the neurological components (chapter 3). When such factors cause delay or difficulty in learning, the child develops psychological problems as a result of failure. For example, long before a boy enters school, he may become aware of the superiority of his contemporaries in such things as playing games; handling crayons, paints, blocks, or scissors. Expressive language may also be more difficult for some pupils than others. Perhaps a child is always chosen last for the team, rejected on the playground, or made to feel like an outsider. Continued negation from parents, brothers, sisters, playmates, and others will lower his self-esteem and heighten his anxiety still further. When he is exposed to instruction and does not learn, his feelings of inadequacy increase accordingly. His original problem may be compounded, making it even more difficult for him to learn.

SYMPTOMATOLOGY OF CHILDREN WITH OR WITHOUT LEARNING PROBLEMS

The dilemma for the educator and specialist is that children can manifest identical symptoms whatever the primary cause of their learning difficulty. Children with psychological problems are particularly vulnerable to the fear of failure and the competitive atmosphere of peers, school, and community. Their characteristic responses to these conditions might include preoccupation, withdrawal, aggression, helplessness, lack of concentration, misbehavior, or cognitive confusion.

It is well known that physical symptoms such as hives, allergies, and appetite loss can result from emotional conditions such as fear and tension. Hyperactivity, distractibility, and impulsivity, considered by some the hallmark of neurological symptoms, sometimes are caused by psychological factors as well.

47

A girl who feels unacceptable, for instance, may react in any number of ways. At one time she may shrink into herself; at another time she may lash out. If she continues to fall below academic expectations, she experiences added disapproval. The vicious interaction of basic and reactive emotional factors has been set in motion.

The same psychological factors can cause learning difficulty in one instance and promote learning in another. We have all known children as well as grown-ups with rugged backgrounds, personality disorders, constitutional handicaps—all manner of burdens considered to cause various problems—who have become scientists or scholars. Indeed, they often tell us that they escaped into learning precisely *because* of their misery. Thus we continue our caution in interpretation.

The Family

The major responsibility for our humanness falls to the family. If a child's parents are rigid, frightened people and she begins to see the world as a fearful place, she may withdraw. If they try to do everything for her (even in her "best interests") and try to prevent her finding out for herself, she can lose much of her curiosity—or she may not.

A child can have parents whose relationship to each other is difficult. They may use the child to give meaning and direction to their lives. If the child has "problems" they may work in unison to alleviate them in order not to face their own disappointment with each other. A mother who feels demeaned through being "just a housewife" might focus on her troubled child instead of facing her own discontent. Conversely, parents who are compatible and reliable can also have children with learning difficulties.

Hank—A Boy of Fourteen Failing in School

The case of Hank, a bright youth, illustrates the interplay between wanting the family's approval and refusing to work effectively in or out of school. Extensive diagnosis revealed that Hank had sufficient intelligence (bright-normal was the category), but he consistently earned only 67th percentile in reading achievement on silent and oral reading tests. School personnel agreed that Hank had mastered some of the basic skills but claimed that he failed his daily work and final exams anyway. Comprehension seemed to be a problem, and his vocabulary was meager. He refused to complete assignments and rarely responded in daily class work.

His mother consulted an educational therapist. It seemed that Hank's attitude was the factor that most seriously interfered with his schoolwork. The reading specialist, who was also trained as a psychotherapist, decided to ask the whole family (mother, father, three sons, and a daughter) to attend a session together. Her philosophy followed family system theory, which considers one member's problem to be part of the family pattern— each one contributing to, as well as being affected by, the others' behavior and attitudes.

On the appointed day, the mother and three of her four children arrived on time. They explained to the therapist that the father was in the lobby waiting for Hank. A few moments later the father arrived and said that he'd called home and discovered that Hank was being detained at the police station. Hank had talked back to an officer and called him an unacceptable name. His mother and father were furious and claimed that this was typical. The therapist said that she was frustrated, too, but admitted she couldn't help admiring Hank's ingenuity in dodging the session so effectively. The therapist went on to say that since they were in the office anyway, they might as well proceed. This would give all of them a chance to see what happens in such sessions. She obtained the family's permission to tape the session for Hank to hear later.

Bob, the youngest, started to talk about Hank and said that he was a real friend to him—that he helped him with his homework and that he was a "good guy." Most members stated that Hank was both likable and frustrating. But the father remained angry and said that he had lost all trust in and respect for Hank. At the end of the session the therapist said to Hank, on the tape, that she was sorry he wasn't there to hear the discussion and that if everyone agreed, including him, she would see them all the next day.

When the whole family appeared, Hank was the first to speak. He said he was angry that he was the one most talked about on the tape, but he was also glad to hear how much everyone cared for him. The therapist asked how it was for him in this family. After much hesitation, he said that he "felt in the middle." The therapist asked him to place each member of the family in tableau form to show how it was for him to be in the middle. He then placed his two brothers on one side of him with his sister on the other and said, "I'm in the middle." There was a pause and Bob said, "But I feel in the middle too." When asked to elaborate he said, "Well, it's very crowded for me. They proceeded to play out a pantomime. Hank placed his father at "work all the time at this desk"; Mom was in the kitchen cooking; Kathy was "out driving the car"; Bob and Sam were playing separately. It turned out that each member felt isolated and ignored.

"Where does that leave all of you?" the therapist asked.

"With my friends" Hank answered. He continued, "I steal in order to show them I can *be* somebody. I make trouble in school, too, to be a big shot."

The father threw his wallet at him and said: "There, take it; you don't have to steal it. What do you want? Should I just give money to you?"

Hank froze. The therapist went over to him and said, "When I did something bad as a kid and my mother made me feel guilty, I felt hopeless and misunderstood."

He answered in a low voice. "I don't want to be this way. I don't want to steal or do bad at school."

The therapist asked if anyone had heard Hank say that he didn't want to be the way he was. There was a long silence and some sighs.

The therapist said it might be a good idea for Hank to have special tutoring for a few months to catch up. He agreed, and after five months he was accomplishing satisfactory work. Although there are still many problems, the family members are trying to work them out without using Hank as the scapegoat. Hank has been freed to strengthen his view of himself. He is also using reading and other academic skills that he always had but refused to implement because he was so angry and resentful.

The School

The school situation can be harsh, especially in light of the pressure for high marks and the shame of not succeeding. The troubled student may have difficulty in overcoming the obstacles of school situations.

Even an understanding teacher may become frustrated with a student who doesn't respond. Classmates of a student with learning problems can add discomfort because pupils find it hard to be kind to a laggard. Sometimes in our competitive society each one is trying hard to measure up. Yet here, too, some students rise above these difficulties and learn despite them.

The cultural milieu also is influential in determining students' attitudes. Those who live among people with high academic standards usually feel failure more acutely than those who live under less intellectual pressure. Parents' attitudes toward the school also lend their weight. Often parents who are frustrated, angry, and bewildered by their youngsters' inability to learn blame the schools and the teachers. Sometimes the student basks in this anger. Perhaps the child thinks, "It's not my fault, it's the teachers', so I don't have to do anything."

Some schools contribute to learning problems by smothering curiosity. Many times we observe kindergartners and first graders with wide eyes and freshly sharpened pencils waiting eagerly to learn. They are enthusiastic about school; they bring home notices to their parents with regularity and reliability. Yet by third grade they often appear tired and bored. They have lost interest in school and consider it drudgery.

The first three grades are crucial in learning. (In some countries these years are considered so important that only the most skillful and experienced teachers are allowed to handle them.) If the readers introduced in first, second, and third grades contain stale, foolish reading matter, children begin to be bored. Bettelheim observes:

> The pre-primers and primers from which [the child] is taught to read in school are designed to teach the necessary skills. . . . The overwhelming bulk of the . . . so-called "children's literature" attempts to entertain or to inform, or both. But most of these books are so shallow in substance that little of significance can be gained from them. The acquisition of skills, including the ability to read, becomes devalued when what one has learned to read adds nothing of importance to one's life.[10]

We cannot say that starting children on charming nursery rhymes and folktales (although that is our wish) will guarantee good readers, but we do consider that such stories will not add the extra burden of dullness.

The Interplay among Multiple Factors

Personality disorders can stem from any of the causes delineated here and in chapter 2. There can be constitutional components that comprise intellectual and neurological deficits; family environments that contribute to the distortion of emotional development; or educational situations that cause or exacerbate a poor self-concept. Any of these can touch off interference in learning, as described in this chapter.

How do we distinguish and handle these intertwined emotional problems? The issue is to try to determine the full nature and degree of prob-

10. B. Bettelheim, *The Uses of Enchantment* (New York: Knopf, 1976), p. 4.

lems in the context of contributing elements. A diagnostician might discover that a student with learning difficulty has personality disturbances and needs psychotherapy. If this choice alone is instituted and the student still does not learn within a reasonable length of time, he or she will fall further and further behind. Even worse, whatever emotional problems were present will be exacerbated through daily academic failure. This does not discredit the psychodynamic stance. It simply states that when other factors continue undetected or ignored, the individual can try, even try *hard*, only to flounder, fumble, and finally despair.

In another case, a specialist might decide that the student's emotional problems are minor and that neurological factors are the cause of the learning failure. He might suggest appropriate teaching procedures to compensate for the student's poor memory, inadequate integrative capacity, or whatever. This may alleviate the problem if the student learns fairly quickly. If not, a reactive emotional disturbance may develop that needs specific attention.

Thus there need never be an either/or decision for choice of treatment. Neither psychotherapy nor remedial work alone is always sufficient to clear up the learning problem. Where psychotherapy is secured (and the high cost of treatment and limited facilities often make it unobtainable), every effort needs to be made to improve school functioning. Few therapists treating neurotic adults would suggest that a patient forgo working until major attitude changes occurred. When the students experience difficulty in school, their academic and emotional problems are likely to intensify. (Chapter 7 elaborates specifics that teachers can use for dealing with pupils who have difficulty adapting to school.)

The following case introduces another kind of difficulty—The phenomenon of school phobia. This problem sometimes puzzles school personnel. Phobias include fear of failure, domestic problems, health difficulties, and other factors. We offer here the experience of one such child.

Marni—A Child with School Phobia*

In some instances a child may refuse to go to school for reasons that are not apparent to parents or school personnel. Marni was such a child. She was seven years old, in second grade and doing well academically; her behavior in class was also satisfactory. One day she woke up and refused

*Abridged from a case provided by Dr. Alma Bond, a psychoanalyst in private practice.

to go to school. No matter how her parents handled her and no matter what the teacher tried to do, Marni would not leave home. She had tantrums and remained unrelenting. Had she been forced to go or had she gone to school and refused to learn, Marni might have developed serious problems. The parents were sufficiently concerned to ask for a consultation with the school counselors and the principal, all of whom recommended therapy for Marni.

Marni lived with her professional parents and three-year-old brother. The parents seemed devoted to their children. There happened to be a brief separation between the parents for a few months, but they were able to reconcile. Both agreed that Marni should have treatment.

In therapy Marni found out many things. For example, Marni discovered that she was refusing to go to school lest she be forgotten by the family and lest her father leave again. The therapist helped Marni reconcile her fears and the jealousy of her brother—who got to stay home all the time. The therapist accepted and empathized with Marni at this stage. She encouraged independence by suggesting that Marni talk to her parents about getting a room separate from her brother. Marni then talked about this with her parents. She also talked with them about waiting until she felt strong enough to return to school. With this kind of self-affirmation, Marni later went back to school willingly and participated productively.

Wise educators realize the importance of exploring the basic causes of a phobia; they respect the child's experience and are patient until the problems are alleviated. In this case Marni was finally able to handle her jealousy and other problems creditably. She continued to be successful in school, eventually completed college, and seemed eager to pursue her life. In a follow-up years later, her mother stated that Marni is now "decidedly her own person."

Suggestions for Further Reading

Abrams, J. C. "Interaction of Neurological and Emotional Factors in Learning Disability." *Learning Disabilities: An Interdisciplinary Journal* 3 (March 1984).

Bettelheim, B. *The Uses of Enchantment.* New York: Knopf, 1976, p. 4.

Blanton, G. H. "Social and Emotional Development of Learning Disabled Children." In Cruickshank, William and Joanne Marie, eds., *Early Adolescence to Early Adulthood: The Best of ACLD,* vol. 5, edited by W. Cruickshank and J. M. Kliebhan. Syracuse, N.Y.: Syracuse University Press, 1984.

Bruner, J. "Development of a Transactional Self." In *New Directions in Studying Children* (Speeches from the Conference of the Erikson Institute, Chicago, April 29–30, 1983).

Freud, S. *An Introduction to Psychoanalysis.* New York: Perma Giants, 1949, pt. 2.

Kernberg, O. *Object Relations and Clinical Psychoanalysis.* Northvale, N.J.: Jason Aronson, 1984, chap. 2.

Kohut, H. *The Analysis of Self.* Madison, Conn.: International University Press, 1987.

Landau, E.; Epstein, S.; and Stone, A. *The Exceptional Child through Literature.* 4 vols. Englewood Cliffs, N.J.: Prentice-Hall, 1978.

Moustakas, C. *The Child's Discovery of Himself.* New York: Ballantine, 1974.

Rosner, S.; Abrams, J.; Daniel, P.; and Sheldman, G. "Dealing with the Reading Needs of the Learning Disabled Child." *Journal of Learning Disabilities* 14 (October 1981).

Silver, A. A., and Hagin, R. A. "A Unifying Concept for the Neuropsychological Organization of Children with Reading Disabilities." *Journal of Developmental and Behavioral Pediatrics* 3 (September 1982).

Sullivan, H. *The Interpersonal Theory of Psychiatry.* New York: W. W. Norton, 1953, pt. 2.

Part II

Diagnosis

5

How Teachers and Learning Specialists Evaluate Reading Ability

---

M OST CASES of reading difficulty are of necessity handled by teachers. Therefore this chapter deals mainly with the approaches a classroom teacher might use in evaluating the difficulty. Only a few cases have problems so severe that they require referral to a psychologist or child study team for diagnosis; chapter 6 describes the type of examination indicated in such cases.

The Investigation of Reading Difficulty

When a teacher suspects that a pupil has a reading problem, he or she tries to identify the contributing factors, find out whether the pupil is working to capacity, and discover the pupil's specific reading deficiencies. On the basis of the findings, the teacher plans a program for remedial instruction.

The teacher confers with any individuals who might be familiar with the child's background, such as former teachers, guidance counselors, or the school nurse. The teacher also consults available records for information regarding intelligence and achievement test results, absences, number of schools attended, physical health, and other relevant matter.

In many instances such exploration might suggest the need for further diagnosis and treatment by specialists. For example, if there are indications of a defect in vision, the teacher might confer with the school physician, nurse, or social worker so that suitable arrangements can be made for an eye examination. Other available specialists, such as a school psychologist or guidance counselor, might be consulted on the advisability of referral for other forms of treatment, including those that deal specifically with emotional and neuropsychological problems.

Whether or not the causative factors are alleviated, the problem of helping the child overcome the reading difficulty remains. Thus the teacher analyzes the available data and administers the tests necessary to understand how the reading difficulty is manifested.

The teacher will need to evaluate the pupil's potential. Where no individually administered test result is available in the child's files, the teacher uses informal measures such as assessing the child's vocabulary development, use of language, general knowledge and understanding, and responsiveness in class. The teacher notes the student's grasp of topics discussed in class, including current events and other types of general information. He or she observes the level of insight displayed during class discussion. Ability in arithmetic computation (not word problems) provides another important measure of intellectual functioning. Intelligence tests that require reading are of minimal use, because the child who has trouble reading cannot earn a valid score. When the estimated intellectual potential is arrived at, the teacher has an approximate measure of the level at which the child might be expected to read. This is generally referred to as the measure of reading expectancy and is discussed further on page 78.

The teacher next estimates the child's reading level—perhaps using a graded series of readers. A comparison of reading level with estimated intellectual level determines whether the child is reading below his or her potential. In primary grades, particularly in grades one and two, for example, a discrepancy of even six months alerts the teacher that the child is having difficulty. A child is considered to be lagging behind in primary grades when there is a gap of one-half to one year in reading level as compared with intellectual potential, whereas in intermediate grades through high school a student needs assistance if the gap is one to two years.

Teachers need to use caution in using such estimates because they are only a rough measure of the student's ability. Our philosophy and experience throughout the years indicate that any student who has difficulty with reading needs the teacher's help. He or she may seek the assistance of a reading teacher or other specialist to strengthen the student's reading, but it is crucial that those who have problems receive the academic assistance that they need in order to avoid demotivation and even failure. Teachers, parents, and all who deal with students need to encourage them through acceptance and the reassurance that they can learn. These adults must also find ways of providing appropriate assistance whenever indicated.

The Analysis of Reading Achievement

Not all pupils will need the extensive reading analysis to be described in the rest of this chapter. The choice of techniques depends upon the severity of the problem and the amount of time the teacher has available. The teacher can make as simple or as detailed an investigation as is warranted. Suggestions are offered for using informal procedures when standardized tests cannot be administered.

In order to obtain a comprehensive evaluation of a pupil's reading ability, the teacher appraises mastery of oral reading, word analysis techniques, silent reading, vocabulary, and written expression. From these tests the teacher decides at what level the pupil can handle different types of reading material. This is discussed further under "Interpreting Oral Reading Test Results" and "Interpreting Silent Reading Test Results" in this chapter.

Remember that the student's age and grade in school will not give a clue of actual reading level; a student of a given age may read at virtually any grade level.

ORAL READING TESTS

Oral reading tests are designed to provide an indication of the pupil's reading level, competence in word analysis techniques; attitudes toward the difficulty; and fluency, articulation, and expressiveness in reading aloud. They also suggest which level of silent reading test to administer; the teacher or psychologist frequently has no other clue to an appropriate silent reading test.

Both standardized and informal instruments are available to test the pupil's ability to read aloud. Whereas standardized oral reading tests yield a grade-level score, results of the informal tests provide an approximation of the grade level at which the pupil can actually handle a book. Neither measure provides information about comprehension, however.

Standardized and informal tests also facilitate detailed analysis of the types of errors a pupil makes in oral reading. For example, examination of

59

errors can reveal whether the pupil used any systematic method for figuring out unfamiliar words, as well as what word recognition skills have been mastered and which still need to be developed.

STANDARDIZED ORAL READING TESTS

Standardized tests are convenient to use because they contain a number of paragraphs of increasing difficulty, from first-grade level to as high as twelfth-grade level (see appendix A). The more familiar the teacher is with a test, the more useful it will be. Therefore the teacher should use the same battery regularly, particularly when retesting a group of pupils. Increasing familiarity will enable the teacher to compare a given pupil's responses not only with the standardized norms but also with the responses of other pupils. This procedure helps to develop an insight into the strengths and weaknesses of the instrument.

INFORMAL ORAL READING TESTS

If standardized tests are not available, the teacher might devise his or her own instrument, choosing appropriate paragraphs from a series of graded readers or from informal reading inventories. If the teacher thinks that the child is reading at about second-grade level, for example, he or she might choose three selections: one at high first, one at low second, and one at high second grade level. (If the teacher has misjudged the pupil's ability, he or she can, of course, add lower or higher level books.) The child reads aloud until there is a book he or she can read with relative ease. How to judge ease of readability on informal tests is discussed in the following section.

Administering the Informal Test

It is helpful to approach the oral reading inventory (or any other testing situation) as a collaborative venture in which teacher and pupil together assess the pupil's strengths and weaknesses in reading in order to bolster the former and remedy the latter. The teacher begins by explaining the test and the reasons for giving it, saying something like: "You know you seem to be having some trouble with reading. By listening to you read, I will be able to tell which books are best for you. After you finish, I can show you where your greatest difficulties lie, and I'll know the kind of help you'll need. *This test has nothing to do with any marks for classwork or for your report card.*"

The teacher might describe briefly the general content of each selection to be read. Then the child begins to read aloud at sight. If there are more than five significant errors per hundred words, the child is given an easier book.[1] Ultimately the examiner should know which book or books the child can read with ease, which with assistance, which with difficulty, and which not at all.

Although many examiners ask content questions after the pupil has read aloud, we do not advise this practice. Many children, particularly those with reading problems, find the mechanics of reading aloud so absorbing that they are unable to attend to content, just as most adults, asked to read aloud during an eye examination, would be unable to answer detailed questions concerning the meaning of the reading matter. Some children experience such anxiety in struggling to pronounce words that they cannot possibly pay attention to their meaning regardless of their ability to understand them. The inability to answer questions on content therefore does not necessarily indicate a lack of comprehension.

RECORDING ERRORS

It is important to establish a systematic method of recording errors to analyze the child's performance and compare it with tests administered previously or subsequently.

When a standardized oral reading test is used, a duplicate copy is usually available on which the teacher can record errors. This convenience is lacking when an informal test is used, but the teacher might request permission from the publishers to reproduce the selected passages so that he or she can mark the copy as the child is reading. The following symbols are those the authors find most convenient:

- If a word or portion of a word is mispronounced or read incorrectly, it is underlined, and the word the child said is written above it.
- A wavy line indicates repetitions. Although not counted as errors, they contribute to qualitative analysis of the child's reading.
- A capital *P* is written over words that the child has failed to recognize. (After a lapse of five seconds, the teacher pronounces the word to minimize the child's frustration.)
- Omissions are circled.
- Parentheses are placed around self-corrected mistakes, with the mis-

1. Significant errors are renderings that are highly inaccurate and distort the meaning—i.e., *wagon* for *capon, family* for *father,* and so on. Mispronouncing the names of people and places is considered insignificant, as is saying *wouldn't* for *would not, a* for *the,* and the like.

pronunciation written above the word. These do not count as errors in scoring.
- A caret indicates insertions made in error.

The lines below illustrate the use of these symbols, but a teacher can devise his or her own.[2]

Mother said, "Now we can go to work. The <u>house</u> is quiet." Tom did (not) want to ˄ work. He wanted to go outside and play.

(The way to evaluate these errors is described in the section "Interpreting Oral Reading Test Results.")

The teacher who cannot reproduce passages from the readers, as we have suggested, can record the child's errors on a separate sheet of paper, as follows:

Word Said for	Word in Book	Non-recognitions	Repetitions	Insertions
how	now	not	he wanted	to go
home	house	outside		

It is sometimes useful to record any unusual aspects of the child's behavior as he or she reads aloud so that the teacher can assess the degree of discouragement that the child has experienced and his or her attitude toward reading. If the teacher is to improve the child's behavior, he or she must be aware of how the child feels, how the child tries to cope with the subject, and what interactions take place. The teacher should understand the meaning of these reactions to handle the child in the most effective way possible.

Interpreting Oral Reading Test Results

As we have implied, some mistakes on oral reading tests indicate relatively severe reading difficulty, while others are considered less important. Merely counting the errors overlooks the most valuable part of the examination. For example, such mistakes as reading *a* for *the* or *Annie* for *Anne* and repeating a word or phrase usually do not alter meaning and can be

2. Adapted from the symbols used in the Gray Oral Reading Tests (see reference in appendix A).

ignored. Children with reading difficulty tend to make a large number of errors of all varieties. It is therefore wise to exercise wide latitude in interpreting mistakes. Weighting all errors equally, regardless of their nature, yields a distorted picture of the child's ability. Naturally, inaccurate reading is not desirable, but if mistakes are interpreted too rigidly, the mature student might be assigned reading material on a much lower level than is desirable in light of individual interests and need for information.

From the specific type of errors that the child makes while reading aloud, the teacher can ascertain which techniques of word recognition the child has already mastered and which are lacking. Does the child know the basic sight words, such as *want, anyone, same*? Does the child have difficulty with consonants, consonant combinations, or vowel sounds? What about the rule for the silent *e* and the rule for double vowels? Is the child able to make sure of context clues, or is he or she just guessing wildly? With a little experience, the teacher will begin to perceive a definite pattern. Based on many students' tests, the teacher might prepare a list of the major skills, make a copy for each student's file, and use it as a checklist to indicate deficiencies and progress.

The teacher can also gain valuable information about the child by observing his or her approach to the reading material. Is the approach markedly different from that to other tests and other situations? Does the student overestimate or underestimate his or her ability? Is the child reluctant to expose what he or she considers poor achievement? Many students attempt to cover up for inadequate skills. For example, a student might read accurately but repeat words or groups of words frequently. This tendency might be due to insecurity; or the student might be stalling for time because some of the words that follow seem too difficult. Perhaps the student gets lost and has difficulty focusing attention on the line. Gladys Natchez investigated children's approaches to oral reading and found that hesitations, interruptions, such as "Is that right?", long pauses with no attempt to figure out the word, and angry outbursts are usually related to the pupil's characteristic reactions to frustrating situations.[3] Readers' anxiety can significantly influence their responses. Thus, observing a pupil during oral reading sessions can yield clues to a personality pattern. In this sense, oral reading tests can be useful projectively.

Fluency of reading is also taken into consideration. However, the rate at which a student "should" read aloud cannot be determined. In an informal test, the teacher simply uses judgment as to the degree of fluency. It is true that the paragraphs in standardized oral reading tests are generally timed. However, the timing usually yields a bonus for fluent reading rather

3. G. Natchez, *Personality Patterns and Oral Reading* (New York: New York University Press, 1959).

than imposes a penalty for slowness. (In any case, timing should be de-emphasized for children with difficulties.)

Tests of Word Recognition Skills

The ability to figure out unfamiliar words is basic to all reading. Students with reading difficulty at all levels, even through high school, are commonly deficient in this ability. Obviously, inaccurate word recognition techniques interfere seriously with reading comprehension, for misreading words changes the meaning of a passage. Although some evidence of the pupil's word recognition difficulties can be gathered from oral reading tests, word analysis tests more precisely specify the skills lacked.[4]

When many pupils have to be tested and the teacher does not have the time to administer a test of word analysis skills to each one individually, it is possible either to use a standard group diagnostic test or to gain some impression of the pupil's basic knowledge of phonics through a group test, which can be made up of initial consonants, consonant blends, and short vowel words.

The teacher can prepare a master sheet with key words to be used in associating the letter sounds to be tested. Each pupil needs a duplicate sheet, subdivided into spaces and numbered according to the way the master sheet is planned.

In presenting initial consonants, for example, the teacher uses key words such as *hill, match, table, lamp,* and so on. As the teacher pronounces each word, he or she asks the pupils to write in the designated space the letter corresponding to the very first sound they hear. The procedure is similar for words that begin with consonant blends such as *spill, tree, blue, stop,* and so on; the children are asked to write the first two letters that represent the sounds they hear. To judge the pupils' knowledge of short vowels, the teacher dictates words such as *bag, top, mud, sip,* and *pet.* The children are instructed to write the whole words.

The results of this informal test will give the teacher a general idea of pupils' needs. For example, errors on the test records will reveal which pupils should be grouped for help with particular initial consonants or consonant combinations and which ones need training with certain vowel sounds. The teacher can plan a word analysis skills program accordingly.

4. Widely used oral tests of word analysis skills include the Durrell Analysis of Reading Difficulty, Gates-McKillop-Horowitz Reading Diagnostic Test, and the Roswell-Chall Diagnostic Assessment of Reading and Teaching Strategies (see appendix A).

Silent Reading Tests

Silent reading tests are used to determine the level at which the student can read silently with comprehension. Among the most widely used are those listed in appendix A. Selected subtests are administered to determine the extent and nature of reading difficulty in the areas of paragraph meaning, vocabulary, and sometimes spelling. As we have pointed out, the results of an oral reading test suggest the level of the silent reading test to be administered subsequently. For example, if the student can read aloud only first-grade material, a silent reading test designed for primary levels should be used, regardless of the student's age or grade. If the student's reading ability is at fifth-grade level, a test designed for children reading at fifth-grade level should be administered, and so on. This method of selecting silent reading tests produces a more accurate assessment of the silent reading skills than does the routine administration of standardized tests chosen on the basis of the child's grade.

Interpreting Silent Reading Test Results

Test results frequently seem to underestimate or overestimate the student's ability. Those whose reading ability is poor may mark items indiscriminately. The results in such cases may be indicative more of their good fortune in guessing correctly than of their proficiency. Conversely, when a student misses many of the relatively easy items at the beginning of a test because of initial anxiety, but gets the harder ones right, or when the child becomes too frustrated and gives up, the score may underestimate reading ability. Grade scores alone do not provide sufficient information about a student's silent reading skills. The test results must be analyzed qualitatively for additional information that may shed light on the nature of the reading problem.

Analysis of test patterns at primary levels is somewhat different from analysis at advanced levels. At primary levels, the tests for the most part measure the degree to which the pupil uses word recognition skills and the pupil's accuracy in using them. The teacher looks for consistent errors. For example, some tests contain illustrations, each followed by a list of words of which one is correct. Students may use a variety of skills in selecting the word that represents a picture. Let us suppose that a picture of a book is followed by the choices, *look, bat, farm,* and *book.* The choice of *look* may

65

indicate the use of similar configuration; *bat* may indicate a reliance on initial consonants; *farm* would probably indicate pure guesswork. Similar errors on sentence and paragraph reading subtests indicate which skills the child has mastered and which are still lacking. Consistency in errors suggests the area in need of instruction.

At higher levels, word recognition is still important, but comprehension plays a greater role. Thus the student's ability to use context influences test results, as does the extent of the student's background information. Previous knowledge of the subject and adept use of context enable a reader to supply a particular word (or one close in meaning) even if the word is not recognized in isolation. For example, a student who uses context skillfully could probably answer questions on the following paragraph, even if the italicized words are unfamiliar.

It's over an hour until the *scheduled* takeoff, but there is plenty for us to do. We don't have any *particular* worries about the plane. After every 900 hours of flying time each engine is *completely* rebuilt.

General background information also influences the ability to use context even when every word is known. For example, each word in the following title is probably familiar to most of us: "Experimental Study of the Quenched-In Vacancies and Dislocations in Metals"; yet without an engineering background, we can't decipher its meaning.

The way in which a pupil answers questions may reveal deficiencies in word recognition, comprehension, use of context clues, or background. If the teacher is uncertain as to the nature of the reading problem, it might be advisable to allow the student to go beyond the time limits of the standardized test and answer as many questions as possible. (The results in this case can be used for qualitative evaluation only, not as actual test scores.) If the student sustains a high accuracy score, the problem is probably related to a slow reading rate. Discussion can help in locating where the difficulties lie if the pupil reads some of the paragraphs aloud.

In analyzing vocabulary subtests, it is important to try to determine whether low scores are due to poor word recognition skills, difficulty in word meaning, or slowness in handling the test. For example, if a student misreads words (such as *profession* for *possession*), he or she cannot possibly find the required synonyms. The examiner can determine whether this is the case by checking some of the incorrect responses orally, after the test has been completed. Students who appear to be deficient in vocabulary are frequently found to know the words very well when they are presented orally; they simply cannot read them accurately. This, then, is evidence of word recognition difficulties—not meager vocabulary. Also, the errors might be analyzed to see whether they tend to occur in highly technical words related to specific subjects rather than in more general words. Even those who have no reading difficulties tend to miss words in areas in which their background is weak. Since many students with reading difficulty have done little or no reading in the content areas, they are likely to miss such words as *resource, ingredient,* and *metallic* with greater frequency than words of a more general character.

Spelling

An evaluation of students' spelling level and analysis of their pattern of performance reveal further diagnostic information. With regard to the importance of spelling in an individual's education, researchers have noted that the mastery of spelling is not a peripheral skill but is central to literacy.[5]

Most standardized achievement batteries have separate spelling subtests from which the teacher can assess the level of spelling proficiency and the types of errors the pupils make. Unfortunately, at upper levels the spelling tests of many batteries consist of multiple choice items that involve choosing the correctly spelled words from clusters of four or five that may be misspelled. This mainly requires recognition of correct spelling and is an entirely different skill from that of writing words. The latter entails revisualization of word patterns, including proper sequencing of letters and recalling the correct numbers of syllables—areas of deficiency for many students who have spelling problems. Therefore, it is advisable to use the tests that require writing words from dictation, such as the Roswell-Chall Diagnostic Assessment of Reading and Teaching Strategies, the Wide Range Achievement Test, and the Durrell Analysis of Reading Difficulty (see appendix A).

An analysis of typical spelling errors and remedial techniques for alleviating spelling difficulties may be found on pages 74–75 of this chapter and on pages 114–15 of chapter 8.

5. E. H. Henderson and S. Templeton, "A Developmental Perspective of Formal Spelling Instruction through Alphabet, Pattern and Meaning," *Elementary School Journal* 86 (1986): 305.

Trial Sessions for Further Diagnostic Information

When formal testing has been completed and the tests analyzed, a fairly clear picture of the student's achievement patterns should emerge. To facilitate evaluation we have devised trial sessions in order to determine which methods are most suitable. Essential as it is to administer standardized tests, the teacher or examiner still does not know, at their conclusion, which methods and materials to recommend for remedial instruction. Also, the student has little understanding of what is actually wrong with his or her reading and in all probability remains apprehensive about the difficulty.

First the teacher tries to relieve the student's anxiety. Then it is vital for the teacher and pupil to discover how the pupil can cope with his or her problem. Not only is enlisting the pupil's participation therapeutic in and of itself, but it serves as powerful motivation for future learning in remedial sessions and in school. Therefore, trial procedures are recommended as an integral part of the diagnostic examination to guide the teacher to the most effective approaches and to demonstrate to the pupil the methods most suited to his or her learning.[6]

In contrast to the controlled standardized test situation, trial procedures are conducted in an informal, spontaneous atmosphere. The teacher tells the student that there are several methods and many kinds of reading matter especially designed to teach those who have similar difficulties. Several appropriate readers or stories are made available to the pupil. The teacher and pupil try them out to decide which ones are most suitable. In presenting reading materials, the teacher encourages the student to react as freely as possible and designate which stories he or she likes and dislikes. When the pupil realizes that he or she can really express an opinion on the selection, even in provocative words, he or she may experience immense relief at finding someone who understands. It is no longer necessary to resist, suffer, or pretend to like meaningless exercises.

The teacher observes whether the pupil is slow or quick to grasp salient points; whether he or she needs a great deal of repetition, support, and encouragement; how well the child recalls what has been read; how much effort he or she puts forth; and so on. However, the whole session is a collaborative one. The teacher explains which techniques seem suitable

6. Trial sessions geared to children reading at primary levels were developed by Albert J. Harris and Florence G. Roswell and published in Harris and Roswell, "Clinical Diagnosis of Reading Disability," *Journal of Psychology* 3 (1953): 323–40. In this volume, the present authors have revised and extended these lessons upward for older students.

and helps the pupil understand his or her problem. The more insight a pupil gains, the more likely it is that he or she will summon the necessary strength to improve. Trial procedures contribute to such insight in a way that the regular test situation cannot. They may be used with pupils at all levels, from beginning reading through high school. The areas to be investigated at the different stages can be divided roughly into reading levels one through three, four through six, seven through nine, and ten through twelve.

Reading Levels One through Three

For a nonreader or one who has mastered few word analysis techniques, the three major word recognition approaches—visual, phonic, and visual-motor—should be tried.[7] If none of these methods is successful, the kinesthetic approach might be used. If it is found that the child can learn by only one of these methods, it is used in treatment merely as a starting point to ensure a successful experience. Before long it must be supplemented by other procedures because a successful reader needs to be able to use a variety of techniques. In addition to finding suitable methods for word recognition, the teacher offers several stories to find the type of reading material that is most acceptable to the child.

VISUAL METHOD

The simple visual approach to word recognition involves learning words by means of picture clues. *If the pupil reads at a second-grade level or above, this procedure is omitted, for it has already been established that he or she is able to use this method.*

Several cards are needed, each with a picture illustrating a well-known object—a book, man, coat, and so on. The identifying noun is printed under the picture. On another set of cards the words are printed without pictures. The pupil is first tested on the cards with the word alone to make sure that they are not already known. After the unknown words are selected, the teacher presents a picture card, pointing to the word and pronouncing it. The pupil is asked to say the word several times while looking at it, then finds the corresponding nonillustrated card containing

7. All these methods are fully described in chapter 8. The teacher should be familiar with the way in which each method is taught. However, for use as a diagnostic technique, they are summarized succinctly in this chapter.

the same word. After five words have been studied in this manner, the pupil is tested with the nonillustrated cards. (If time allows, he or she is retested after a short interval.)

If the pupil can grasp a visual procedure readily and shows some knowledge of letter sounds, the teacher immediately proceeds with step 1 of the phonics approach.

PHONICS APPROACH

STEP 1: WORD FAMILY METHOD. A rudimentary blending technique, sometimes called the word family method, is especially useful with children who are not yet able to cope with a letter-by-letter blending procedure. It affords a limited degree of independence in word analysis. For example, a known word such as *book* may be changed into *took, look,* or *hook* by substituting different initial consonants. Several initial consonants are taught, studied, and combined with the appropriate word ending. Other words learned in the visual lesson may be developed in the same way: *boat, goat.* If the child cannot learn initial sounds readily, it will be necessary to practice the auditory discrimination of letter sounds.

STEP 2: COMBINING SEPARATE SOUNDS. To master the phonics method, the pupil must be able to combine separate sounds to form whole words. To determine whether that skill has been mastered, the teacher first tries an informal auditory blending test without written words. The teacher pronounces one-syllable words slowly and distinctly, emphasizing each sound. The child tries to distinguish other words in this way. If the child can figure them out, he or she has the ability to combine sounds, and it is safe to try the phonics approach.

The teacher reviews the sounds taught under step 1 and then introduces a short vowel sound, for example, by printing the letter *a* and telling the pupil its name and short sound—"ă" as in *apple.* Then the teacher prints a suitable word, like *fat,* to demonstrate how the vowel can be blended with known consonant sounds to form words. Several different consonants are then substituted at the beginning of the word, as in step 1. After the child practices them sufficiently, the teacher changes the final consonants—that is, *fat* to *fan, mat* to *man, sat* to *sad,* and so on—and asks the pupil to sound them out. If the pupil has difficulty, he or she is assisted in blending the sounds together. The teacher then proceeds to a more difficult step: interchanging initial and final consonants alternately. Finally, the teacher presents the most difficult step of all—reading words in mixed order: *mat, fan, sad, bat,* and so on. The degree to which the pupil is able to recognize the words in these progressive steps indicates the kind and amount of phonics work that will be needed in remedial sessions.

VISUAL-MOTOR METHOD

The visual-motor method is tried when students have difficulty reading words that have irregular letter-sound relationships. Essentially, it involves visualizing and writing words from memory. This method, which can be presented in small groups, is fully described on page 100.

KINESTHETIC METHOD

The kinesthetic method has been found useful in helping students recall the spelling of particularly troublesome words because they seem to profit from the added tactile or kinesthetic clues. However, as a method for teaching reading it is applicable only in cases where students have failed to learn by other methods. It is laborious and time consuming because it involves repeated trials in tracing each word taught, and furthermore requires an individualized tutoring situation. This approach is explained on pages 101–2.

Reading Levels Four through Six

For students reading at fourth- through sixth-grade levels, regardless of age, trial sessions include investigation of advanced word analysis techniques, comprehension skills, and reading materials best suited to the student's reading level and interest. As already stated, it is especially important to have appealing reading material so that the student will become genuinely involved in helping to improve reading ability. If the results of standardized tests indicate deficiencies in phonics, the student is shown how he or she will be taught any sounds and combinations that are unfamiliar. If the student has difficulty with spelling, several approaches are tried, such as the visual-motor method, kinesthetic method, or calling attention to distinctive spelling patterns.

The teacher also evaluates the student's knowledge of specialized vocabulary (the technical words connected with the separate subject areas). He or she selects about ten words from the student's texts. Words from a social studies text might include *hemisphere, glacier, technology,* and *primitive.* If the student is unfamiliar with them, the teacher shows how they can be learned through various methods. The meaning is explained, if necessary, through graphic illustrations or vivid explanation. The student finds out how learning the specialized words connected with different subjects can

71

be a big boost to understanding them. He or she realizes that to some extent at least it was not the text but the special vocabulary that was difficult.

A number of workbooks that contain interesting articles to be used for developing comprehension skills are available. The teacher chooses material at a level determined by the student's performance on standardized tests. The student is told that reading these selections will help with understanding the factual material of textbooks. As soon as the student learns how to get information from the articles, he or she will be shown in future lessons how to transfer these skills to textbooks. It is important to discover which workbooks a student likes and which ones may already have been used in school. Since there is a wide choice of appropriate materials, the student is encouraged to find those that he or she can readily accept.

In the same way, the student samples recreational reading that has been carefully chosen. The experienced teacher usually has a few excellent books that he or she knows from past experience are apt to arouse the student's interest.

Still, at times the student may not like any of the selections presented. It is possible to have developed such intense distaste for reading that everything seems tiresome and uninteresting. In such a case, the student needs immediate reassurance, perhaps being told that others sometimes feel the same way. Certain procedures may help the student. For example, very short passages may be used at the start. Also, many different topics should be chosen; sooner or later something will be appealing.

In the end, the student should have a clear idea of which word analysis or comprehension skills are needed and the kinds of material that will be used for remedial instruction. At the end of the session, the student should have become fairly confident that, with help, he or she can improve in reading and progress with less difficulty in school.

Reading Levels Seven through Nine

Students with reading problems whose scores on reading tests range from seventh- through ninth-grade levels vary in age, intelligence, maturity, and interests.

A brief period might profitably be spent answering the questions that must be uppermost in the student's mind. Even more than a younger child, a child in the middle years wants to know the outcome of the evaluation, the meaning of test scores, and above all how he or she can be helped.

The structure of the session and the procedures used are essentially the same as those described for students reading between fourth- and sixth-grade levels. However, the presentation is on a more mature level, and the materials selected are those designed for the student's level of functioning.

Reading Levels Ten through Twelve

The older student is also very much interested in receiving an interpretation of test results and finding out how he or she might be helped.

The major problems are likely to be a slow rate of reading and a lack of flexibility in handling different kinds of material. The teacher will describe what methods and materials might be used to good advantage. Looking over the workbooks, the student will find that they contain articles condensed from high school and college texts. He or she sees how practice with factual articles followed by pertinent questions will prove valuable in handling school texts, as it will teach skills in extracting information quickly and efficiently.

The student is usually struck by the abundance of material available for high school and college students. The effect is usually electric. He or she wants to know what has helped others and how to proceed. Perhaps it has never occurred to the student that so many others have similar problems.

The teacher explains that articles with different formats, varying lengths, and many types of questions will help shift the pace from one kind of reading matter to another. Rate of reading will be guided by purpose, and the student will thus develop flexibility. Time limits may cause anxiety, but the student can be assured that this is a fairly common concern; after a while students become accustomed to a stopwatch and do not notice it. The teacher will give the student some idea of the methods to adopt to speed up reading. (These are discussed in chapter 13.)

At the conclusion of the session, both teacher and student have an overview of the program that will be devised on the basis of individual needs. The student knows where to begin and how to go ahead, aware of how much depends on his or her own efforts even though assistance will be given. Having his or her problem interpreted and described in concrete fashion often offers added incentive and encouragement.

Trial sessions at all levels are extremely helpful in preparing the student for remedial instruction. Instead of leaving the examination with a vague feeling of "something's wrong with my reading," the student knows *what* is wrong. He or she has been shown where help is needed. The teacher has demonstrated how to alleviate the difficulties, and the student has seen the specific methods and materials that are available. Gradually, as the student recognizes the problem and understands what to do about it, he or she becomes more hopeful. Anxiety is lessened, and the foundation is laid for effective remedial treatment.

Trial Sessions in Spelling

Trial sessions in spelling are always included in evaluation. The student learns to be flexible in approaches depending on the spelling pattern of the word. To begin with, the teacher selects four or five misspelled words with different types of errors, either from the student's notebook or from a recent spelling test. Fundamental errors such as *jast* for *just* or *bik* for *bike* suggest the need for basic phonics instruction. There are other common categories of error. For example, if the word in question is *really* and the student writes it as *realy,* the teacher shows the student that the base word is *real* and that the *ly* is a suffix that comes at the end of many words, such as totally, finally, and so on. Such words have a base word that the student can find; the base word needs to be retained in its entirety when *ly* is added.

In the next example the teacher uses the appropriate procedures and explains why different approaches are indicated. For example, when *doesn't* is misspelled *doesent,* the teacher explains that the two words *does not* are put together with an apostrophe to show that a letter is omitted. Other words that illustrate this principle are *don't* for *do not, can't* for *cannot, couldn't* for *could not, you're* for *you are.*

With *understand* written *unnerstan,* precise pronunciation would eventually eliminate the error. Teacher and student try to figure out ways in which to develop more effective listening skills, not only to improve spelling but also to acquire more accurate pronunciation. Sometimes students come up with original procedures that they find helpful in correcting their own spelling.

In the case of irregularly spelled words that do not follow any rules, such as *league* misspelled *leeg,* techniques might include the visual-motor method, the kinesthetic method, and even spelling the word aloud.

Other techniques that the teacher briefly illustrates, depending on the student's spelling level and ability, are how to divide long words, such as *newspaper, nominate,* or *destination,* into syllables. As the student's competency develops he or she will be able to distinguish unique features that aid recall. Also, most spelling books offer simple rules that can clear up certain confusions. The well-known rule of *i* before *e* except after *c* has aided many a person puzzling over spelling.

Students become responsive during trial sessions when they see that they begin to spell correctly the words that they used to miss. In this connection mature students are advised to keep a notebook of alphabetized words that are especially difficult to remember. They are also made aware of available inexpensive paperbacks that list the most frequently misspelled words.

Trial Sessions in Written Expression

For students from about fourth-grade through adult levels, some time is spent evaluating the ability to write. In trial sessions the teacher attempts to show the student ways to improve writing in school assignments. The teacher might elicit several topics from the student, or he or she might ask the student to write a summary of a brief reading selection. The teacher assesses how the student handles the task. If necessary, the teacher provides suggestions. These introductory procedures give the student a preview of ongoing sessions. If successful, such a process usually stimulates a degree of motivation that is absent when the student contemplates wading through more schoolwork. If there is not sufficient time to allow for written work, the student is asked to bring writing samples connected with schoolwork.

The written work produced by the student, whether during the session or at home, is analyzed with regard to coherence, content, sentence and paragraph structure, style, spelling, punctuation, and other relevant features. The teacher discusses these aspects with the student and inquires about any other problems that seem to be interfering with writing ability.

Taking into consideration the student's own assessment of his or her needs and the teacher's analysis of the work, the teacher outlines an appropriate program for future sessions. Since most students need a great deal of reassurance about their writing ability, the initial discussion can be particularly meaningful.

During the trial sessions realistic goals are set and the teacher chooses the procedures to be followed according to the student's instructional needs. If the student genuinely feels that he or she has profited from the varied approaches, he or she leaves with a hopeful outlook and in most cases is eager to obtain the recommended help.

75

Diagnosis

Suggestions for Further Reading

Chall, J. S., and Curtis, M. E. "What Clinical Diagnosis Tells Us about Children's Reading." *Reading Teacher* 40 (April 1987).

Feuerstein, R., et al. "Learning Potential Assessment." *Special Services in the Schools* 2 (Winter/ Spring 1985–86).

Goodman, Y.; Watson, D. J.; and Burke, C. L. *Reading Miscue Inventory: Alternative Procedures.* New York: R. C. Owen, 1987.

Harding, L. M. "Reading Errors and Style in Children with Specific Reading Disability." *Journal of Research in Reading* 7 (September 1984).

Harris, L. A., and Lalik, R. M. "Teachers' Use of Informal Reading Inventories: An Example of School Constraints." *Reading Teacher* 40 (March 1987).

Jansky, J. "The Clinician in the Classroom: A First-Grade Intervention Study." *Bulletin of the Orton Society* 31 (1981).

Sapir, S. G. *The Clinical Teaching Model: Clinical Insights and Strategies for the Learning Disabled Child.* New York: Brunner-Mazel, 1985.

Silver, A. A., and Hagin, R. A. *SEARCH: A Scanning Instrument for the Identification of Potential Learning Disability,* 2d ed. New York: Walker, 1981.

Vellutino, F. R., and Shub, M. J. "Assessment of Disorders in Formal School Language." *Topics in Learning Disorders* 2 (September 1982).

Weinstein, C. E. "Fostering Learning Autonomy through the Use of Learning Strategies." *Journal of Reading* 30 (April 1987).

Ysseldyke, J. E., and Algozzine, B. "Where to Begin in Diagnosing Reading Problems." *Topics in Learning and Learning Disabilities* 2 (January 1983).

6

Diagnostic Procedures and Recommendations for Treatment

THIS CHAPTER describes how the reading examinations discussed in chapter 5 can be extended for students with more serious learning difficulties. Most students who come to the attention of the specialist either have not responded sufficiently to educational procedures or have displayed deviant behavior. The term *specialist* refers to anyone responsible for the diagnosis of students with reading and related problems. Usually it is social workers and psychologists who investigate those factors for which they are professionally trained, such as personality disturbance, intelligence level, and neurological components.

Diagnosing Learning Difficulty

OBTAINING BACKGROUND INFORMATION

The social worker or psychologist gathers background information for a complete case history. The specialist also determines the possibility of neurological dysfunction, basic emotional disturbance, or other factors related to educational difficulties. The evaluator must obtain as complete a history as possible, paying special attention to (a) conditions at birth, early infancy, and childhood with special reference to the possibility of central nervous system dysfunction, (b) speech development, (c) school experiences and attitudes toward reading, (d) the possibility of converted handedness, (e) attitude of the family toward the difficulty, (f) the amount and kind of help that has been provided by the family and the school, and (g) the presence of related difficulties in other members of the family.

Evidence of severe emotional difficulty is investigated, particularly of any disturbance that developed before the child entered school. Such symptoms as bed-wetting, feeding problems, recurrent nightmares, stuttering, excessive fearfulness, and phobic reactions offer important diagnostic clues as to the possible origin and degree of the emotional problem.

School attitudes are important, too, beginning with the child's reaction toward nursery school, kindergarten, first grade, and so forth, as well as the teacher's impression and the child's attitudes toward his or her teachers. It is also useful to know the parents' attitude toward the child's difficulty, teachers, and current educational methodology. Parents' attitudes also may reveal the ways in which the child is handled at school and at home.

INTELLIGENCE

It is important to establish as valid a measure of intelligence as possible. Verbal and performance tests such as the Stanford-Binet Intelligence Scale, the Wechsler Intelligence Scale for Children, and the Wechsler Adult Intelligence Scale (appendix A) are usually selected at appropriate levels. In order to arrive at a rough approximation of the difficulty, a comparison is made between the child's reading achievement and potential. This indicates a measure known as *reading expectancy* (see page 58). Reading expectancy scores must always be interpreted broadly since they are influenced by the amount of schooling and the degree of experience of the child as well as the probable errors of test measurements. For example, a seven-year-old boy with a mental age of ten years can only in theory be expected to read as well as the average ten-year-old, because he has not had the same amount of academic exposure or comparable years of experience. He would, however, be expected to read considerably better than the average seven-year-old.

PHYSICAL FACTORS

Physical problems may directly or indirectly influence a child's ability to focus attention on learning. Therefore, a medical examination is frequently indicated to determine whether any physical condition may be causing or contributing to the learning problem. The school nurse or the social worker needs to be consulted for such referrals.

It is important in any case that relevant findings be reported to the specialist in charge of the case so that he or she can integrate all diagnostic information.

NEUROLOGICAL FACTORS

The psychologist as a member of a team or as an independent specialist undertakes the evaluation of neurological development according to his or her professional training and expertise. The areas to be assessed are clearly designated in chapter 3 and generally include language development, visual-motor coordination, integrative capacity, sequencing, orientation, visual and auditory memory, abstract thinking, information processing, and attention span. If according to the examiner's judgment further investigation is indicated, the student is referred for neurological examination.

A precise differential diagnosis between neurological and psychological problems is frequently difficult to ascertain because symptoms are often similar. The case of Paul, which follows, shows how hard it is to distinguish between psychological and neurological causes.

PAUL—THE DIFFICULTY OF DIAGNOSIS

It was eventually discovered that Paul's difficulty was neurological in nature. However, because of the unmistakable presence of psychogenic factors, Paul's reading disability was at first treated primarily as an emotional problem.

Paul was nine years old when he was first referred for diagnosis. He was repeating second grade because of his extreme difficulty in learning to read. (His reading was at high first grade level.) His birth and developmental history were within the normal range. His speech had been somewhat immature until the age of seven. There was no indication of neurological impairment on any of the psychological tests. The reading tests revealed that he had marked difficulty in synthesizing sounds to form words, a strong tendency to reverse letters such as *b* and *d,* and a tendency to confuse left and right. Projective tests revealed Paul to be very dependent and immature, with a great deal of anxiety and an extremely weak ego. In addition, it was learned that Paul's mother was overprotective and very controlling. Because the problem seemed to be primarily due to emotional factors, psychotherapy was instituted.

After one year, no appreciable improvement had taken place in his schoolwork. Paul still read at a high first grade level, although he was scheduled to enter third grade the following fall and was close to ten years of age. Diagnostic instruments that previously had not been used were administered to search further for possible causes. His poor performance on some of these tests strongly pointed to the possibility of neurological impairment. Most revealing of all was Paul's continued inability to blend sounds, his faulty memory, and his tendency to confuse and reverse letters in reading and writing. He repeatedly transposed sequences in writing, such as *rnu* for *run, hwo* for *who,* and even *Plau* for *Paul.* Therefore, a complete neurological examination was undertaken. The findings of this examination, which included an electroencephalogram, were positive. The results of this investigation further suggested that Paul's emotional problems—his insecurity, immaturity, weak ego, and anxiety—were probably reactions to a neurological disorder. Paul was subsequently placed in a class for children with learning disabilities in which special educational techniques were employed.

This example is but one of many that show the advantage in using all the means at the psychologist's disposal to ensure an accurate estimate of emotional factors and their possible causes. Such a combination of symptoms supports the advisability of a referral for a neurological examination.

EDUCATIONAL FACTORS

School has a major influence on our development because we spend so great a portion of our life there. Experiences such as frequent moves from school to school, absences, or shifts in teachers may have an adverse effect. In considering other school influences it is advisable to observe children of all ages while they are engaged in academic and free-time school activities, with particular focus on interpersonal relationships in the classroom.

During a school visit the social worker or psychologist needs to observe whether pupils show poor concentration, restlessness, or difficulty in recalling recently obtained information. Does the teacher perhaps label them dyslexic or learning disabled and believe that he or she does not have sufficient background to cope with the problem? Does the teacher show concern, or does frustration impede constructive efforts? Has he or she used materials that are suitable to the pupils' maturity and reading level? Is the teacher free to devise an individualized program for the child? Is the classroom atmosphere so permissive that it lacks appropriate structure, or is it so inflexible that pupils exhibit tension under stress? Other factors to be observed are the role played by covert attitudes and dynamic interactions in the classroom. Observation aids in gaining perspective about the weight of each contributing factor.

What part do parents play in all the interactions related to school? Are they resentful of what they regard as the school's role in their youngster's failure? As one mother complained, "Why can't the school teach my child to read?"

If the child is receiving remedial instruction, how is he or she reacting to it? Are sound procedures being used? Does the problem lie in the child, the teaching techniques, or the teacher? What can be done? How can the teachers help? School personnel need to be aware of the situation and see that assistance is made available.

Making Recommendations in Relation to the Diagnosis

Beyond specific suggestions for remedial instruction, as outlined in chapter 5, recommendations need to be as useful as possible. The examiner needs to consider the possible causes of the reading difficulty and then emphasize the student's strengths. In this connection additional services need to be considered.

Many diagnoses must of necessity remain tentative. Children continue to grow and develop, and their present difficulty may gradually disappear due to a number of intervening factors. It has been found, for example, that many disturbed children who are given remedial instruction but no psychotherapeutic treatment make substantial progress in emotional adjustment as well as in reading. And some individuals who show extreme difficulty in learning are eventually able to read adequately despite their handicaps.

Mainstreaming and Supportive Services

Schools now provide various possibilities for students who have learning difficulties. This is the result of Public Law 94-142 (1975), which mandated an appropriate educational program in the least restrictive environment for all students with handicapping conditions. This practice is called *mainstreaming*. In mainstreaming the focus is on the learning needs of the child and how they are best met in existing programs of regular education and support services.[1] This means that most children remain in general education but if special services are required, such as counseling, speech therapy, physical therapy, or help with academic skills, they receive such services to the extent feasible. Included in mainstreaming are students who have

1. K. Kavale, *Exceptional Child* 20 (March 1979).

been in special education classes and are now considered ready for general education.

THE RESOURCE ROOM*

The resource room is a place to which students with academic difficulties are referred. There can be one or more resource rooms in a school depending on students' needs. The teachers are trained in the discipline of special education. Students recommended for this resource must demonstrate significant academic difficulties. Generally students must be one or two grade levels below their expected achievement in one or more of the following areas: reading, communication, mathematics, and study skills. Students in need of special services are usually identified by the classroom teacher, a member of the educational staff, or a family member.

When appropriate the student is referred to an interdisciplinary team known by a title such as the student based support team (SBST), the child study team, or by a similar designation. The team consists in the main of a social worker, educational evaluator, and psychologist. Additional consultants may be called in where indicated. The most suitable member of the team meets with the classroom teacher or parent to decide if a special education service is indicated. If referral to the resource room is advisable, a social history is taken from a parent, who also signs a release for the student to be tested. The educational evaluator and psychologist collaborate in administering a comprehensive examination. Subsequently the findings of the examination and plans for treatment are discussed with the parent.

If the student is eligible for resource room services he or she is certified by the team. Scheduling and other factors are spelled out. Students attend the resource room for at least three hours a week but no more than three hours a day. An IEP (individual educational plan) is prepared for each student by the team. This is followed by a long-term plan drawn up by the classroom teacher. These plans are reviewed yearly by the classroom and resource room teachers. At the end of a three-year period the student is reevaluated by the team. Where space permits, resource room services are available for short-term treatment of at-risk students.

THE READING TEACHER

Reading teachers are another available resource for students with reading problems. The kinds of services they provide depend on administrative

*The information pertaining to the resource room was kindly supplied by Peggy McNamara, Teacher Consultant, Special Education Support Program, Board of Education of the City of New York.

directives from states, cities, or school districts. These might include special assistance for classroom teachers to help students individually or in small groups, either in pull-out programs or in the classroom. Paraprofessionals who help students with reading difficulties might also profit from these services. It is not within the scope of this book to discuss those children who need to learn English as a second language (ESL); the administrative staff is often able to see that available services are open to these children. ESL teachers, for example, are an invaluable source for helping classroom teachers work effectively with children who have difficulty reading and writing English.

Additional alternatives include referring certain students to outside clinics connected with mental health centers or to colleges that have training practicums for teaching children with reading difficulty. In addition, there may be occasion to refer some students to private clinicians who will coordinate their work with the school.

THE REGULAR EDUCATION INITIATIVE

During the past few years a movement that is finding support among educators is the regular education initiative, commonly referred to as REI. Its advocates are critical of the way educational problems of mildly handicapped students are handled through current mainstreaming practices. For example, such students are selectively removed from their regular classes for instruction in either resource rooms or for other services (referred to as pull-out programs). They maintain that these practices set such students apart from their classmates and stigmatize them.[2]

Furthermore, through mainstreaming there are large numbers of students who need extra services but are not eligible for them under the terms of a categorical program.[3] (Such requirements are described in this chapter's section on resource rooms.) Besides, labels or categories are often irrelevant to instructional needs and may prevent more meaningful understanding and treatment of students' psychoeducational needs.

Stephen Lilly suggests that there are more effective ways to deal with the education of mildly handicapped children in their regular classrooms, thereby limiting the use of special placements[4]: "Supportive services are needed that are based in regular education. . . . A single coordinated system

2. M. C. Will, "Educating Children with Learning Problems—A Shared Responsibility," *Exceptional Children* (February 1986).

3. "A Statement of the National Coalition for Students and the National Association of School Psychologists," *Education Week*, December 4, 1985.

4. S. M. Lilly, "The Relationship between General and Special Education: A New Face on an Old Issue," *Counterpoint* (March 1985): 10.

of service delivery is preferable to the array of special programs currently offered in the schools."

Critics of the REI proposal suggest that the issues raised are highly complex and need careful examination. They express doubts as to whether the present educational system, so widely criticized in national surveys for its failure to handle the general population, would be able to cope with students with special needs.[5] They further point out that since learning disabled students comprise such a heterogeneous population, regular classroom teachers do not have the training to be able to handle them.[6] Even those teachers who possess such expertise would rarely be able to find time to do justice to the rest of the class. Still others note that there are teachers who are competent in regular education but who may resent having to work with children who are so difficult to teach. Furthermore, many reformers who advocate curriculum changes stress the need for greater demands on pupils for achievement. Such approaches frequently go counter to programs that require pacing the instruction according to students' ability to process information and grasp what is being taught. Whether all students with learning difficulties whose problems range from mild to severe can be adequately served in general education is open to question.

In summary, how to improve services for students with learning difficulties presents many complex issues. The problems currently posed by the present system of mainstreaming and proposed changes in REI require thorough exploration. We need continuing research and experimental trial programs. Any recommended reforms need to be based on sound research findings. And the results will need systematic and periodic reevaluation.

Suggestions for Further Reading

Abrams, J. C. "Interaction of Neurological and Emotional Factors in Learning Disability." *Learning Disabilities: An Interdisciplinary Journal* 3 (March 1984).

de Hirsch, K., and Jansky, J. "Patterning and Organizational Deficits in Children with Language and Learning Disabilities." *Bulletin of the Orton Society* 30 (1980).

Gartner, A. "Disabling Help: Special Education at the Crossroads." *Exceptional Children* 53 (1986): 72–76.

Madden, N. A., and Slavin, R. E. "Mainstreaming Students with Mild Handicaps: Academic and Social Outcomes." *Review of Educational Research* 53 (1983): 519–69.

Paratore, J. R., and Indrisano, R. "Intervention Assessment of Reading Comprehension." *The Reading Teacher* 40 (April 1987).

5. B. Keogh, "Improving Services for Problem Learners: Rethinking and Restructuring," *Journal of Learning Disabilities* 21 (January 1988).

6. T. Bryan, M. Bay, and M. Donahue, "Implications of the Learning Disabilities Definition for the Regular Education Initiative," *Journal of Learning Disabilities* 21 (January 1988).

Robinson, Alan H., and Schatzberg, Kathleen, "The Development of Effective Teaching." In *Becoming Readers in a Complex Society,* edited by A. Purves and U. Niles. Chicago: University of Chicago Press, 1984.

Schumaker, J. B., and Hazel, S. J. "Social Skills Assessment and Training for the Learning Disabled." *Journal of Learning Disabilities* 17 (August/September 1984) and (October 1984).

Sizer, T. *Horace's Compromise: The Dilemma of the American High School.* Boston: Houghton Mifflin, 1988.

Snow, R. E. "Individual Differences and the Designs of Educational Programs." *American Psychologist* 41 (1988): 1029–39.

Wang, E. C., and Baker, E. T. "Mainstreaming Programs in Design Features and Effects." *Journal of Special Education* 19 (1983): 503.

Ysseldyke, J. E. "Current Practices in Making Psychoeducational Decisions about Learning Disabled Students." *Journal of Learning Disabilities* 16 (April 1983).

Part III

Treatment

7

Interweaving
Psychotherapeutic Principles
with Teaching Procedures

Good TEACHING has far-reaching therapeutic results. Throughout the ages, teachers such as Moses, Confucius, Plato, Rousseau, and Dewey have had immeasurable influence on their students. As Henry Adams said, "A teacher affects eternity; he can never tell where his influence stops."[1] Teachers who work with students with learning difficulty also have effected remarkable changes in the lives of their pupils. Their influence is crucial and can make the difference between the success and failure of an entire life. It is not the techniques of instruction that are of such lasting influence; it is the attention, inspiration, and understanding the students receive that help them overcome the massive frustration, despair, and resentment they have stored for so long. When positive feelings come to the fore, students are finally able to use capacities that had been misdirected or lying dormant.

We realize that those who work with students with reading difficulty apply many of the basic principles of psychotherapy, perhaps without being aware of them. To make the process more conscious and perhaps more effective, we shall elaborate some of the fundamental principles that are inherent in any good teaching situation.

1. *The Education of Henry Adams* (New York: Modern Library, 1931), p. 300.

Establishing a Relationship

One of the cardinal principles of psychotherapy is to develop a good relationship. The teacher achieves this through accepting the student as a human being worthy of respect, regardless of his or her "failure." A good relationship also encompasses a collaborative spirit within a planned structure, compassion without overinvolvement, understanding without indulgence, and a genuine concern for the student's development.

Teachers are troubled by pupils who do not learn satisfactorily. Not only do they consider it a burden to deal with the "slow" ones in their classes, but they feel that lack of progress is somehow their fault and a reflection on their teaching ability. It is understandable that teachers frown on problem cases because they require extra attention. In addition, their low test scores bring down the class average. Remedial teachers also share some of these feelings. Although they do not have to worry about lowered class averages, they are under pressure to have their pupils improve because they need to justify their very existence to administrators by showing overall gains. Hence, concern over pupils' improvement can undermine teachers' confidence. When a teacher's confidence is impaired, it is difficult to show approval to the poor achiever. As a result, the pupil feels uncomfortable and fearful of the teacher. This can cause an even greater drop in performance.

Anna Freud has commented on children who equate receiving good grades in school with being loved and failure with being unloved and worthless. Even if such drastic comparisons are not made, certainly children who get poor report cards again and again lose status with all those on whom they depend for affection and approval. They may develop a kind of free-floating anxiety toward schoolwork—always dreading it, always anticipating failure. Since pupils with learning problems live in an atmosphere of rejection and disapproval, they often conclude that they have no ability or talent, that they are good for nothing, and that they rate no recognition whatsoever.

If these pupils feel so defeated and teachers feel so burdened by them, what can be done? Teachers need to realize that they are not personally responsible for lack of progress. They must understand that pupils' weaknesses are simply a reality that must be remedied. When teachers realize that their own status is not threatened, they are in a better position to accept the pupils. They can recognize pupils' ultimate potentialities, not present achievement. To paraphrase Goethe, the child is treated not as he is but as he can become.

Collaboration

Teachers may know the best methods and materials but need to find those most suitable for a particular reading program. They try many approaches, and as the teachers and students work together, the teachers can determine by the students' responses which work well and which do not.

In reading, for example, teachers choose the grade level of the materials, but the choice of subject matter may often be left to pupils—would they prefer sports stories, science fiction, or folktales? At the lower levels, perhaps students may be permitted to make a selection from two or three suitable readers. If teachers wish to use certain books for specific reasons, the choice will be up to them. But pupils continue to participate even when teachers assume full leadership. For older students, the choice of materials depends on their expressed needs with regard to vocational goals, subject matter, or other aspects of functioning. Thus teachers do not insist on preconceived plans and students participate in the collaborative experience.

Treating poor performance in a matter-of-fact way, as something that will eventually respond to one alternative or another, often relieves pupils' anxiety. Problems that heretofore have been vague and mysterious become evident and tangible. Pupils may be able to view their problem more objectively and accept a reasonable responsibility for it. The tone of a session should remain cooperative throughout, with pupil and teacher entering into a give-and-take relationship.

Structure

Besides knowing what is expected, students become aware of what is acceptable behavior and what is not. Although strong reactions during the sessions are welcomed, students are not allowed to be destructive or unrestrained.

Structure is even more important than limits in teaching disturbed individuals, since it introduces order into their chaotic lives. Children who come from unstable, inconsistent environments, where they do not know what to expect from one minute to the next, can be transformed from perverse, boisterous pupils to orderly, manageable ones as soon as they get accustomed to a routine that they understand and appreciate. However, if they are not adequately prepared for a shift in plan, they may revert to their former agitated behavior.

Planning also eliminates discussion and disagreements over which activities should be performed and in what order. For example, children lose respect or become confused by being asked what they want to do next or which activity they wish to choose.[2] A child's natural reaction is, "If you don't know which book I should read, how am I expected to know?" Lack of direction and continued floundering of the teacher must be very disappointing to one who comes for remedial instruction hoping for help. Moreover, if students are given considerable leeway, too much time may be spent on unimportant activities. Lack of direction also places unwarranted responsibility on children. Furthermore, in an unstructured setting, either their aggression may get out of hand or they may sit and do nothing.

Therefore the atmosphere should be neither too permissive nor too rigid. As a criterion, teachers use rational authority based on competence. Children are given freedom within reasonable limits.

After the sessions have been planned by a teacher in the best interests of the child, the question arises, "What happens if the pupil does not abide by the plan?" In a good teaching program, in which methods and material are suited to the child and a collaborative spirit prevails, this difficulty rarely occurs. When it does, the teacher can shift to one of the child's favored activities. If this is insufficient, a frank discussion that reveals the teacher's acceptance of occasional deviant behavior not only relieves the pupil's guilt but enhances the human element in the relationship. Continued lack of cooperation, however, needs to be understood and treated.

Sincerity

Students detect immediately whether a teacher has sincere and honest attitudes. In discussing this subject, one of our graduate students exclaimed that she knew one "must never display annoyance or disapproval." However, children soon catch the insincere undertones of this attitude, no matter how much the teacher tries to conceal them. Thus honest appraisal is necessary. If the child's work is poor, the teacher tries to minimize anxiety about errors and inconsistencies by telling him or her that many children have had similar difficulties and that they are unavoidable at his or her present stage. The teacher might add that it is not the errors that are so important but how to overcome them. He or she assures the student that ultimately most students improve. Children often appear incredulous when they are treated in this way, because they are so used

2. C. Dahlberg, F. Roswell, and J. Chall, "Psychotherapeutic Principles as Applied to Remedial Reading," *Elementary School Journal* 53 (1952): 213.

to being corrected, reprimanded, or given poor grades because they do not respond to instruction.

The teacher should also encourage children to work mainly for themselves, not for anyone else. It is their life that will be affected if they do not learn. Particularly in cases of learning difficulty, where motivation is so important, children must be led to recognize the importance of work. They benefit from the support of a friendly, sincere ally with whom they share their efforts and their difficulties. But in the long run, they must become totally involved in the task.

Success

Obviously, achieving success in reading or other subjects is paramount for children in remedial treatment. But can a teacher provide experiences that engender these feelings merely by preparing a suitable program and materials? With reading difficulty, for instance, it is not simple. Although all competent teachers know that materials must be within the range of pupils' ability, they know, too, that they dare not risk permitting them to fail. Does that mean that the material students are given must be so easy that they will never miss a word? Does it mean that children should never be permitted to falter? Many teachers reflect accepted pedagogy when they answer, "Children with learning difficulty should be given material at least one year below their reading level; they must succeed!" Yet a feeling of success is not always achieved through giving children easy materials that can be completed without error.

Building up feelings of success in these defeated children is a complex problem that has long been oversimplified by learning specialists and educators. Ted, for instance, is ten years old, in the fifth grade. He is of average intelligence but is reading at the third-grade level. A book one year below his reading level will be a second-grade book. Will reading this make Ted feel successful? It will be hard enough to find even a third-grade book that will be sufficiently mature. More important, Ted needs to know that reading words incorrectly is not fatal, that a certain amount of unevenness is to be expected, and that he will not be reprimanded for his mistakes. As long as the teacher supplies unknown words while he reads aloud, Ted can use third- or possibly fourth-grade books (although for independent reading it would be advisable to suggest books at third-grade level, which he can read with little or no assistance).

Children need stimulation. Their curiosity and interest need to be constantly aroused and furthered. Handling easy material perfectly is less rewarding than making errors in stimulating stories—provided, of course, that the children are receiving instruction in developing the necessary reading skills.

Are there cases in which offering more difficult material may be harmful? Yes, very definitely. As in all remedial work, nothing is ever absolutely right or wrong. Everything depends on the needs and the vulnerability of the students. One must assess their capacity for making mistakes without becoming extremely upset. There are some individuals who have suffered so drastically because of their failure that misreading words arouses the dread of failing. Furthermore, nonreaders who are fourteen or older cannot possibly be given materials sufficiently challenging for them. In these cases, the teacher explains that the simple books will be put aside as soon as possible.

Interests

The chances of success are increased through providing reading materials that are based on children's interest. However, determining true interests is not easy. Many children with reading difficulty have only transitory interests or no interests at all. Sometimes the teacher uses an interest inventory or asks pupils what activities they especially enjoy—sports, horses, doll or stamp collecting, movies, and so on. In order to please the teacher, a pupil may name one at random. Unsuspecting teachers may attempt to find materials based on this false response. They try hard to find exciting articles about the topic, but to get information within the desired reading level is almost impossible.

In fact, these students' knowledge, based on television and other visual media, so far surpasses what they can read that they are utterly bored with the selections presented. We have observed teachers, in their attempts to coordinate material with interests, exhaust all available resources, only to end up exhausting themselves and, no doubt, the children.

Even when appealing selections on a specific interest are discovered, they are useful only for a short while or as an introduction. If pursued, they become too narrow and confining. Reading competency cannot be built merely on sports, mystery stories, or any other single category. Gradually, children need to read varied materials. Careful observation of actual reactions offers the best and safest clues about their true interests.

The Use of Bibliotherapy

For many years, the authors have been closely observing students' reactions to the themes of stories. They have noted their sheer delight and excitement with particular material. They have been impressed, too, with the opportunity for the development of personality and of the pupil–teacher relationship afforded by these stories.

Certain themes seem to have universal appeal for children as well as grown-ups. For instance, the Cinderella story has been woven into adult and children's plays, novels, and movies throughout the years. It has maintained its appeal because so many of us can identify with ill treatment, and our wishes are fulfilled in the happy ending.

In children's books, there are various versions of the pathetic figure who is victorious in the end. One story that is especially satisfying is "Boots and His Brothers," in which Boots is always the underdog—the child rejected by his brothers as well as his parents. The king is faced with an impossible situation. He becomes so desperate that he offers half his kingdom and the princess in marriage to the one who solves his problem. Boots inevitably performs all the difficult tasks and conquers all obstacles in the end. Boys and girls are intrigued with this story. Frequently they ask to read more like it and their resistance to books begins to lessen.

Humorous stories often help children to relax. When the teacher and pupil share genuine laughter, a free and easy situation conducive to learning is encouraged.

Biographical sketches are apt to provoke dramatic reactions, particularly those that depict a hero who rises above disaster. These and other moving themes have a profound effect on those with reading difficulty because they identify so strongly with those who suffer misfortune.

The term *bibliotherapy* sometimes refers to reading as a means for promoting personality development. Sometimes a child identifies so strongly with a character in a story that dramatic changes take place. Thus the psychotherapeutic principles in remedial reading are not something diffuse and intangible. Developing contact with others, achieving academic success, and inducing constructive attitudes toward work for its own sake diminish feelings of failure, discomfort, and misery. Then dormant attitudes such as perseverance, hope, and application can come to the surface. This type of remedial treatment can be one of the most provocative, stirring experiences in the child's life.

We do not focus so much on "success." There is enough pressure for that. We try to mitigate such pressures by emphasizing the child's reactions to his or her predicament. Perhaps the child can accept not being near the top of the class. The child may even come to understand that being on top is precarious—that one can so easily be toppled. We encourage the child to make a contribution in his or her own way and to accept himself or herself as much as possible. If we as adults condone our own strengths and limitations and gain some peace thereby, perhaps the child or adolescent may catch our attitude and learn to deal with life in a satisfying and fortifying way.

Suggestions for Further Reading

Bohning, G. "Bibliotherapy: Fitting the Resources Together." *Elementary School Journal* 82 (November 1981).

Cornett, C. E., and Cornett, C. F. *Bibliotherapy: The Right Book at the Right Time.* (Bloomington, Ind.: Phi Delta Kappa Educational Foundation, 1980).

Edwards, P. A., and Simpson, L. "Bibliotherapy: A Strategy for Communication between Parents and Their Children." *Journal of Reading* 30 (November 1986).

Larrick, N. "Random Notes on Recent Research Reflecting on Children's Reading." Paper presented at the International Reading Association Conference, Anaheim, Calif., May 1983.

Pardeck, J. T., and Pardeck, J. A. "Helping Children Cope with the Changing Family through Bibliotherapy." Paper presented at the Annual Meeting of the National Association of Social Workers, January 31–February 3, 1985.

———. *Young People with Problems: A Guide to Bibliotherapy.* Westport, Conn.: Greenwood Press, 1984.

———, compilers. *Books for Early Childhood: A Developmental Perspective.* Westport, Conn.: Greenwood Press, 1986.

Schrank, F. A. "Bibliotherapy as an Elementary School Counseling Tool." *Elementary School Guidance and Counseling* 16 (February 1982).

Strupp, H. H. "Psychotherapy: Research, Practice and Public Policy (How to Avoid Dead Ends)." *American Psychologist* 41 (February 1986).

8

Teaching Word
Recognition Methods

COMPETENCE in word recognition methods is basic in learning to read. There is no one method that is more effective than others. Indeed, the overreliance on any one approach impedes the ability to develop fluency in reading. Therefore, children need to learn a variety of strategies: whole-word recognition, sound blending techniques, identification of larger units within words, and ways to figure out words using context clues.

Innumerable cases have come to our attention of children who were so firmly attached to one particular method that they were completely at a loss to handle words that did not conform to the only approach they knew. This was especially apparent when teachers or parents had stressed the learning of letter sounds as the key to mastering reading. Despite their good grasp of basic phonic skills, many of these children could not handle even a pre-primer; as soon as they met phonically irregular words, their single strategy led to confusion and frustration. Furthermore, in the course of remedial instruction, it was extremely difficult to help them overcome this firmly entrenched approach. Therefore, from the outset, flexibility in word recognition skills needs to be emphasized.

The objective in teaching word analysis techniques is to help children learn to read and derive meaning from what they read. This chapter describes the basic word analysis skills that are necessary for pupils of any age and grade level to develop competence in reading. Chapter 9 shows how these skills may be adapted for pupils of varying ages, both individually and in a classroom. Although word recognition is never separated from understanding, for purposes of clarification we elaborate comprehension techniques separately in chapter 10.

The Sequence of Word Recognition Instruction in Remedial Reading

Although many word recognition skills in remedial reading are the same as those in a regular program, there are certain major differences. In the usual program, sometimes known as the developmental reading program, a large number of skills are presented according to a systematic plan. In remedial reading, however, instruction is simplified. The number of skills is cut to a minimum to make it easier for those who have already been unsuccessful for at least a year.

Reading authorities disagree about which skills in remedial reading are most important and which sequence is most effective. The authors favor the sequence of skills listed in table 8-1. Of this sequence only the skills

Table 8-1

Word Analysis Skills for Remedial Reading
(In Suggested Sequence for Teaching)

---

1. *Sight words*
   a. The ninety-five most common nouns (see appendix C)
   b. The basic sight vocabulary of 220 words (see appendix C)
2. *Initial consonants—s, d, m, t, h, p, f, c, r, b, l, n, g, w, j, k, v, y, z.*
   Four or five initial consonant sounds are taught at a time, along with one vowel sound.
3. *Short vowel sounds—a, i, o, u, e* (one at a time)
4. *Consonant digraphs—sh, ch, th*
5. *Consonant blends—sp, st, sk, tr, gr, cl, fl*
6. *Long vowel sounds.* These are taught in conjunction with the two vowel rules that follow.
   a. *The silent e.* When *e* is added at the end of a one-syllable word, it usually is silent and makes the first vowel long, e.g., *at, ate; bit, bite.*
   b. *Vowel digraphs.* When two vowels come together, the first is usually long and the second silent, e.g., *paid, seat.*
7. *Syllabication.* The two major rules follow.
   a. In case of two adjacent consonants, the syllables are divided between them, e.g., run-ning, bas-ket.
   b. When two consonants are not found together, the word is divided after the first vowel, e.g., ta-ken, mo-tor.

NOTE: Examples suitable for older students, using the same methods of word recognition, are presented in chapter 12.

that the pupils do not already know are taught. Thus we first identify the gaps in the pupils' word recognition skills and adapt the program accordingly. This streamlined procedure keeps pupils' discouragement to a minimum while it promotes rapid and effective progress. Instead of being given an undue number of lessons on rules and techniques, pupils are allowed as much time as possible to read stories and books. The pride of continued accomplishment—even though the reading may remain somewhat uneven—often encourages children to develop more proficiency.

The specific word analysis skills form a basis for figuring out many unknown words. Poor readers who do not know fifty to a hundred sight words, such as *were, always,* and *same,* learn those that are introduced in the easy materials they are using. More advanced readers learn any of the basic sight words that they do not already know—perhaps five to ten at a time. In addition, the teacher introduces letter sounds that need practice. The teacher presents one vowel sound simultaneously with the sounds of four or five consonants. This allows practice with the phonic approach as soon as possible. Once the children learn the additional skills listed in table 8-1 and apply them in their reading, they seem to learn more rapidly any other word recognition skills they may need.

Teaching Word Recognition

In introducing word analysis skills, sight words are usually taught first. These words make up a large part of the material children meet in their books—for example, *this, their, what, whose, come, many.* They are called *sight words* because the pupil must learn to recognize them at a glance. They occur so frequently that the inability to recognize them prevents fluency. Pupils are encouraged to recognize such words in their entirety rather than sound them out. Many of them cannot be figured out phonically; many are similar in configuration; many are abstract and elusive in meaning. Often they are difficult to learn.

The teacher can refer to any one of the several published lists of sight words to decide which words warrant special study. Dolch's lists of the 220 words that comprise the basic sight vocabulary and the most common nouns are reproduced in appendix C. Other widely used word lists are those of Robert Hillerich,[1] and Albert Harris and Milton Jacobson.[2] There

1. R. L. Hillerich, "240 Starter Words: A Basic Reading Vocabulary, Getting It All Together," *The Reading Teacher* 27 (January 1974): 353–60.
2. A. J. Harris and M. Jacobson, *Basic Reading Vocabularies* (New York: Macmillan, 1982).

are several ways of teaching sight words: the visual, the visual-motor, and the kinesthetic methods.

THE VISUAL METHOD

The visual method consists of exposing words again and again until the pupils learn to identify them by their general configuration. Children with reading difficulty tend to have problems perceiving accurately and are likely to confuse words of similar shape. Such pupils frequently can learn words in isolation and yet be unable to recognize them in context. They may know the words one day and forget them the next; they may recognize them in one sentence and mispronounce them a few lines later in a different context. Adults often show similar difficulty in associating faces and names. For example, one may know the face and name of one's letter carrier, yet be unable to recall her name or to identify her if one sees her at the movies. Pupils need to see sight words in a variety of contexts until the word is firmly fixed in their minds. For this reason, sight words are presented in as many different ways as possible—in picture cards, stories, games, workbooks, and worksheets.

Picture Cards   In presenting sight words, teachers may use commercially prepared or homemade picture-word cards. They choose nouns that are unfamiliar to the children but that represent well-known objects. Each word is printed under a picture. (If the teacher makes the cards, the pictures may be cut from magazines.) Another set of cards is made with the words alone. The children look at the picture card first, pronouncing the appropriate words. Then they match the word-only card to its illustrated counterpart. The picture card is then removed and the children try to say the printed word. This is repeated several times.

Each child can keep a pack of picture-word cards and practice them alone until they are learned. The illustration serves as a self-checking device. The child can also compile an individual picture dictionary, drawing or cutting out pictures corresponding to the words.

Stories   To improve carry over from isolated word practice to recognition of the same words in context, emphasis is placed on sentences and stories that use these words. The children are given the most interesting books that can be found at their level and asked to read aloud. The teacher should supply unknown words as quickly and as unobtrusively as possible so that the reading proceeds smoothly. Often the child can remember these words if they appear again. If not, the teacher supplies them as often as necessary until they are recognized. Appropriate support during reading and constant repetition of the same words apparently help the children to learn as they read. The joy of completing story after story adds immeasurably to the child's positive feelings toward reading and the reading itself reinforces recognition of the words.

THE VISUAL-MOTOR METHOD

Words that children have not been able to learn by the simple visual approach or sight method can sometimes be mastered by the visual-motor method. This method is particularly useful in learning irregular words. But some individuals have considerable difficulty visualizing words, because of either poor visual discrimination or poor memory. In such cases, the use of the method should be discontinued.

The teacher chooses three words, each about five to eight letters long, that are unfamiliar to the pupils. The words are clearly printed on cards or the chalkboard and presented one at a time. The teacher says: "This is the word *fruit*. Look at it carefully. What is the word? Now close your eyes. Can you see it with your eyes closed? Look again. What is the word?" The word is covered and the children write it. They then compare their written word with the model. If the written word is incorrect, the procedure is repeated. No erasures are permitted. If a child makes a mistake, he or she starts over again. Sometimes it is necessary to show the word several times before the children are able to write it correctly. When the word is reproduced accurately, they write it several more times, covering up each previous sample to make sure that they are recalling the word from memory rather than merely copying it. The teacher checks carefully to see that it is written correctly each time. Another word is then introduced, and the procedure is repeated. After some time, the words are reviewed.

THE KINESTHETIC METHOD

The kinesthetic approach, developed by Grace Fernald, is relatively arduous and burdensome and is most effective for individual cases under careful supervision.[3] It is recommended only when all other methods fail. In this method the teacher writes or prints all unfamiliar words on unlined paper in letters approximately two inches high. The child is told that the method will be an entirely new one—using his or her fingers.

The child looks at one word, is told what it is, and traces it with his or her index finger, simultaneously pronouncing each sound of the word. If there is error or uncertainty, the child retraces the word, again saying each part of it aloud. Then the child tries to write the word without reference to the model. Erasure is not permitted. He or she continues to trace and

3. G. Fernald, *Remedial Techniques in Basic School Subjects* (New York: McGraw-Hill, 1942), pt. 2.

say the word over and over until it can be written easily without any consulting of the sample.

As soon as this child can write the list of words adequately, he or she begins to make up stories, asking about unknown words. Each of these words is written out and taught as just described. Whatever the child writes is typed by the teacher so that it can be read in printed form while still fresh. Pupils keep their own alphabetical file of words to practice on their own and refer to them in writing additional stories.

GAMES AND DEVICES

After the teacher introduces sight words, systematic practice is afforded by games and devices based on reliable word lists and by workbooks or made-up materials that use these words in different contexts. The teacher can make up games, use commercial games, or refer to published compilations of classroom games.

WORKBOOKS

Workbooks must be used with caution since they often do not fulfill the pupils' needs. Few workbooks are designed just for teaching sight words. Therefore the teacher selects exercises carefully. The most useful exercises use such features as picture dictionaries for ready reference, simple riddles, or sentences that include the words to be practiced. The exercises may be selected from any standard workbooks for primary-level reading.

Although the separate skills for teaching sight words have just been described in sequence, the authors always experiment until we find the approach most suitable for helping a particular child learn to read. Remember that we are dealing with children who already have been exposed to these skills at least once. Until we investigate, we do not know which skills they may have retained and which we need to stress. José, for example, had had a surfeit of phonics instruction with no success. He could not distinguish letter sounds despite his classroom teacher's conscientious persistence. When he was exposed to sounding out words once again by his reading teacher he became so frustrated that she considered suspending reading sessions for a while in favor of nonreading activities with a special emphasis on language development. How José's teacher helped him is discussed in chapter 9.

The Phonics Method

The learning of sight words must be taught concurrently with, or soon supplemented by, phonics so that the child gains greater independence in word analysis. This knowledge is then used immediately in sentences and reading matter. Unfortunately, many children with reading disability have difficulty blending sounds together to form whole words. In most cases, this difficulty is overcome at about eight or nine years of age, at which time a systematic phonics approach may be used. In rare cases the child is ten or older before being able to synthesize sounds. If, despite all the teacher's ingenuity, the child is still unsuccessful with the phonics method, it must be discontinued and alternate methods used until the child is able to profit from phonics instruction. However, the teacher does not merely wait without trying to demonstrate from time to time how sounds can be combined to form words. Sometimes a little assistance in this direction can help the child use the procedure. For instance, the teacher might encourage fitting sounds together the way links of a chain are combined. Also, the teacher can encourage the right sensation by pronouncing the separate sounds along with the student, in the procedure known as *choral blending.*

In the phonics procedure the pupil learns first the sounds of letters, then how to change the initial consonant of a known word in order to figure out new ones, and finally how to blend separate sounds together in words. Remembering that most of the children who have reading difficulty have been exposed to similar procedures many times before, the teacher seeks to minimize embarrassment by choosing material and techniques suitable for older pupils.

CONSONANTS AND CONSONANT BLENDS

The teacher introduces the selected sounds by presenting them in upper and lower case letters along with pictures. Some children can learn as many as four or five sounds in a single lesson. The consonants listed below have suggestions for illustrations that the writers have found appropriate.

s	sun	*b*	boat
d	door	*l*	ladder
m	matches	*n*	nest
t	television	*w*	window
h	house	*j*	jacks
p	pencil	*k*	key
f	fish	*v*	violin
c	cake	*y*	yellow
g	gate	*z*	zebra
r	radio		

103

The teacher should have the children name each picture to avoid possible confusion—as in *fence* for *gate* or *boat* for *ship*.

When teaching several sounds in succession, the teacher is careful to group those that differ markedly in appearance and sound. (For example, *b* and *d* are easily reversed and hence confusing in the same lesson.) The order in which the letters are listed in table 8-1 follows this principle, but the teacher always chooses the order most suitable to pupils' needs. For the letters *g* and *c*, the hard sounds are introduced first (*g* as in *good*, *c* as in *cup*). The soft sounds (*g* as in *gem*, *c* as in *circle*) are best delayed until later as they occur less frequently. The letters *q* and *x* have not been listed because they do not have single sounds (*q* in words is generally followed by *u*, sounding as *kw*; *x* usually sounds like *ks*). Pupils are less confused if they are taught these sounds when they meet them during their reading.

Auditory Discrimination

The children are told the name and sound of one letter at a time. Beginning sounds should be emphasized. (Of course, extraneous vowel sounds, such as *huh* for *h*, should be avoided.) Vivid associations are given wherever possible. In teaching *h*, for example, the teacher might say, "You can make steam on a window pane or mirror when you go 'hhhh.' " The children listen to words beginning with *h* and then are asked to distinguish a word that begins with a different letter sound. The teacher shows them a picture of a house with an upper and lower case *h* printed alongside it. The children pronounce the name of the letter and its sound. The teacher then pronounces other words that begin with *h*, such as *hat, hit, hose,* asking the children to listen carefully to the beginning sound. Then the children are asked to volunteer additional words beginning with the same sound. (They often have difficulty thinking of examples.) The teacher might ask riddles:

Here are some riddles that give you hints of the word that I am thinking of that begin with *hhhh.*

- You have two of them. You use one to write with. (*hand*)
- You climb it. (*hill*)
- In the summer it is sometimes very (*hot*).
- You do it when you go up and down on one foot. (*hop*)

The teacher might develop the children's auditory discrimination further by pronouncing groups of four words, three of which begin with the same sound.

hat	hit	miss	hope
fake	hose	here	him
have	card	help	hero
hot	hall	head	bear

The children are asked to listen carefully to the words and to indicate the one that does not begin with the sound being taught by clapping or raising their hands. The teacher does not proceed to a new group of four words until the children have correctly identified the word that begins differently. This is continued until sufficient auditory discrimination has been attained. Other letters are taught in the same way. When children learn letter sounds easily, the teacher can dispense with training in auditory discrimination.

When the children have learned several consonants and one short vowel sound, they are shown how to blend them together into words. The picture clues for the separate sounds are kept for ready reference as long as necessary.

Consonant blends are taught in the same way as single consonants. The teacher points out how two consonants already learned can be combined to form blends. There is no need to dwell on teaching a large number of blends because many of them tend to fall into similar patterns, such as *tr, gr, br.* However, the consonant digraphs that represent a single sound such as *sh* and *ch,* do have to be taught as entirely new sounds. *Th* has two sounds, as in *thimble* and as in *those.*

Rudimentary Blending of Sounds

If the child can grasp a visual procedure readily and shows some knowledge of letter sounds, a rudimentary phonics method, the word family method, may be tried. This technique is especially useful for those who are not yet able to blend sounds letter by letter. However, it affords only limited independence in word analysis. The word family approach consists of changing a known word into many new words by substituting for the first letter other letters being taught or reviewed. Thus the known word *cold* is changed to *gold, hold, sold,* and so forth.

A variation of this method is to substitute the same initial consonant in several words that the pupils already recognize, thus changing them to

105

entirely different words. For example, if the pupil knows the words *sat, fill, Sam, like,* and *day,* the teacher says to read the list aloud, substituting the letter *h* for the initial consonant in each word and pronouncing the new word that has been formed. (The words in which the substitution is made must be carefully chosen and familiar, so that the pupil has only the new sound to deal with.)

Practice in word families is presented to children in context instead of in isolated lists wherever possible. For instance, the child is shown how to extend his or her sight vocabulary while reading by noting similarities in words and applying the knowledge of sounds accordingly. That is, if the pupil comes across the word *hike* in reading, he or she is encouraged to figure it out from familiar elements—the sight word *like* and the sound of *h.*

TEACHING VOWEL SOUNDS

Vowel sounds are taught in the same way as consonant sounds, but they are much more difficult to distinguish and hence usually take longer for the pupils to master. Although there are many different sounds for each vowel (dictionaries may list six or more separate sounds for *a*), only the short and long sounds are taught at the outset to children with reading difficulties. The authors recommend that the short vowel sounds be taught first because words of one syllable—as *tag, mat,* and so on—are readily sounded out and written from dictation. As the pupils' mastery of reading and writing increases, diphthongs and other vowel combinations are taught. The pupils can begin to draw their own generalizations from their growing familiarity with the construction of words.

In learning the vowel sounds, many children have considerable difficulty distinguishing between the short sounds of *a* and *e.* Therefore, it is advisable to postpone teaching the short *e* until the other vowels are learned. Whatever sequence is followed, however, vowel sounds are presented one at a time, interspersed among the teaching of consonants. All the while the sounds are used in words, sentences, and stories. As for *y,* the children learn that it is sometimes a vowel, sometimes a consonant. Its use as a vowel is given little emphasis; instead, the children discover its function in connection with words that they encounter in reading.

The vowels might be illustrated by the following words:

Aa	Ii	Oo	Uu	Ee
Apple	Igloo	Octopus	Umbrella	Elephant

106

Auditory Discrimination of Short Vowel Sounds In introducing vowels for the first time, the teacher shows the children the five vowels and explains that every word in the English language has at least one vowel in it. They might next be challenged to suggest a word without a vowel. The teacher then presents the vowel sound. The teaching procedure is similar to that for consonants, except that only one vowel is taught at a time. (As already stated, a vowel may be taught with four or five consonants in one lesson.)

For example, the teacher presents the letter *a* and says, "This is *a*, and the sound is *ă* as in *apple.*" The use of an accompanying picture may serve as a cue for remembering the sound. The children learn to hear it at the beginning of other words (*absent, answer, after*). Then they listen to groups of words, one of which has a different sound at the beginning (*act, ill, am, add*) and try to distinguish the one word in the group that begins differently. After the pupils have distinguished the sounds satisfactorily, one-syllable words are presented with the short *a* in the middle (*fat, can, lap, pat*). Then one word in each group is changed to a different medial sound, and the pupils indicate the word that does not have the *a* sound in the middle (*fan, but, tag, had*).

After pupils have learned the short vowel sounds and can apply them in figuring out consonant-vowel-consonant words, the long vowel sounds are taught.

Blending Separate Sounds To determine whether blending sounds can be used successfully with children who have reading difficulty, an informal test of auditory blending is given. The teacher pronounces a word *set*, for example—first quickly, then slowly, *s-e-t*. Similarly, the word *fat* is pronounced naturally and then slowly as *f-a-t*. The pupils are then asked to identify other words that are said only slowly (*s-i-t, p-e-t, t-o-p*). If they can learn to recognize words from hearing the separate sounds, the phonics approach can be introduced. It should be remembered, however, that these children often need encouragement and help in understanding what they are expected to do.

In introducing blending, the pupils are shown several letters that they have learned. For example, the consonant sounds of *s, d, m, t, h,* and *p* are reviewed along with the short vowel sound of *a*. The letters might be printed on the chalkboard or a sheet of paper or selected from a set of lower case letter cards.

A word such as *hat* is printed for the children. The teacher illustrates how the separate sounds *h-a-t* may be blended together to form the word *hat* and gives as much assistance as necessary in helping the children synthesize the individual sounds into a whole word. The teacher then illustrates how *hat* may be changed to *mat, sat,* and *pat* in word families.

This makes the introduction to synthesizing separate sounds fairly easy. The next step, which involves substituting final consonants, is much more difficult to learn—changing *hat* to *had, mat* to *map,* and so on. The hardest step of all is reading words in mixed order, as *sap, pan, had, mat.* Frequently much practice is needed before children master the last two steps. To reinforce learning of letters and their associated sounds, the teacher may dictate words that the children sound out and write simultaneously.

Dictation The dictation of simple phonically regular words can help the pupils connect letters with the corresponding sounds. This usually helps their reading as well as their spelling ability. The teacher dictates word families first since they are easier. If the pupils know the consonants *h, t, n, f, l, d,* and *s* and vowels *i* and *a,* for example, the teacher dictates *fit, hit, lit, and sit;* then *sin, tin, fin;* and finally *fat, hat, sat, tan,* and *fan.* During the next stage, the teacher dictates the words in mixed order: *lit, tin, sit,* and *fin.* Later still, he or she might try more difficult dictation, such as *fin, fan, sat, had, lit,* and so on, interchanging initial and final consonants and vowels. The pace, of course, depends on the pupils' progress. Sufficient practice is given throughout so that when all the consonants and vowels are learned, the children can write or sound out accurately any phonically regular words in whatever order they appear, as *pet, map, hid, rug,* and *job.*

In presenting phonics exercises, the teacher avoids using nonsense syllables and words that children rarely meet. Exercises are not used merely as isolated drills but are applied immediately in sentences, poems, limericks, or stories. A collection of poems and limericks may be gradually developed as the teacher comes across them in books and anthologies of children's literature. Words of some folksongs and stories that have rhyming, such as those by Dr. Seuss, may provide additional sources for practice. Phonics exercises are presented systematically at each session, but the presentation remains brief lest the children become resistant or satiated.

TEACHING LONG VOWEL SOUNDS

Once short vowels have been mastered, the sounds of the long vowels are introduced. These are simple to learn since the long sounds just make the vowels "say their names." It is unnecessary to go through auditory discrimination training. Nevertheless, the rules governing their use are more complex and depend to a large extent on knowledge of the short vowel sounds. Long vowels are taught in connection with the two major rules governing their use.

Rule of the Silent e In one-syllable words ending in a consonant with the vowel in the middle, the vowel is usually short—*mat, bit, cut.* However, when *e* comes at the end of such a word, it can make the first vowel say its own name. The pupils are then shown familiar words that change vowel sounds because of the silent *e*—for example, *can, hid,* and *mat* change to *cane, hide,* and *mate.* The children should be encouraged to formulate the rule for themselves; a rule stated in their own words is frequently more meaningful.

Rule of the Double Vowel When two vowels come together in a word, the first one is usually long and the second one silent, as in *paid, coat,* and *seat.* Again, it is good practice to present words and encourage the children to figure out the rule for themselves; however, children should be told the rule if they do not see it for themselves. The important point is that they understand how it works and how to use it.

Vowel Combinations

It is usually sufficient for children with reading difficulty to be taught the short and long sounds of the single vowels. However, if pupils have difficulty with vowel combinations, these must be taught as well. Vowel variations are taught in the same way as are single vowel sounds. The teacher need not waste time teaching rare combinations. The most common combinations are listed below.

$\overline{oo}$ as in *moon*	*ay* as in *say*	*ow* as in *how*
$\breve{oo}$ as in *good*	*y* as in *my*	$\overline{ow}$ as in *slōw*
oi as in *spoil*		*au* as in *fault*
		aw as in *saw*

Workbooks and games help to lighten the tedium in learning phonics and can be a supplementary device for practice. As already stated, phonics must be applied and used in reading as much as possible after any isolated practice is completed.

In teaching phonics to children with reading problems we must be careful not to overemphasize its applicability to reading, as it is only one of several approaches needed to develop competence. The case of Neil in chapter 9 shows how he used the letter sounds he had learned but applied them indiscriminately.

Structural Analysis

Structural analysis is the way we identify parts of a word. It therefore supplements the methods described previously in this chapter and includes the teaching of such word endings as plurals, compound words, syllabication, roots, prefixes, and suffixes.

Word Endings For children with reading difficulty, it is generally sufficient to point out the normal changes of word endings; overemphasis should be avoided, and time should not be spent on endings that occur rarely. The children are shown the base word and add several endings to see how the word changes. The most common endings are *s, ed, ing, er, est, y,* and *ly.* Once in a while, children become confused because *ed* sometimes sounds like *t* as in *liked,* at other times like *ed* as in *parted,* and at other times like *d* as in *roared.* If pupils do not grasp the sound from reading the word in context, the teacher must take time to explain the differences.

Compound Words Compound words are fairly easy for children with reading difficulty to master. In most cases they need only be shown that some words are made up of two separate words, as *up stairs, blue bird,* or *pea nut.* Authorities sometimes recommend that the child "find little words in big words." If this technique is used, it is advisable to conduct it orally because finding the short word can actually hinder recognition. For example, focusing on *get* in *together* or *cat* in *locate* is very confusing.

Syllabication Stressing too many rules of syllabication can diminish rather than promote reading fluency. Deemphasizing rules is advisable. Pupils need to know how to divide words into identifiable small units. At first the teacher exaggerates the pronunciation of words so that the separate syllables are easily distinguished. Until the pupils learn to recognize the number of syllables in a word and understand that each syllable always contains one vowel sound, they cannot determine how to divide words into syllables. Oral work must be undertaken with the teacher until it is established that the children know where the separations come.

Root Words, Prefixes, and Suffixes Knowing that certain base words can be combined with prefixes and suffixes may be an aid to word recognition. However, for the child with reading difficulty, this concept must be simplified.

In teaching base words and suffixes, the teacher might point out that whenever a standard ending appears in a word, a suffix has been added. Pupils are then shown how to distinguish between a root and its suffix, as in *jump-ing, fast-er, quick-ly.* Prefixes are taught in the same way. The base words used in teaching should be complete in themselves. For example, pupils quickly grasp that the prefix *dis* (meaning *not*) placed before the word *believe* results in *disbelieve,* and the change in meaning is clear. Obviously, it would be confusing to use such words as *disdain* and *revoke,* for which there is no independent base word in English. Finally, the relationship between the prefix, the root word, and the suffix is demonstrated, as in *re-fill-ing, re-work-ing,* and so on. From their knowledge of the base words, the pupils may be able to discover the meanings of prefixes, for example, that *re* means *again.*

The suffixes and prefixes that are taught should be chosen on the basis of consistency of meaning and frequency of occurrence. The following prefixes and suffixes fulfill these criteria:

Prefixes: *com dis ex pre re sub*
Suffixes: *tion ment ful less*

As the foregoing discussion implies, extensive practice with root words, prefixes, and suffixes is more suitable for pupils at upper levels. Methods for older pupils are presented in chapter 12.

LINGUISTIC METHODS

Some children who do not learn easily through the sight word, phonics, or other methods sometimes profit from linguistic approaches as an introductory measure. The consistency of the word structure in the special linguistic readers helps students experience success and they may proceed to regular readers when they are ready.

Certain linguistic approaches resemble phonics procedures in that they introduce words that follow regular spelling patterns. However, in the linguistic methods we have examined, the children are expected to discover the sound–spelling relationships and are therefore not given instruction in separate sounds of letters and are never taught sounds in isolation.

According to the teacher's handbook in one series, the teacher writes a word on the board, reads it aloud, and has the children repeat it. The teacher then writes other words illustrating the same pattern directly below the first, such as *man, Dan, ran.* Pupils are asked to spell and then read each word as it is added to the list. These words are subsequently incorporated into sentences: *The man ran. Dan ran. I ran.* The presentation of the spelling patterns is controlled so that regular correspondences are introduced first. The children progress gradually from simple to complex patterns.

Linguists do not agree on whether the direct teaching of sounds should be omitted from beginning instruction; they also differ in methodology. Therefore, teachers who wish to employ these methods need to refer to the original sources from which the programs have been derived and also to follow carefully the instructions in the teacher's handbook for the particular linguistic reader.[4] A word of caution: Most children need only limited practice when they use such specialized books. They should be transferred as soon as possible to regular readers.

4. Linguistic readers include the following: C. Fried, *Merrill Linguistic Readers* (Columbus, Ohio: Charles E. Merrill, 1986); R. F. Robinett, *Miami Linguistic Readers,* 2d ed. (Lexington, Mass.: D. C. Heath, 1987).

Dictionary Skills

Children benefit from learning to use a dictionary efficiently for pronunciations, meanings, and word usage. Dictionaries are now available at all levels, starting with the very easiest picture dictionaries. The teacher gives practice in any skills the pupils lack, such as finding entries, identifying word meanings, and using the pronunciation system. Among the excellent simple dictionaries are *The Dictionary for Children* (Macmillan), *The Thorndike-Barnhart Beginning Dictionary* and *The Thorndike-Barnhart Junior Dictionary* (Scott-Foresman), and *Scholastic Dictionary of American English* (Scholastic). They all include instructions for use. Teacher's guides and workbooks are available from the publishers. Furthermore, dictionary exercises are incorporated in most of the workbooks that accompany basal readers.

Context

Usually children with reading difficulty have previously learned how to figure out a word from context. Too often, time that might profitably be spent on foundation skills is wasted on teaching the use of context. Many students come to overemphasize the skill, with the result that they tend to rely on indiscriminate guessing. Their eyes flit back and forth from the word to the picture; they use the initial consonant, general configuration, or other means to help them. If the students are not familiar with the use of context, merely pointing out that words can sometimes be ascertained from the rest of the sentence or other clues is usually sufficient.

Overcoming Reversal Errors and Inaccuracy in Reading

The group of skills described in this chapter constitutes the minimal word analysis techniques needed by individuals with reading difficulty. Children with reading disability, for example, may tend to reverse letters, words, or phrases. They may add, omit, or substitute words when reading a paragraph aloud. They often phrase poorly and have little expression in their oral reading.

Reversing such letters as *d* and *b, p* and *q,* is common in children with reading problems. In the case of confusion between *p* and *q,* it can be pointed out that *q* is usually found with *u.* For a problem with *b* and *d,* it is sometimes helpful to show the pupil that small *b* can be changed to capital *B* by adding another loop in the same direction.

Another technique has also been found useful. Children rarely reverse the *d* or *b* in cursive writing. Therefore, when they are puzzled as to which letter begins a word, they might be told to trace the letter with their forefingers. A cursive letter *d* can be traced over a printed *d,* and a cursive *b* can be traced over a printed *b.*

Reversing letters in such words as *was* (*saw*) is also common. Sounding the first letter of the word should act as a correct clue. For example, sounding *n* at the beginning of the word *no* should help to distinguish it from *on.*

A large arrow drawn at the top of the page may remind the children to read words and sentences from left to right.

Placing a zipper over a line of print to open from left to right is another useful method. Young children especially enjoy opening the zipper to see the letters or words appear. Beyond these simple devices, the frequency of reversals can be lessened by practice in reading.

Finally, two additional characteristics of children with reading disability—inaccuracy and lack of fluency in oral reading—may become habitual patterns of performance because of the insecurity and anxiety inherent in the situation. Development of rapport with a competent teacher, improvement in word recognition, and experience in reading suitable material usually alleviate these difficulties.

Encouraging the Use of Word Analysis Skills

The skills outlined in this chapter can be incorporated in regular classwork, as described in chapter 9. The teacher's relationship with pupils who have reading difficulty is of the utmost importance. Spending even a short time with an individual or small group can make an enormous difference in their progress. According to a study made by the New York City Board of Education: "Even five minutes a day of . . . individual contact which engrossed the child's real attention was worth much more to him than one-half hour a day in a group reading situation which merely tapped his surface attention. Moreover, the teacher's concern and efforts in his behalf seemed to convince the child that she understood his difficulties and meant to help him."[5] Children with learning difficulty need the satisfaction of being singled out as individuals in positive ways, since too often they have been ridiculed or reprimanded.

5. New York City Board of Education, *Teaching Guides: Language Arts,* no. 2 (New York: Board of Education of the City of New York, 1955).

Spelling Difficulties

Most children with reading difficulties have even more trouble with spelling than with word analysis. Teaching spelling along with letter sounds acts as an effective reinforcement for using phonics. Before beginning instruction with children who have spelling problems, the teacher administers a standardized spelling test. Spelling subtests are included in most standardized achievement batteries.[6]

The basis of spelling is the knowledge of sounds. Pupils must be made aware of the connection between hearing a sound and reproducing it accurately in writing. In teaching spelling by the phonics method, for example, the instructor points out the connection between sounds and visual symbols. For irregularly spelled words, the visual-motor method can be tried; for the many children with spelling problems who have difficulty recalling words visually, kinesthetic clues are useful. Furthermore, any approaches that draw special attention to spelling patterns or to roots or parts of words can also be helpful. For example, once children learn *could,* they can be shown the resemblance to *would* and *should.* (One student who wrote *mudgarity* for *majority* had no further trouble after he was shown that *majority* included *major.* Similarly, he found it useful to find the word *science* in *conscience.*) Many students need to be reminded of the correct pronunciation of words, such as *government, probably,* and *environment,* to eliminate common spelling errors.

Still another approach that students at all ages have found helpful is keeping their own alphabetized lists of words that they have repeatedly misspelled. Also, there are published lists of words most frequently misspelled by children in various grades, as well as spellers that facilitate studying particular words. Such lists are much easier for children with reading difficulty than looking words up in the dictionary, for the lists contain fewer words and are much less confusing. Dictionaries are important, but they can prove discouraging to individuals with spelling difficulties. A pupil once asked one of the authors, "How on earth do you spell *pearl?*—and don't ask me to look it up in the dictionary because I've already looked under 'pir,' 'pur,' and 'per' without finding it."

Pupils may also be taught spelling in connection with written compositions. The teacher should not correct misspellings in written work by underlining the mistakes, for that calls attention to the *incorrect* spelling. Instead, misspelled words should be crossed out and the correct spelling

6. Including the Roswell-Chall Diagnostic Assessment of Reading and Teaching Strategies, Wide Range Achievement Test, Durrell Analysis of Reading Difficulty, and Test of Written Spelling II (see appendix A).

written above them. The child keeps a record of these words and tries to learn them.

Students who wish to become better spellers must continue to use whatever approaches are most suitable for them. Despite conscientious effort, some of them have extreme difficulty in this area for many years. Whether this is due to a general language disorder or other factors is not known. Students and teachers who realize how long spelling and reading disability sometimes persists can at least view the difficulty constructively by using every means of compensation rather than feeling apprehensive and guilty if practice and application are not entirely successful. If available, typewriters and computers that have programs to signal misspellings can be extremely helpful to individuals with persistent spelling difficulties. However computers cannot always understand what a student has written. With the word *pail,* for example, the computer will not know which of the following is correct: "He has a pail" or "He has a pale face"; "It is right" or "It is a rite." "Allowing a spelling checker to become a speller correcter may be a major mistake since the spelling checker does basically what most teachers do: it notes possible spelling errors but does not correct them. . . . This means that the student must still be the judge of whether to correct the word or not."[7]

Teaching Word Recognition Techniques with a Word Processor

Computers can be of help in teaching word recognition. Since special programs are being modified and expanded all the time, it is imperative that the school's personnel investigate available programs and try them out to see which ones are suitable for their pupils.

It goes without saying that those who are unaccustomed to using word processors need time to master the mechanics. However, motivation is usually high and soon the pupils want to try the computer. The computer often improves concentration, particularly for those with learning problems who are restless, hyperactive, or diffuse. These highly distractible pupils, who have real problems in sitting still for any appreciable length of time, begin learning letters, sight words, sounds, and even practice techniques while focusing on a computer. A talking computer that has pictures for a story sometimes helps the pupils to understand the text more easily. Children can also make up their own stories and illustrate them.

7. D. Rodrigues and R. Rodrigues, *Teaching Writing with a Word Processor, Grades 7–13* (Urbana, Ill.: National Council of Teachers of English, 1986), p. 19.

Computer programs for word recognition techniques emphasize immediate feedback and stress positive learning because the child can go at an individual pace. This emphasizes the child's power to manage alone. The computer is also an asset for original written work, particularly for those with poor penmanship, because the mistakes are so easily corrected.

Teachers who use the computer for word recognition techniques such as sight words, vowel and consonant sounds, and context clues agree that it is a useful tool. Although commercial computer programs offer novelty and variety at different levels, teachers who do not find suitable programs can tailor word processing programs to make up their own teaching disks.[8]

Although the computer is not actually a diagnostic tool, the alert teacher can discern pupils' strategies while they are working. The teacher can make notes on the skills the pupils are using to see which techniques or reading skills are needed. This can eliminate the harrassment of test taking because the computer stresses *positive* feedback, thereby avoiding the students' focus on their deficiencies. Finally, pupils using a computer enjoy it because it is a "grown-up" tool that promotes their self-respect.

* * *

Remedial treatment covers a wide range and variety of diagnostic problems. The remedial specialist coordinates with other workers in the field whenever indicated, helps in any way possible to foster competency in schoolwork, and, above all, promotes the very best qualities that are present in every individual. Remediation is more than imparting techniques; it is more than therapeutically oriented treatment. It is a situation that is personal and unique in all cases. Such positive experiences can make the difference between a life of failure and a life of acceptance and harmony.

Suggestions for Further Reading

Anderson, K. F. "The Development of Spelling Ability and Linguistic Stages." *Reading Teacher* 39 (November 1985).

Balmuth, M. *The Roots of Phonics: A Historical Introduction.* New York: Teachers College Press, 1982.

Chall, J. *Learning to Read: The Great Debate,* 2d ed. New York: McGraw-Hill, 1983.

Durkin, D. *Teaching Them to Read,* 4th ed. Newton, Mass: Allyn & Bacon, 1983.

———. *Phonics, Linguistics and Reading.* New York: Teachers College Press, 1972.

Ehri, L. C., and Wilce, L. S. "Does Learning to Spell Help Beginners Learn to Read Words?" *Reading Research Quarterly* 22 (Winter 1987).

8. Ibid.

Frith, U., ed. *Cognitive Processes in Spelling.* London: Academic Press, 1980.

Gough, P. "Word Recognition." In *Handbook of Reading Research,* edited by P. D. Pearson. New York: Longman, 1984.

Hall, M. *Teaching Reading as Language Experience,* 3d ed. Columbus, Ohio: Charles E. Merrill, 1981.

Heilman, A. *Phonics in Proper Perspective,* 5th ed. Columbus, Ohio: Charles E. Merrill, 1985.

Read, C. *Children's Creative Spelling.* New York: Routledge & Kegan Paul, 1986.

Smith, F. *Understanding Reading: A Psycholinguistic Analysis of Reading and Learning to Read,* 3d ed. New York: Holt, Rinehart & Winston, 1982.

Stauffer, R. G. *The Language Experience Approach to the Teaching of Reading,* 2d ed. New York: Harper & Row, 1980.

Taylor, B. M., and Nosbush, L. "Oral Reading for Meaning: A Technique for Improving Word Identification Skills." *Reading Teacher* 37 (1983).

Templeton, S. "Synthesis of Research on the Learning and Teaching of Spelling." *Educational Leadership* 43 (March 1986).

9

The Application of
Word Recognition Methods

In THIS CHAPTER we will describe some of the general approaches that may be used in the actual teaching of word recognition to a group and to individuals in or out of the classroom.

Oral Reading

Although rarely considered a method, oral reading is one of the best means for practicing word recognition. In the course of reading, many words, especially sight words, are repeated again and again. The teacher can supply those that the child does not know. The child repeats them in the course of reading and, in this way, gradually learns to recognize them. The process is sometimes called incidental teaching; but the teacher can also help the child sound out the words and use structural analysis and context while reading. In this way, the pupil learns new words not just as an entity but embedded in many different contexts. For example, he or she may know the word *there* in isolation, but it seems to be less recognizable when woven into different sentences where its context is altered. Therefore, as long as the oral reading is not allowed to become laborious, the pupil has a better chance of strengthening word recognition ability in a natural and

118

less taxing setting than in straight drill. Oral reading also enables the teacher to determine the pupil's progress in word recognition and to decide which skills are still needed.

PHRASING AND EXPRESSION

Eventually oral reading must be done with proper phrasing and expression. But first the child should be reading within the scope of his or her ability and have mastered all the needed word recognition techniques. Otherwise there are too many skills to consider at once. In any beginning foreign language class, for example, it takes a high degree of mastery before the pupils—regardless of their age—can read a text fluently or with expression.

To improve performance in reading, several procedures can be tried. The teacher might alternate with the pupil in reading paragraphs or pages, or he or she might try choral reading (reading simultaneously with the pupil). Thus the pupil may be able to imitate the teacher's example. Using a tape recorder will let the pupil hear how he or she sounds; however, taped renditions may be threatening, particularly for those whose performance is very poor.

The most effective means of all is to encourage as much supplementary reading as possible. Most children with reading difficulty shy away from independent reading and therefore rarely gain the practice needed for a fluent performance. They should be guided toward exciting stories at a level that they can handle. Many high interest, low vocabulary books with mature content are readily available.

COMPREHENSION

For children with reading difficulties who are functioning on a primary level, the authors do not treat comprehension in connection with their reading in the manner recommended by the standard manuals. Since these pupils are usually reading material containing concepts designed for much younger children, they rarely have trouble with the meaning unless they have a language problem or an extremely limited experiential background. Their major problem stems from difficulty in recognizing words. Therefore, to follow the widespread practice of answering questions about content, looking back to substantiate answers, and finding explanatory phrases or paragraphs to elaborate specific points, is not only inappropriate but smothers any spark of interest that may have been aroused. In fact, some of the deep resistance to reading that the authors have encountered

119

with such children has been due to their experience of being asked endless questions, which ruined any delight in the story itself. Imagine how someone feels who is struggling with word recognition, feeling clumsy in reading aloud, and worrying about sounding utterly absurd. Then at the end of this wretched experience this student must think up answers to comprehension questions! Instead of being concerned about understanding the material at this stage, the teacher should seize every opportunity to promote pleasure in completing the story. Wherever there are strong reactions to the ideas themselves, the teacher of course should encourage spontaneous discussion. More often than not on the lower reading levels, however, the teacher and children will finish a story with brief comments and go on to the next procedure.

Word Analysis in the Remedial Program

After oral reading and discussion have been completed, some extra practice on the separate skills may still be needed. The children learn consonant sounds, vowel sounds, consonant combinations, and so on by the methods described in chapter 8.

As we have noted, only the most essential word analysis techniques are emphasized with children who have reading difficulties. Because they usually have become discouraged as a result of previous failures and tend to carry over these negative attitudes, the teacher attempts to show them that certain basic skills will increase their reading ability quickly and effectively. The teacher names the skills to be learned and explains how they are used. This encourages a collaborative spirit and sets concrete and realistic goals. Rather than plowing through endless lists and countless exercises, the pupils can learn a streamlined version of word analysis and proceed as rapidly as possible.

In working with such children, the teacher should not expect complete accuracy. These students have a prolonged tendency to mistake sight words and confuse letter sounds. Whether this is due to word-finding difficulty, perceptual disorder, dysfunction in storage and retrieval of linguistic information,[1] or other factors related to reading disability is not known. Instead of expecting perfection, the experienced teacher strives for steady improvement. If the teacher shows understanding and acceptance of the fluctuations in the children's progress, their anxiety about making mistakes usually lessens. This in turn tends to decrease errors and gradually results in smoother and more proficient reading.

1. F. R. Vellutino, "Dyslexia," *Scientific American* 256 (March 1987): 36.

The Classroom Library

The ultimate objective of teaching word recognition is to develop pupils' reading ability. To promote this aim, the teacher should have a large selection of appropriate reading materials on hand in the form of a classroom library.

Children with reading difficulty usually are reluctant to use classroom libraries. They have long been discouraged by their unsuccessful attempts to read any of the volumes. When these children are assigned outside reading, their major criterion is the slenderness of the book. In order to try again, they need a great deal of encouragement.

The teacher can foster more positive attitudes toward reading by providing a wide variety of materials with controlled vocabulary but high interest. If only a limited amount of money is available, books can sometimes be borrowed in quantity from the public library. Another possibility is to purchase a number of short story collections at varying levels. These can sometimes be cut up into their separate selections. The children can help to prepare the material and make suitable covers for each story. The result is hundreds of attractive booklets that offer pleasurable reading to many children at different stages of reading competency.

To facilitate the pupils' choice of suitable reading matter, the teacher might code the books according to level, marking them conspicuously on the cover or back binding with an appropriate symbol. For example, if letters are used, the pupils are told which letter represents the books that are most sensible for them to read at present. A similar system uses different colors to represent the different levels. If such a procedure is used, the children should be told the reason for it: it is good to find books that are enjoyable; they cannot be appreciated if they are too difficult; therefore, they are coded for convenience just as in regular libraries.

The teacher might check on the pupils' reading by asking them to tell what part of a story they liked best or found funniest. If a story seems suitable for other children as well, she might ask them to share it with the class. This practice is accepted enthusiastically by most children. It seems to effect an improvement in the attitude of the poorer readers in particular. Disheartened readers often become interested in exploring the possibilities of the library when they find out they can really read and derive pleasure from books.

The following pages describe children at various ages who read at beginning levels.

A Group of Fourth Graders Reading below Grade Level

Ms. T was the corrective reading teacher for grades one through four in an elementary school.* Although the variety of materials she used made the program attractive to younger children, one particular fourth-grade group presented problems from the very beginning of the school year. Some of the students had been in her twice-weekly class for several years and had become bored by the format; others resented being singled out to leave their own classrooms; a minority enjoyed working independently on programmed material but had made only minimal reading improvement. Clearly, a new approach was needed for this fourth-grade corrective reading class.

Placement in Ms. T's class had been determined by the previous spring's test scores as well as by teacher recommendation. The range of achievement as represented by grade equivalents was 2.3–3.8. Informal assessment of the students indicated many special needs with regard to strategies for word recognition as well as comprehension and writing. Most of the children had mastered basic decoding skills, although syllabication skills were very uneven. Some were reluctant readers and had to be coaxed into action. Many could identify details when reading silently, but these were not connected to larger concepts and therefore lacked significance. Several students were having difficulty with word meanings since they were not native speakers of English. Across the board, all class members were unwilling to write and thereby expose their spelling and syntax deficiencies. This heterogeneity of students' strengths and weaknesses further complicated the program planning since the children did not seem to fit into the traditional pattern of having similar reading needs.

Eventually Ms. T decided against normal grouping and arbitrarily set up two boys' and two girls' groups. Meeting alone with each group, she managed to elicit some commonality of interests from the six children and very generally framed a project that the group might undertake. It was understood that each child would contribute to the overall activity but that their work would vary according to their strengths as well as their reading needs. Working with the group, Ms. T assigned roles to each child and made up a schedule for task completion. Aside from setting up a detailed system of record keeping, the hardest job was to find appropriate material for each task. As a corrective reading teacher Ms. T had rarely used the school library, but now she found herself working closely with the librarian and sending children, in pairs, to get the necessary books.

*Supervised by Prof. Joan Raim, City College of the City University of New York.

The fall projects dealt with gliders and kites, cooking, folk dances, and rockets. In the spring, there was a travel journal, a book about Puerto Rico, play writing, and transportation stories. In each case there was a culminating activity, such as a play presentation, the writing of a book, or a demonstration. The range of language arts tasks included oral and silent reading, note taking, summarizing, making outlines, using the dictionary, drawing pictures, answering comprehension questions of all types, and writing dialogue and stories. Ms. T spent her classroom time conferring with the groups, observing the children working, and intervening when necessary. As specific problems with individual students became obvious, she would provide individual instruction and assign workbook pages for practice. The infrequent and judicious use of the workbooks resulted in more positive responses from the children. Ms. T did fear that in her concern for the group project she might overlook the needs of some children, particularly those with more severe problems. Although she tried to observe closely and confer with each child at least once a week, she was not totally secure in her assumption that activity-oriented reading could provide the same proficiency as directed skill practice. She also had concerns about how the regular classroom teachers would view her projects; consequently she had frequent contact with them to justify her new procedures as well as her class organization. Outsiders could observe that her classroom was busy and somewhat noisy but also that the children maintained a relatively high level of enthusiasm.

Evaluation of the spring reading test scores from this class indicated that 75 percent of the students would not need to return the next fall, a somewhat higher percentage than in previous years. As Ms. T had suspected, it was the children with the most severe reading problems who would require additional remediation. According to the achievement tests, regardless of the initial level of reading performance the youngsters whose decoding skills were weak or whose reading lacked fluency made less progress. She observed that her program was most successful with those children whose skills allowed them to work independently. What was especially gratifying to Ms. T was that most of the children *wanted* to return to her class and that their regular teachers reported more positive attitudes toward all reading-related activities. She concluded that her project approach to corrective reading had proven successful in enhancing growth in reading achievement as well as in motivation.

José—A Total Nonreader in Third Grade*

At eight years, six months, José was in third grade and could not read at all when he was referred to a reading clinic for help. His intelligence was in the borderline range and his marked tendency to fantasize interfered with his ability to sustain attention. Very often he went off on a tangent in the middle of instruction. He came from a non–English-speaking family of very low income and poor educational background. His parents were separated and he had siblings who showed signs of serious emotional disturbance. His problems were exacerbated by recent severe traumatic experiences.

José was handsome, well-coordinated, and physically well-developed but pale, obviously fatigued, and poorly nourished. His expressive language was meager; his vocabulary was limited, and his naming of objects was often inaccurate. He could barely retell a narrative coherently. Any book read to him had to be paraphrased into short, declarative sentences in the present tense. Most illustrations were hard for him to understand. He could not grasp any material that he himself had not experienced, no matter how simply an explanation was presented.

Because of José's severe language deficit, it was important to use language directly, to communicate feelings verbally, and to tell stories so that he would learn to understand the function of language. Before he received any reading instruction, José needed to understand the connection between letter and sound, print and speech, reading and speaking, and speaking and feeling. So, for about one month José drew pictures, told stories, dictated stories, and chose pictures from magazines and made up stories about them.

José could not identify the name or give the sound of any letter, nor could he point to the appropriate letter if given its name or sound. He seemed unable to hear initial consonant sounds or to rhyme words. He could match letters, words, and shapes (while unable to read or identify them), and he could write his name and copy letters. His visual perception seemed adequate, as did his fine motor control; however, his insecurity and imagination made it very difficult for him to concentrate on any task.

Since José sang the alphabet song with great pride, energy, and gusto, he was taught the names of the letters. A felt board and felt letters were used. He traced the letters on his hand, tried visual clues for reinforcement, and wrote the letter while saying its name. However, José could not re-

*Reported by Catherine Lipkin, a reading specialist.

member the name of a letter for even a short time. A phonics approach was tried. His tutor used the accepted method of associating letters with familiar objects. This was discontinued after a month because it proved ineffective. Since he could not retrieve the names of objects, he could not associate or find the proper initial consonant sound. José's learning style was so chaotic that he forgot the items almost immediately after they were introduced.

José was never angry or belligerent. He tried very hard but he knew that something was desperately wrong.

Because of José's extreme difficulty in grasping reading instruction, it was considered advisable to discontinue instruction temporarily and give José a sense of mastery, perhaps by having him construct things with wood and glue.

However, when one of the authors (Florence Roswell) was consulted, she said that it was imperative for José to feel a sense of mastery in the reading itself. If he could learn to read despite his previous failures, he could gain confidence and satisfaction. There were several alternatives: perhaps he could learn street signs such as *Walk, Don't Walk, Danger,* and *Columbus Avenue.* Or he might be able to read simplified pre-primers in which a minimum number of words were introduced gradually. This would emphasize the visual approach and would give José a chance to understand what he read in contrast to sounding out words from which he derived no meaning. (Phonics could be reintroduced much later, after he had a solid beginning.)

Accordingly, the Detroit Reading Series was introduced and José began to read. This series uses a sight approach. It is easy to use visually and conceptually and the pictures are extremely simple. The vocabulary is controlled and introduced very slowly. There is a reassuring aspect to this series, due to its pace, consistency, and vocabulary repetitions.

Because José learned so slowly, all words had to be reinforced with many techniques. For example, pictures were found from magazines to illustrate words such as *cat* or *run.* He matched the words on index cards with the illustrations or wrote the appropriate word under the illustration. He constructed little books himself and used the words that he had just learned. He was introduced to varied activities that would reinforce the words in visual, auditory, and kinesthetic procedures.

In retrospect, it seems that the first advance occurred when José could communicate feelings orally. Second came his understanding that print carries meaning. Finally came his ability to recognize and read and write words himself. With this last step came a tremendous sense of pride and desire to improve.

125

The sessions then essentially followed this structure: (1) José read aloud from the series; (2) new words were written on cards; (3) words and sentences were dictated; (4) we drew, or wrote stories, or José was read to. After finishing the Detroit series, José was unable to go to a higher level. Therefore other simple stories on the same level were located.

Work dealt with communication of experience and expression of feelings. Once José had talked to me about things in his life that mattered to him, he began to read; once he began to read, his concentration increased. Previously his responses were automatic. Now he could read for as long as thirty minutes. His physical manner changed. At this point he seemed more confident, more energetic, more in control. He had gained self-esteem.

Of course, his deficits were still glaring. His sight vocabulary was limited and he had trouble learning new words. His language problems were still significant and profound. He was often difficult to understand. He continued to lack basic information such as the names of the days of the week, and he could not even give the names of most letters. But he could read, and of that achievement he was very proud. He enjoyed reading to people and would take his pile of word cards and read to whomever would listen. He was attentive and cooperative and eager to achieve. He loved to be read to. He was beginning to hear initial consonant sounds and at one point he suddenly recognized *run* and *read*: "They start the same." He gradually developed auditory skills and it seemed that he was ready for a systematic phonics approach to reading.

In spite of his hyperactivity and his massive emotional and environmental disadvantages, José had been reached and had begun to enjoy reading.

Randy—Reading at Pre-primer Level in Second Grade

Randy's problem was different from José's but almost as severe. He did not seem able to remember most sight words despite his being well into second grade. He got the idea that he had "no memory." Randy was examined by one of the authors, who also served as consultant. Treatment was carried out by a reading specialist in collaboration with his classroom teacher.

Randy could read a simple pre-primer, but his ability to learn was markedly impeded by his conviction that he had a severe memory problem. His recurrent comments during the testing session were, "I don't know; I can't remember." In a very amiable way he conveyed a feeling of helplessness, almost as if by engaging the examiner's sympathy she might not expect too much of him, nor push him too hard. Yet, his intelligence was about average, with his highest scores on tests involving memory for digits and memorization of new symbols. On the other hand, his fund of information was very low. He did not know how many pennies there were in a nickel or the number of days in the week, and he could not even name the day of the week on which he was tested.

There was no doubt that this child's learning problem needed a many sided approach. It seemed important first for Randy to find out that he could learn and retain what he had been taught. This was accomplished during trial learning procedures at each of the testing sessions, in which there was careful control of the level and amount of material introduced.

For example, he was given a simple pre-primer containing only eleven words, in addition to names of characters. These words were presented gradually and the special features of each word were emphasized. Whenever proper names proved troublesome, they were supplied. Soon Randy began to recognize that he could read and remember the words taught. Even though there were only a few words on a page, Randy reacted with a sense of achievement as he read page after page successfully. He was encouraged to apply any meaningful clues, such as letter sounds, visual impressions, or tactile-kinesthetic senses that could facilitate recall. By the third session he was able to handle a second pre-primer which included the words in the first pre-primer plus a limited number of new ones. As the trial lessons proceeded explanations were given to Randy regarding how the various methods could help him retain what he had learned. Much to Randy's satisfaction, he found that he could remember.

At the conclusion of the examination, a conference was held with both his classroom and special reading teachers. It was apparent that even though they were using suitable materials at an appropriate level, they were bombarding this child with too many workbooks and too large a vocabulary load. Therefore, they were advised to introduce new words and materials very gradually and wait until previous work had been mastered so that Randy could develop a sense of having grasped what he had been taught. Both teachers were asked to coordinate their programs and to ensure that expectations were being kept within their proper scope.

The last recommendation was made to the parents. Because of Randy's striking deficiency in his fund of knowledge and lack of awareness of what was going on around him, it was suggested that his parents keep bringing everyday events into sharp focus and call his attention to aspects of time and space such as the days of the week, the months of the year, and special features of places they visited. In other words, they should attempt to fill

127

the gaps in his experience and information in order to bring them more in line with those of his peers.

Follow-up after several months disclosed that Randy had made decided progress and no longer mentioned his faulty memory. In a short period of time he had mastered the Dolch Basic Sight Vocabulary and was handling a high first grade reader. His teachers reported that they had worked together to carry out the suggested program. For example, to help Randy build up a sight vocabulary, they presented only a few words at a time in easy steps as follows: (1) Randy matched words so as to sharpen his perception of similarities and differences in word forms; (2) the teacher named words and Randy identified them; (3) Randy read the words; (4) Randy wrote selected words and simple sentences from dictation; and (5) the teacher presented words in different sizes, colors, and types because of his difficulty in shifting from one format to another. Thus, the gradual stages of teaching word recognition apparently helped Randy grasp and recall what was taught.

In addition, his teachers emphasized the learning of such information as Randy's address, telephone number, and date of birth, as well as the names of the days of the week and concepts such as *before* and *after.* For connected reading, both storybooks and linguistic readers proved suitable. Games were used mostly for reinforcement of sight vocabulary.

Because of the satisfactory progress that Randy made, his parents and teachers asked about the poor memory with which everyone had been so concerned. Apparently Randy initially had somewhat of a problem learning to read because of some lag in maturational development. When instruction was offered at a pace too fast for him, he stated that he could not remember. His parents and teachers attributed his difficulties to a severe memory deficit. This led Randy to retreat into a state where he felt justified in not learning.

This case illustrates one of the many negative adaptations that failing children can unconsciously develop, as well as the risks inherent in teachers' and parents' accepting a particular label without further investigation of its solidity. Fortunately, Randy's problem was recognized early and appropriate remedial measures rectified his rationalizations for not learning.

Neil—Reading at Second-Grade Level in Third Grade

Neil, an alert, articulate, appealing boy, came for testing toward the end of second grade because he was among the poorest readers in his class. He was keenly aware of his low status, because his classmates ridiculed him constantly and called him stupid. He was socially at ease, spontaneous, and keen during the administration of the intelligence tests. However, his demeanor changed perceptibly when he encountered items on reading tests with which he could not cope. At such times, his profound discouragement and anxiety were paramount.

Neil's developmental history was reported to be entirely normal, so that there was little in his background that could throw light on the reasons for his reading problem. Yet test results showed a marked discrepancy between his functioning in reading and his superior intellectual level on the Wechsler Intelligence Scale for Children. Reading scores were as follows:

	Grade Scores	Percentile Scores for End of Grade Two
Oral Reading Test	2.3	
Silent Reading Test		
Word Knowledge	2.3	22
Reading	1.7	11

The Diagnostic Reading Scales showed a fairly good grasp of basic phonics skills.

Neil did particularly poorly on both the sentence and paragraph reading portions of a primary reading test because of his limited sight vocabulary. When left to his own devices, he used a phonics approach for all unfamiliar words. Thus, both phonically regular and phonically irregular words were handled the same way. This led to enormous frustration when the sounds did not correspond to their visual symbols.

The examination covered three one-hour sessions with one of the authors. Part of each visit was devoted to working with Neil in a typical learning situation where methods and materials were presented that he could handle with a fair degree of success, as described in chapter 5, in the section "Trial Sessions for Further Diagnostic Information." During these periods, Neil's spirits lifted considerably. He was interested in the test findings and their interpretation, when his needs were pointed out and

129

suitable methods for helping him cope with his deficiencies were discussed.

In this connection, he was told: "You're a very bright boy, but like many others, you have some problems with reading. You know your consonant and vowel sounds, and you can usually put them together to form words. Sometimes you don't do it when you read parts of words like *c-at-ch* and *m-us-t,* and then stop making whole words out of them. You also try to sound out all words you don't know and frequently this doesn't work, because some words, called 'sight words,' have to be learned by looking at them and remembering them." Then it was explained how we would use the Dolch Picture-Word Cards and the Dolch Basic Sight Vocabulary, among other materials, for this purpose. Typical stories that would be presented were shown to him so that he got some idea of procedures and materials that would be used to help him overcome his reading problem. In this way, his problem was concretized, thereby lessening his feeling of having vague, overwhelming difficulties.

At the conclusion of the examination, Neil requested to be tutored by the author and seemed most eager to get started. Accordingly, we got off to a good beginning. At the outset, something had to be done to discourage Neil's overuse and misapplication of the phonics method. Therefore, emphasis was placed on his learning quickly to recognize commonly used words. Games and other materials were used along with a considerable amount of story reading, starting with a simple second grade reader. However, games were employed judiciously to avoid the impression that the purpose of the sessions was merely fun.

Neil was so enchanted with the folktales and other stories he was reading that he begged to be permitted to take books home for supplementary reading. The author rarely makes home assignments because this can be counterproductive. But self-initiated activity is conducive to growth. Because of the wide amount of recreational reading Neil did, his competency improved to the point that it was possible to introduce silent reading exercises in various workbooks at third-grade level. New vocabulary was presented and concepts that were likely to be unfamiliar were discussed.

Occasionally Neil's anxiety became apparent when tasks appeared challenging and his fear of failure loomed. He frequently remarked, "That's too hard" during the earlier sessions. Thus, the author was constantly alert to this child's low tolerance of frustration and his resistance to difficult materials. He was repeatedly assured that assistance would be forthcoming if necessary. It was further pointed out that dealing with unknown factors is how one learns, and that not knowing an answer was to be considered not as failure but as part of a process of exploring something new. This led Neil to feel free to try to handle questions without concern as to the number of right or wrong answers. In this type of trusting relationship, where the tutor showed confidence in Neil's basic capacities and he showed faith in her ability to teach, he progressed extremely well.

After forty sessions, work was discontinued. Comparable test scores were as follows:

	May	December
Oral Reading Test	2.3	4.4
Achievement Tests	For Grade Two	For Grades Three and Four
Word Knowledge	2.3	5.0
Reading	1.7	3.9

These satisfactory changes within a few months were probably due to the interaction of many factors. The constructive relationship between instructor and child was of paramount significance. The well-planned sessions with a definite structure promoted learning and lessened Neil's wish to control the situation by requesting only the activities he preferred. He frequently asked for games and frowned when he was given work materials. Nevertheless, he responded well to the limits that were set, especially since there was a balance during the session between materials that were highly appealing and those that demanded concentrated, independent effort. His need for structure and gentle firmness were observed by his classroom teacher as well. Our coordinated efforts helped the boy cope with his feelings of inadequacy so that he was able to try challenging assignments without complaining.

From the beginning, Neil was helped to overcome his tendency to rely solely on a sound-blending method. Other strategies were stressed, such as the acquisition of a sight vocabulary, the use of large units within words, and the finding of words through context. At the outset he read books containing folktales and fairytales at low second grade level. By degrees, he progressed to high second-, third-, and then fourth-grade levels with materials always carefully chosen for their high interest value. Silent reading exercises in workbooks at third- and fourth-grade levels promoted independent work while they increased his word recognition ability, broadened his vocabulary, and provided subject matter similar to that found in textbooks at school. At each session, spelling was introduced in connection with simple tasks involving expressive writing.

As implied throughout this account, the atmosphere during the sessions was informal and friendly, but basic concern for this child's need to function in a mature, effective manner precluded the prolonged use of games.

Thus, they were introduced first for motivational purposes, but their use was decreased gradually and then discontinued in order to place the major emphasis on oral and silent reading. The reasons were twofold. First, there is little carry over from isolated words presented in games; and second, the main goal is to encourage independence in handling meaningful activities. Many children with reading difficulties are immature and not at all task oriented. Therefore, the overuse of games and other game-type devices only prolongs the period of dependency and are of questionable effectiveness in instruction. Instead, we believe that the inner satisfaction that a child derives from accomplishment and enjoyment in reading books is a more powerful and significant incentive.

Frank—A Serious Reading Disability

Frank was referred to one of the authors for evaluation and treatment of his severe learning problems. In describing his history, Frank's mother reported that her pregnancy was normal but labor was prolonged and difficult. During Frank's first years, there was delay in all areas of development, including teething, sitting, standing, walking, and talking. Frank's parents considered him a nervous and restless child. He did not play well with others.

Although Frank had been in first grade twice, he still could not grasp even the simplest instruction in schoolwork. His experiences in school had been most unfortunate. An extremely unsympathetic teacher demanded work that was far beyond his capacity. She was impatient with him because "he refused to learn."

Psychological test results showed that Frank had low average intelligence. His language patterns were immature, and deficits in memory areas were apparent. In addition, there were many indications of possible neurological involvement; a neurologist's examination did reveal impairment. The neurologist recommended that Frank receive individualized instruction from a specialist who would understand Frank's needs and that the educational program in school be adapted to his level of functioning and his adjustive needs.

In interpreting the findings of the psychological and educational testing to the parents, the author indicated that the tests confirmed that Frank was a nonreader and could not carry out even the simplest arithmetical computations. The type of educational program that he required was explained. Tasks would be given that he could handle successfully. Furthermore, the author would interpret test findings to the school and try to work out a coordinated plan of instruction.

One could not predict at this point the pace at which Frank could learn. However, his ability to relate well to the author and his expressed desire to receive help were favorable factors in the learning process.

Frank's parents agreed not to put pressure on him for achievement. He had had too much of that already. They were assured that their concern regarding his progress or any other aspects of his functioning could be discussed during regular conferences with the author. She suggested that they could contribute to his educational development by heightening his self-image through the enhancement of any of his strengths. They could also offer explanations about people, places, and things in his environment. In fact, encouraging Frank to become more aware of his surroundings by pointing out events, discussing movies, or doing anything to enrich his background knowledge would be of positive value. Last, it would be important that they listen attentively to whatever he tried to communicate and to guard against criticism of any negative characteristics. In short, he needed acceptance and supportive help on many fronts.

The following is an account of Frank's remedial instruction between the ages of seven and a half and thirteen years.

Frank was seen individually for remedial reading twice a week. On the Stanford-Binet Intelligence Scale his mental age was six years, eight months at the beginning. Each session lasted about forty-five minutes and was divided into brief activities so as to maintain Frank's interest and attention. He reacted favorably from the outset. A good relationship was established easily and was maintained throughout the years. The author who worked with him continued as educational consultant to Frank and his family. Re-evaluation was undertaken annually long after remedial instruction was discontinued.

Consultations with Frank's school were held regularly. His ability to grasp instruction during the early grades was initially very slow but developed gradually. Despite this, all of Frank's teachers commented on his cooperation and the considerable effort he exerted along the way.

When remedial work was started, Frank was given very simple materials at pre-primer level. It was evident almost immediately that he could not cope with them, and reading readiness materials were substituted. These he accepted readily. Because of Frank's extreme immaturity, he responded enthusiastically to such materials. He would clap his hands like a young child to show his pleasure and delight as he performed the simple tasks required in these readiness books. He experienced success at each session and was most responsive to encouragement.

Because of Frank's poor muscular coordination, readiness activities were an integral part of the program. Exercises in visual discrimination were introduced at the simplest level. Gradually he was given more difficult items until he was able to recognize words through matching them with pictures. Exercises in auditory discrimination were also presented to integrate work in both visual and auditory perception.

A typical session would include (1) cutting, pasting, drawing, and matching exercises in readiness books; (2) work in auditory and visual discrimination presented through game-type procedures; and (3) reading to Frank, which he enjoyed immensely. The tutor's reading served many purposes. It provided experiences of sheer delight in listening to stories, thereby engendering awareness that books contain something pleasurable and worthwhile. This served to counteract the traumatic experiences related to reading that he had had in school. Furthermore, some of the stories offered therapeutic possibilities, as discussed in chapter 7. The tutor noticed that Frank was particularly delighted with stories such as "The Lion and the Mouse," in which the little mouse comes off victorious; "Jack and the Beanstalk," in which Jack conquers the giant; and "Drakesbill," in which a little duck eventually triumphs over a king. Apparently Frank identified in each instance with the helpless creature who became a hero in the end, and he seemed to sigh with relief as each one overcame his lowly status.

Each session provided feelings of success and well-being for Frank. He came for his sessions regularly and willingly. He always put forth excellent effort and felt he was gaining in achievement. Along with the reading, he got help with arithmetic.

Gradually, Frank developed a sight vocabulary. He also learned to read the names of colors connected with concrete illustrations. But abstract words such as *here, the, get, this, will,* and so forth, were impossible for him to learn as yet.

Difficulty in recalling names and in associating words with pictures persisted for the first two years of tutoring. Frank frequently groped for names of animals or objects with which he was completely familiar. For example, he looked at a picture of a cow and after being unable to name it, said, "Eats hay"; for "top" he said, "Spinning thing"; for "barn," "You find it on a farm." And vice versa when he saw the word *cow* in print, he said, "I can't think of its name, but I'll find its picture," which he quickly did. Also, when he saw the word *elephant* in print and could not name it, he said, "I know what it is, let me draw it." He sketched it hurriedly and then suddenly called out, "Elephant!"

Words that had seemed thoroughly learned were forgotten. Sometimes

Frank could read a word correctly in four successive sentences and then fail to recognize it in the fifth. In fact, various kinds of memory defects had been manifested repeatedly. He could not remember names of the characters in the books he read. (They were always quickly supplied.) When he could not recall a word, he would say: "Don't tell me what the word is. You're supposed to think of the right word." He would try to remember by such means as closing his eyes and trying to visualize the object. He would try very hard and become upset when he was unable to recall words. Again encouragement was given. The word would be supplied to him while he was told, "Soon you'll be able to remember it."

During this period, many methods of word study were tried, including the kinesthetic, but the only successful one was the visual, and this to a limited degree. Since he had no other means of figuring out words, he would continue to confuse words of similar configuration, such as *doll* for *ball, pig* for *big, pig* for *dog, little* for *kitten,* and so on.

After nine months, there was improvement in his visual and auditory discrimination. At this time, a pre-primer in a graded series was introduced, along with its workbook. He continued with the other pre-primers in this series, and by the end of one year, he was ready for his first hardback book, a primer. He was also beginning to learn the names and sounds of letters. Correlated with this was work in writing, using material from the same publisher as his reader and sentences that were made up for this purpose. Even though Frank had been placed in a special class following the neurological examination, school still presented problems. Frank reported: "The other kids make fun of me. The teacher gets angry with me. Then I go home and pester my mother and father because I get so angry about what the kids did to me. My mother and father have a right to scold me because I pester them so much."

Frank continued to learn very slowly. There was much fluctuation and variability in his performance, but nevertheless learning gradually took place. When Frank was nine years six months of age and after two years of work, he was able to handle a high first grade reader in most series. He enjoyed this and found it " 'citing." His infantile speech patterns persisted as an integral part of his language disability. He was even more pleased when he could read by himself a first-grade book that contained folktales. When he was ten years three months of age, he was given an easy second-grade reader. At this point, he was capable of reading himself the folktales that he had enjoyed hearing so much, and he remained enchanted with these stories. He took home supplementary reading material at first-grade reading level.

Around this time it was possible to introduce the word family approach.

He had learned letter sounds somewhat, through practice in the remedial sessions and in workbooks, but mainly he learned them by playing Go Fish. As soon as he learned these sounds, he discovered how new words could be formed by changing the initial consonants.

Some phonics workbooks were used in connection with the teaching of word analysis skills; and the Group Word Teaching Game, played like Bingo, helped reinforce his learning of the Dolch 220 Basic Sight Words.

By the age of eleven years, one month, Frank could read *Aesop's Fables* at third-grade reading level. Word analysis skills were improving. He was able to learn consonant combinations. But he still experienced difficulty in blending sounds together. Through the use of exercises in many different phonics workbooks, he was able to learn some means of figuring out phonically regular words—probably through word comparisons, even though he could not blend auditorily. Also, he was able to write regularly spelled words that were dictated to him. By the age of eleven years, six months, he was able to read a high third grade book.

Between the ages of twelve and thirteen, there was considerable improvement in his word recognition skills. He was at last able to use a phonics approach. In all probability, some integration in the central nervous system had taken place to facilitate this ability. In addition, silent reading materials at third-grade level were introduced. He showed decided interest in materials found in various workbooks and enjoyed reading them. The comprehension questions were simple enough for him and resulted in a high degree of success. His persistence and effort were maintained at a high level throughout the sessions.

When Frank was thirteen years of age in seventh grade, reading at fourth-grade level, the regular weekly remedial sessions were discontinued, but contact was continued with the school. Thereafter, Frank was seen about twice a year, then once a year until the age of eighteen. Progress continued to be apparent, as evidenced in the test results that follow:

Age in Years		Grade Score
8–10	Too low to be measured by standardized tests	Nonreader
10	Achievement Test Primary I	2.3
12	Achievement Test Primary II	3.3
15	Achievement Test Elementary Grade Level	4.6
17	Achievement Test Intermediate Grade Level	7.5
18	Achievement Test Advanced Grade Level	10.1

In retrospect, this case shows the snail's pace at which severely impaired children learn and confirms Martha Denckla's contention that maturation continues well beyond childhood, probably into the thirties and even into later years. Had Frank been given up as hopeless during the period when progress was almost imperceptible, it is difficult to predict what might have happened. It might be surmised that school and work would have been closed to him.

When Frank was eighteen years old and finishing high school, he was reading at tenth-grade level. Apparently he had attained sufficient proficiency in reading and related skills to be admitted to a community college. He was able to cope with the requirements and obtained an A.A. degree. Judging by his academic performance in high school and college, the IQs found on tests at earlier levels had markedly underestimated Frank's intellectual potential. And Frank's ability to use all of his capabilities effectively helped him to overcome his difficulties. Another significant influence in Frank's success was the cooperative spirit exhibited by all those concerned with Frank—his parents, his teachers, and the author. A follow-up when Frank was thirty-four years old revealed that he continued to show growth in all aspects of intellectual development. He had managed his own small business responsibly for years and showed good adjustment in his personal and family life.

What caused the acceleration of his reading especially after preadolescence can only be conjectured. Heightened neurophysiological development immediately suggests itself. This is in line with findings of Denckla, who suggests:

> Focus upon negatives and deficits alone appears to be misleading; success does not imply "catchup" of negatives and deficits but rather a gradual process of compensation or even a sudden leap to a different way of succeeding. . . . Not only are regions in the cerebral cortex known to be necessary for reading . . . but there is evidence that the *connecting* and *associating* areas of the cerebral cortex show the longest period of myelination. . . . This form of physical maturation continues well past childhood, at least until the thirties, possibly up to senescence.[2]

Figures 9-1 through 9-4 are reproductions of four Bender Visual-Motor Gestalt Tests administered to Frank between the ages of eight and seventeen years. Marked changes in visual-motor coordination, perceptual development, and integrative capacity are apparent on his successive records.

2. M. B. Denckla, "The Neurological Basis of Reading Disability," in *Reading Disability: A Human Approach to Learning*, 3d ed., by F. G. Roswell and G. Natchez (New York: Basic Books, 1977), pp. 35, 36.

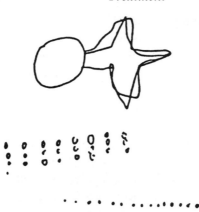

FIGURE 9-1

Frank, age eight years.

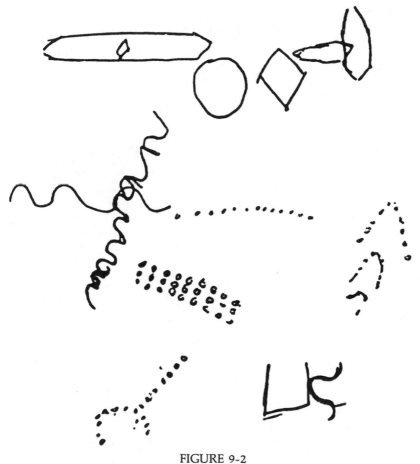

FIGURE 9-2

Frank, age ten years, three months.

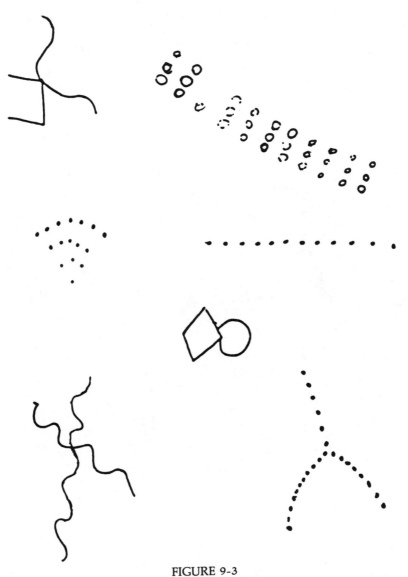

FIGURE 9-3

Frank, age fourteen years.

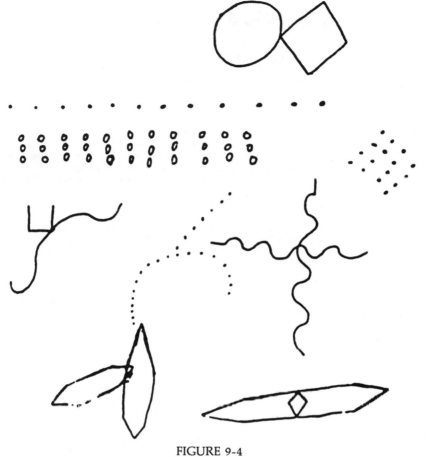

FIGURE 9-4

Frank, age seventeen years, one month.

Treatment

Suggestions for Further Reading

Green, F. "Listening to Children Read: The Empathetic Process." *Reading Teacher* 39 (February 1986).

Harris, A. J., and Sipay, E. R. *How to Increase Reading Ability,* 8th ed. New York: Longman, 1985.

Henk, W. A.; Helfeldt, J. P.; and Platt, J. M. "Developing Reading Fluency in Learning Disabled Students." *Teaching Exceptional Children* 18 (Spring 1986).

Herman, P. A. "The Effect of Repeated Readings on Reading Rate, Speech Pauses, and Word Recognition Accuracy." *Reading Research Quarterly* 20 (Fall 1985).

Hoffman, J. "The Oral Recitation Lesson." In *Issues in Literacy: A Research Perspective,* edited by J. A. Niles and R. Lalik. Rochester, N.Y.: National Reading Conference, 1985.

Johnson, D., and Pearson, P. D. *Teaching Reading Vocabulary,* 2d ed. New York: Holt, Rinehart & Winston, 1984.

Johnson, D. J. "Using Reading and Writing to Improve Oral Language Skills." *Topics in Language Disorders* 5 (June 1985).

McCoy, K. M., and Pany, D. "Summary and Analysis of Oral Reading Corrective Feedback Research." *Reading Teacher* 39 (February 1986).

Raim, J. *Case Reports in Reading and Learning Disabilities.* Springfield, Ill.: Charles C Thomas, 1982.

Ross, E. P. "Classroom Experiments with Oral Reading." *Reading Teacher* 40 (December 1986).

Stanovich, K. E.; Nathan, R. G.; West, R. F.; and Vala-Rossi, M. "Children's Word Recognition in Context: Spreading Activation, Expectance and Modularity." *Child Development* 56 (December 1985).

10

Comprehension, Study Skills, and Vocabulary

COMPREHENSION means the application of thought processes to reading; there are as many ways to teach it as there are variations in pupils and teachers. Pupils with reading problems who are reading at high third grade level or above usually have difficulty handling textbooks and understanding information found in reference books, newspapers, and magazines. They are less likely to have trouble comprehending simple narrative material. Thus, at this stage, the focus of instruction shifts. Instead of dealing with narrative material and word analysis skills, the remedial program becomes concerned more with comprehension and study skills. Work on word recognition continues as necessary, but greater stress is placed on reading to gain information. Oral reading skills are no longer emphasized because eventually most reading is done silently.

This chapter will discuss components of comprehension and remedial procedures for developing comprehension and study skills. Cases illustrate how some teachers present these skills in their classrooms. The next chapter will address teaching students of all ages how to handle expository texts.

In teaching comprehension and study skills, two broad goals are kept in mind. One is to overcome the aversion for schoolwork that most older pupils with reading difficulties have developed over the years; the other is to help pupils apply basic comprehension and study techniques wherever they are needed. Of course, adequate evaluation, as described in chapters 5 and 6, should be undertaken as early as possible to determine ultimate expectations and suggest areas that need special attention.

The factors that interfere most with comprehension are limited intelligence, insufficient familiarity with the basic concepts of the subject matter, paucity of background knowledge, lack of interest in the material, and meager vocabulary.

Comprehension should be taught in its entirety according to the demands of the topic. However, for purposes of clarification and emphasis, it is discussed here in terms of separate processes.

Schema Theory, Prior Knowledge, and Experiential Background

Schema theory depends on a pupil's prior knowledge of the subject matter. According to David Rumelhart, schema theory describes how knowledge is represented and how that representation facilitates its use.[1] Experienced teachers have long been aware of the relationship between adequate background information and depth of comprehension. Schema theory provides a structure to help the reader organize the information in the text, determine which information is important, and draw inferences about unstated information.[2] It also helps the reader to integrate new information with previous knowledge and emphasizes that reading is an interactive process that involves both the reader and the text, working in concert to reveal meaning.[3] Schema theory has refined our notions of how background knowledge affects comprehension and has shown teachers how they can facilitate students' approach to new topics.

Comprehension is further improved through instruction in *metacognition*—or awareness of one's own thought processes. R. Y. Nolte and H. Singer suggest that "in learning active comprehension students are gaining knowledge and developing the ability to regulate and monitor their cognitive processes and evaluate the outcome. In addition, metacognitive ability

1. D. E. Rumelhart, "Schemata: The Building Blocks of Cognition," Center for Human Information Processing, Technical Report No. 79 (San Diego: University of California Press, 1978).
2. I. L. Beck and P. A. Carpenter, "Cognitive Approaches to Understanding Reading," *American Psychologist* 81 (1986): 1104.
3. M. Strange, "Implications of a Conceptual Theory of Reading Comprehension," *Reading Teacher* 33 (January 1988): 391–97.

enables students to know what they need to learn and what kinds of strategies to activate."[4] Thus not only is such training of great value to students in general but it can be especially important to students with learning difficulties who exhibit passive attitudes toward learning.

In teaching specific subskills the teacher needs to be alert to students' approach to reading matter. He or she notes whether they are able to apply critical, inferential, and reflective thinking. When pupils seem to grasp only literal meanings or if they accept uncritically whatever is printed, more effective techniques are taught. For example, most readers at even the lowest levels who read or hear Aesop's "The Boy Who Cried Wolf" are able to infer why the men did not come to help the boy when he cried "wolf" the third time. However, if inferential thinking presents a problem at any reading level, the teacher points out how conclusions can be drawn from the text even though explicit information is not directly stated. Pupils with such a problem often require a step-by-step method, proceeding from the concrete information given to the implied meaning.

Another aspect of inferential thinking that may need to be developed is the understanding of metaphorical language. The following is an illustration of a simple metaphor that most pupils can understand. A mother says to her child, "You are my sunshine." The teacher elicits from the group their associations with the word *sunshine.* Their responses will probably be brightness, warmth, comfort, happiness, and so on. The children might conclude that the mother's use of the word *sunshine* meant that the child made her feel good or happy.

Older students might read in their social studies text, "In Brazil, coffee is king." For those who have prior knowledge of the relationship between the production of coffee and the amount of money it brings to Brazil, the concept is readily understood. For others, the metaphor might need clarification.

The level and complexity of the materials increase gradually as examples are chosen from the student's own texts. The teacher might also find it convenient to choose interesting selections on a variety of subjects from workbooks or other materials to illustrate the skills being taught. Because inferential thinking and abstract reasoning pose a great problem to students of all ages, there is usually a need for continued guided instruction.

In encouraging critical thinking, the teacher might present materials conveying multiple or differing points of view. Examples of these might be found in movie and theater reviews and in investigative articles in

4. R. Y. Nolte and H. Singer, "Active Comprehension: Teaching a Process of Reading Comprehension and Its Effects on Reading Achievement," *Reading Teacher* 39 (October 1985): 29–30.

newspapers. Propaganda is another useful source for helping students to differentiate fact from opinion. Reflective and creative thinking can be fostered as the reader compares his or her own knowledge with the writer's statements. The mature reader forms opinions and also creates ideas to build on those already stated. According to Jeanne Chall, the reader creates his or her own "truths" from the "truths" of others.[5]

Subskills to be taught include finding the main idea and important details, identifying cause and effect, following a sequence of events or ideas, predicting outcomes, using signal words, following directions, and adjusting reading rate according to the reader's purpose and the nature of the text. The reader needs to use skills appropriate for the structure and organization of the particular reading material.

FINDING THE MAIN IDEA AND IMPORTANT DETAILS

In discussing a main idea and its supporting details, the teacher might start by showing the pupils a picture or even by having them look around the room to describe what they see. The teacher tries to get them to condense their thoughts into a few words or a sentence, such as, "I see a country scene." This is the main idea. Then the teacher asks the students to list more specific aspects of the concept, for example: "Two boys and two girls are going on a picnic. They have a Thermos jug and a basket filled with food." These are the details. The pupils are helped to distinguish between the general concept and the details by identifying the essential differences in the statements. Then the teacher explains that authors have written down the main ideas and details that they wish to convey. Selections are then used for illustration; short paragraphs are best for purposes of clarity. For instance, the teacher might choose a paragraph similar to the following:

Millions of years ago, when dinosaurs lived on the earth, the North American continent was very low-lying. It was made up of seas and swamps. The climate was warm and perfect for lush plant growth. The plant-eating dinosaurs would creep through the hot swamps continuously eating this vegetation. They required a tremendous amount of food for their huge bodies.

The teacher first explains any words that might be unfamiliar, in this case perhaps *continent, low-lying, continuously,* and *tremendous.* He or she might ask

5. J. S. Chall, *Stages of Reading Development* (New York: McGraw-Hill, 1983).

146

if the students have ever been near a swamp and what they know about dinosaurs. After they have read the paragraph, the teacher asks them to state the main idea and supporting details. The teacher can next introduce short selections in workbooks in similar fashion and later show how to use the technique with books and reference materials.

Another way to practice finding the main idea and details is to locate the topic sentence and examine its relation to the rest of the paragraph. As is well known, however, the topic sentence may be the first or last sentence in a paragraph or come somewhere in-between. This variability often confuses students with reading difficulty. Hence, if taught at all, the topic sentence approach should be delayed until students show evidence that they can profit from such practice.

IDENTIFYING CAUSE AND EFFECT AND FOLLOWING A SEQUENCE OF IDEAS

To read well, students must also be able to identify cause and effect and follow a sequence of ideas or events. For students in intermediate grades a good practice selection is Longfellow's poem "Paul Revere's Ride." Students are asked to follow Paul Revere's routes and to find out what eventually happened. The presentation can be both informative and absorbing as pupils take turns reading successive stanzas. They follow the sequence of Paul's midnight ride to deliver his message to every "Middlesex village and farm." The students read about the British attack and the American victory. This historical event can engender a lively discussion, and the skills are incidentally elicited. For older students more mature subject matter is chosen.

PREDICTING THE OUTCOME OF EVENTS

Prediction lends itself to active participation with pupils. In the course of reading a story or selection, the teacher at an appropriate point asks the pupils what they think is likely to happen next and why they think so. Are their answers drawn from information in the text, from their background, or from their own thinking?

USING SIGNAL WORDS

A very important aspect of comprehension is the significance of signal words and their influence on the meaning. These would include the words and phrases *however, nevertheless, in spite of, on the other hand, moreover, yet, finally,* and many others. The teacher guides the students by pointing out the words in stories and texts and showing how they signal an opposite opinion, an additional thought, an ending, or a conclusion.

FOLLOWING DIRECTIONS

Those who correct students' examination papers are well aware of how often points are lost because students made mistakes in following the directions. Pointing out this fact, plus offering striking examples such as what happens when sugar is used instead of salt in a recipe, usually alerts the students to their problem. A variety of practice directions can be obtained from cookbooks, magic books, mathematics problems, science experiments, and so on. An example of how an experiment might be used follows:

Squeeze a lemon into an ordinary dish. Dip a toothpick in the juice and write a message. The toothpick won't hold much juice. You must dip it after every word. You can use any kind of white paper. To read the message, put the paper near a warm electric light bulb or iron.

The teacher can have the materials for the experiment on hand and have one pupil come to the front of the room for demonstration. Words such as *ordinary, message,* and *electric* are explained and pronounced when necessary. The students then read the experiment silently. The teacher asks them to watch those who will demonstrate and check to see whether they are following directions correctly.

ADJUSTING READING RATE

Adjusting the rate of reading to the material being read is usually one of the last skills to be taught. It is important to delay this skill until problems in word recognition, comprehension, and fluency have been largely resolved. After students have relatively little difficulty in these areas, the teacher can consider how to use their reading skills most effectively. Not rate per se but rather flexibility in reading is stressed. For example, even a "fast" reader does not read a technical report at the same rate or in the same way as a mystery story. We consider, even if not consciously, what we want to get out of a selection and then read it accordingly. The rate that students may have used in narrative materials will be inefficient for handling more mature types of reading matter. Thus students may have to be cautioned to read carefully and guided in ways to read more rapidly without sacrificing comprehension.

At every opportunity the teacher gives practice in reading for a variety of purposes. When the class is studying social studies, for example, the teacher can ask for particular information and guide the students in deciding where and how to look for it, as well as how to approach the subject matter. For instance, finding out how many people live in the Soviet Union and where most of them live will require skimming, whereas discovering the major changes from feudalism to communism requires reflective, concentrated reading. Such contrasts dramatize the flexibility that must be developed for efficient reading.

Using Textbooks

Textbooks are an important part of schooling and require special attention from the teacher. The teacher might begin by familiarizing the students with the organization of the textbook. They might examine the table of contents, chapter headings, illustrations, and the index to develop an overall conception of the major information that is offered in the book. Then the pupils might begin to practice using these aids to locate specific information.

In introducing a particular topic the teacher builds up understanding through extensive discussion. He or she explains unfamiliar concepts and vocabulary that appear in the selection. Then they turn to the portion of the book under consideration. They are encouraged to use any aids the author supplies in the form of headings in different type, italicized words, maps, and so forth. It is sometimes useful to consider each subheading as a main idea and have the pupils turn it into a question.

The teacher is specific in making assignments. That is, he or she asks questions, the answers to which can be easily found in or deduced from the text. This sets the purpose for reading and helps students work more efficiently. The more success they gain and the more adept they become, the more advanced can be the materials they use and the skills they can learn. Additional skills will be identified by teachers according to the structure and organization of the texts that are in use.

Teaching Comprehension in a Classroom

When teachers are faced with a class of pupils who show a wide variation in their ability to master comprehension techniques, they often do not know how to provide for those whose foundation skills are weak. Some teachers form teams of two or three pupils, each team with one good reader, to read the material that has been assigned. After discussion in class, the pupils are given questions for which they must find the answers. The good reader serves as a resource to help with words or passages that present difficulty. Of course the teacher uses his or her ingenuity in forming teams so that the more proficient member remains helpful and does not become domineering or superior.

Other teachers handle the problem by having a collection of books, texts, and other material at different levels. Through the years they have developed a resource file on the main topics in the course of study. It includes sufficient variety to provide reading matter for both good and poor readers. Often teachers ask, "Doesn't this take a great deal of preparation?" It does. But, as one teacher said, "I'd rather spend one hour a day preparing materials and reap the sense of satisfaction of a happy, responsive class than be miserable five hours a day, five days a week."

Individualized Teaching for a History Unit in Sixth Grade

One teacher whose sixth-grade class was studying the American Revolution used such a file to good advantage.* He first discussed the lives of the people and the government of that time. Then he raised these questions: "Do you think the American people treated England so unfairly that they were responsible for the events that followed? If you had been in the English Parliament would you have supported King George?" This led to research in which the more able pupils consulted English as well as American texts and had the startling experience of discovering that reputable English authors presented a strong case against the colonists. The less able pupils, in the meantime, read history texts at fourth- and fifth-grade levels and numerous simple pamphlets and articles that the teacher had collected in the past. Later, when the pupils decided on the unusual procedure of having a trial in the classroom to investigate whether King George and his

*Donald Lonergan, Mamaroneck, N.Y.

government should have been held responsible for the American Revolution, all the pupils were able to acquire sufficient information to participate and contribute according to their ability. Thus comprehension skills were developed at different levels to accommodate each pupil. Since appropriate materials were provided to everyone, poor readers could gain as much knowledge and skill as the others.

Individualizing Reading Materials

Even though comprehension and study skills are best taught through using the actual textbook material in connection with a topic under consideration, this is not always feasible. When working with students who have difficulty in comprehension, the teacher or reading specialist does not always have time to use the regular text, which may be broad in scope and coverage. Comprehension workbooks, which contain a variety of interesting selections, offer a convenient shortcut in developing understanding and study skills. Also, they simulate other types of informational matter that the students will use. They are available at all levels from second-grade level through college. The wide range of subject matter covered by these workbooks makes them especially valuable for pupils with reading difficulty, for it helps them to build up, in a relatively brief period, the foundation that so many of them lack because of their history of sparse reading. The brevity of workbook selections is inviting to poor readers. In addition, workbooks provide a basis for a systematic, periodic record from which the student can gauge progress.

Workbooks were used as the initial resource for developing comprehension skills in a sixth-grade class supervised by members of the staff of the City College Education Department.* The students in the class varied in cultural, racial, and socioeconomic background. There was a wide range in intelligence and in reading levels. The class was divided into two groups: those reading between high third and high fifth grade level and those reading above sixth-grade level. The pupils spent three one-hour sessions a week reading selections from a wide variety of informational articles in workbooks and pamphlets at suitable reading levels. In the lower reading group, pupils had simpler materials and read two selections at each session. At the beginning of the session the teacher presented new vocabulary and concepts.

The more competent readers needed only a little direction from the

*This project was carried out by Profs. Florence Roswell and Jeanne Chall.

151

teacher. They finished the exercises more quickly than the other group, at which point they read library books. For this group it was not necessary to purchase a workbook for each one. Instead, two copies of each book were cut up into individual exercises, thereby providing a larger number of selections. The exercises were mounted on construction paper with answers recorded on the reverse side. The pupils prepared the material under the direction of the teacher, and they took charge of distributing it. At every session pupils chose two new selections to read. They did the appropriate exercises, checked their answers with the key on the back, and kept a record of which exercises they had read.

Whenever workbook exercises are employed, a plan is followed similar to the one described in the section "Using Textbooks"; that is, the teacher builds up background, explains unfamiliar concepts and vocabulary, and so on. However, the teacher must be careful to preread articles in order to select those most appropriate in content and format. After each selection is read, the pupils can answer questions orally or silently. If the work is written, the teacher must look it over so that pupils have comments and suggestions to guide them in subsequent exercises. It is important to make certain that pupils understand the types of errors they make and that they are shown ways in which to avoid the errors in the future. Incidentally, the answer key supplied with the workbook is not sacrosanct; sometimes questions are ambiguous no matter how carefully they are selected, and more than one answer may apply. Therefore, if pupils can defend their answers, the teacher should make allowances for them.

With very severe cases of comprehension difficulty, the teacher may need to participate more actively and introduce silent reading in gradual stages. For example, he or she might start out by reading an article to the pupils and have them answer the questions orally, so that he or she can see where they are confused and can clarify meanings immediately. In subsequent sessions, the teacher can guide them to read the selection silently and answer questions orally so that he or she may keep a close check on their progress in comprehension skills. Finally, they can be encouraged to work independently and be given help only as needed.

Teaching Research Skills to Junior High School Students

In one junior high school teachers complained that the students did not know how to use library references in connection with writing reports. Not only were the pupils having difficulty finding information, but when they did come across relevant material, they tended to copy it indiscriminately. Although they had all been introduced to the use of the library, it was apparent that they could benefit from further guidance. They also needed work on practical research skills.

The reading consultant and the librarian undertook a joint venture to teach research skills to these pupils.* They formed several groups according to reading level. (The minimum reading level for the lower group was 5.0; below this level the program would have been too difficult. More advanced groups ranged up to eighth- and ninth-grade reading achievement.) The groups met for approximately seven lessons; the slower groups had more, and the faster groups fewer, sessions. Some lessons emphasized where to find particular information, others how to keep notes of information obtained, and others how to use particular reference material. All the lessons were given in conjunction with regular reports that the children were required to write. After reports were submitted, the reading consultant and the classroom teacher evaluated them and looked for possible weaknesses in specific skills. These skills were taught later. The reports were discussed with students when indicated, but grades were omitted.

Some lessons emphasized how to use a skimming technique to gather information quickly and accurately, using the *World Book Encyclopedia*. Two sets of encyclopedias, fourteen volumes each, were available in the school. Every pupil received a volume. After an orientation period in which skimming was explained and illustrated, the pupils worked individually on their assignments. Assistance was available when needed.

After the sessions, students reported that they were better able to handle their research and homework assignments in all their classes.

---

*Ruth Gottesman, Albert Einstein College of Medicine, New York, was the reading consultant; Urania Fuller, Greenburgh Junior High School, New York, was the librarian.

Ann—A Junior High School Student Reading at Fifth-Grade Level

Ann, aged twelve years six months in seventh grade, was referred to one of the authors for evaluation and treatment of her reading problem. Her schoolwork in the elementary grades had been satisfactory, even though she had never done voluntary reading. Now, in junior high school, she was experiencing difficulty with social studies, English literature, and written expression.

Outwardly, Ann appeared happy and poised, but this impression was quickly dispelled as Ann revealed her anxieties and concerns regarding her school difficulties and her parents' lack of understanding of her problems.

Evaluation of Ann's functioning revealed that she had at least high average intelligence, but her reading ranged between fifth- and sixth-grade levels. Her oral reading was highly inaccurate, and on the silent reading test she skipped over difficult passages rather than risk failure. Nevertheless, during the trial learning session Ann was cooperative and seemed eager for help.

In order to develop a coordinated plan of remedial treatment with Ann's school, the author conferred with Ann's homeroom/social studies teacher by telephone. However, the teacher indicated that there was no way in which the school could modify its requirements for Ann while she was struggling to deal with her reading and writing problems. In fact, the teacher's curt reply to suggestions for any such consideration was: "I am not concerned when I see adolescents fall apart as this girl is doing. She will have to pick herself up again. It is my duty to prepare them. . . ." Thus it was clear that working with the school in Ann's interest would be difficult.

The only choice that remained was to help Ann accept the school's mode of functioning. Despite the teacher's attitude, the author urged Ann to give her wholehearted efforts to the proposed remedial program designed to meet her special needs, so that she would eventually be successful. The author promised Ann her full support. Ann was given an explanation of what the program involved and the specific measures that would be employed to help her.

Remedial instruction included the development of oral and silent reading skills and written expression. For oral reading Ann was started on a humorous story at about fifth-grade level. Using such materials at the outset has many values. It causes anxious students to relax, while those who are resistant become more amenable to treatment. Furthermore, it fosters a good relationship between teacher and student, as they share the humor. After a few sessions it was possible to use adapted versions of materials that paralleled the school curriculum in English literature.

With regard to social studies it was clear that Ann's approach to learning was unproductive. Her idea of studying was to read the number of pages assigned and try to remember whatever facts she might be quizzed about in class the following day, regardless of whether she could recall them at a later time.

To improve her study skills, Ann was shown how to approach her textbook. She learned how it was organized and how to use the table of contents, chapter headings, index, and glossary. Ways to improve her understanding of the text were also discussed. For example, before beginning to read an assignment, she needed to try to recall what she already knew about the topic under consideration. Wherever her knowledge was vague, she was provided with further background information so that the material would be more meaningful. She also learned to preview the chapter for clues such as subheadings, boldface type, and illustrations. Gradually she was able to grasp a modified SQ3R approach to studying (discussed on page 207). In addition, analyzing paragraph structure helped Ann organize her thoughts when reading and in written work.

Another area that required emphasis was vocabulary. Improvement was approached through (1) general vocabulary development; (2) the study of prefixes, suffixes, and Latin and Greek roots; and (3) the learning of words specially related to the subject matter.

Selected passages from comprehension workbooks were occasionally used to provide reading matter on a wide variety of topics and to further develop comprehension and vocabulary skills.

Even though there was noticeable improvement there were also occasional setbacks. Lack of flexibility in the school's expectations kept Ann's morale uneven. Her performance depended to some extent on her teachers' or parents' attitudes. When they were critical, rejecting, and demanding, her functioning was impeded. One day Ann came in particularly distraught, exclaiming, "I am a failure; I got a D in social studies." I pointed out to her that she needed to differentiate between *being a failure* and having failed to measure up to certain standards. The latter we could do something about. Since Ann had a grasp of the subject matter, the author suggested that she could discuss some of her knowledge in class when it was appropriate.

We also talked about ways that Ann might reduce her anxiety with regard to speaking up in class. For example, in our time together we could role play, simulating the kind of situation she faced daily in school. She

155

could review what she read and recite a summary, or she could raise questions herself that needed further clarification. After all, even the president of the United States and other prominent people receive a great deal of help in preparing for press conferences. Ann was surprised to hear this and was intrigued with the idea of trying it out herself.

Thus oral recitations were practiced regularly. However, the goal was not merely for Ann to rehearse correct answers but also to discuss what she had learned in greater depth and from several points of view. Then, as she gained more knowledge, she could incorporate this into what she already knew. This, in turn, would engender increased confidence and effectiveness in presenting her ideas and responses.

As Ann's role-playing sessions promoted her self-assurance, she gradually dared to volunteer in class and even to consult her teacher about something she did not fully understand. Ann reported that it took a great deal of courage to carry out these acts, but she admitted that perhaps now her teacher might not see her as an uninterested pupil and a failure. Thus a beginning was made in helping Ann assume responsibility for her own achievement.

The type of supportive handling described in this case can have a therapeutic effect. It can make the difference between prolonged failure where the student appears frozen in a pattern of defeat and the beginning of improvement. When some degree of success is achieved the process of failure is gradually reversed and the student begins to adjust in school.

At the completion of the remedial sessions Ann was in eighth grade, functioning generally at ninth-grade level. Follow-up in tenth grade revealed that she was adjusting well and even read an entire book voluntarily now and then.

High School and College Students with Marked Comprehension Difficulties*

Some high school and college students carry with them the burden of years of persistent failure. In such cases the task of the instructor is to build on limited skills while giving the support students need to approach learning with confidence. Such students need concrete procedures for dealing with reading and study skills; expository materials have proved the most useful

*Contributed by Ruth G. Nathan, Albert Einstein College of Medicine, New York.

in developing these skills. Textbooks and articles from newspapers and magazines make relevant and interesting material.

One college instructor begins a process of class orientation by using concrete examples. Producing a newsmagazine, she introduces a discussion of the cover picture. Parts of the picture are considered and weighed. Simple questions, such as, "What is the artist trying to tell us?" and "What makes you think so?" encourage analytic thinking. The goals of the orientation sessions are twofold. First, it is important to establish that communication involves ideas. Second, access to these ideas is facilitated by the ability to break them down into parts and put them together again.

Cartoons are useful in reinforcing the same principles. Analyzing the parts of cartoons, especially those with no written captions, can provide entertaining and useful insights into how the parts of an idea function. Covering up an essential part or detail of a cartoon and asking if it is still funny dramatizes the relationship of the parts to the whole.

In another class, the instructor distributed the words of a current popular song. The students read the words as they listened to the record. The lyrics reiterated a simple lament about man's destructive effect on his environment. Students were able to grasp the idea quickly, sort it into key ideas and supporting details, and repeat it in their own words. At subsequent sessions, the students brought in their favorite songs and enjoyed figuring out meanings in similar ways. Students and teacher alike discovered that seemingly absurd lyrics proved to be about ideas and could be analyzed.

Illogical thinking may become apparent in work with songs and cartoons. For example, one student looked at a cartoon depicting a presidential candidate debating with his opponent and said, "All politicians are crooks." Needless to say, this concept was not implicit in the cartoon. Such irrelevant interpretations suggest that many students need fundamental orientation to arrive at sound conclusions. Lyrics and cartoons provide a concrete way to analyze material and separate logical inference from one's own opinion or bias.

Another teacher asked her students with low reading levels to make a collage to illustrate a complete thought without using words. The works were presented to the class for response and discussion. Some of the students with limited verbal skills were able to communicate visually on a highly sophisticated level. Among the collages submitted, for example, was one depicting the economic difficulties of a large city. Tumbling skyscrapers were surrounded by a shower of torn dollar bills. The concept and its supporting details were clearly thought through and beautifully executed. In contrast, another student submitted elegant pictures of natural phenomena. The content was so generalized that the only possible response from the class was "nature." The assignment vividly demonstrated the difference between fully developed concepts and vague generalizations.

When students realize that ideas are communicated in many ways, the next step is to analyze factual material. Paragraphs are introduced as the smallest unit of written communication. Good sources for practice paragraphs include the students' texts, current magazine and newspaper articles, and commercial workbooks. As they learn that each well-constructed paragraph is about one idea, students are often relieved. As they begin to feel more confident about finding the key ideas in single paragraphs, short selections composed of several related paragraphs are introduced. Current literature often provides good sources for such material. In one college remedial class, students subscribe to a weekly newsmagazine, which provides relevant, adult material for outside reading assignments.

Students are responsive to material that suggests provocative questions about human behavior. One example that elicited strong emotional reactions and lively discussions was a newspaper story about an infamous incident in which a large group of neighbors watched as a woman was murdered, without calling for help or coming to her aid. Another effective selection is a passage from the book *Alive,* which describes the plight of the victims of an air crash and their extraordinary moral dilemma.[6] The question "What would you have done?" always provokes strong reactions. Reading about dramatic real-life events encourages involvement and motivation and provides interesting possibilities for written work. Students discover that reading can deal with serious and significant questions relevant to their own lives.

Through their remedial classes, older students have been helped to develop a more positive attitude toward their abilities, and they have learned ways to approach their schoolwork more constructively.

Jeanne Chall has developed a view of the progression of the entire reading process that is known as *stage theory* (see table 10-1, reprinted from *Stages of Reading Development*). Stage theory can contribute to better understanding of how reading is acquired at different ages and levels. It can also contribute to a deeper grasp of the implications for teaching comprehension skills. (Chapter 14 presents ways to apply the theory to teaching underprepared students at the college level.)

6. A. M. Rosenthall, *Thirty-eight Witnesses* (New York: McGraw-Hill, 1964); *Alive* excerpted in E. Spargo, ed., *Topics for the Restless* (Providence: Jamestown, 1974).

Table 10-1

Stages of Reading Development: An Outline of the Major Qualitative Characteristics and How They Are Acquired

1 Stage Designation	2 Grade Range (Age)	3 Major Qualitative Characteristics and Masteries by End of Stage	4 How Acquired	5 Relationship of Reading to Listening
Stage 0: Prereading, "pseudo-reading"	Preschool Ages 6 months–6 years	Child "pretends" to read, retells story when looking at pages of book previously read to him/her; names letters of alphabet; recognizes some signs; prints own name; plays with books, pencils, and paper.	Being read to by an adult (or older child) who responds to and warmly appreciates the child's interest in books and reading; being provided with books, paper, pencils, blocks, and letters.	Most can understand the children's picture books and stories read to them. They understand thousands of words they hear by age 6 but can read few if any of them.
Stage 1: Initial reading and decoding	Grade 1 & beginning Grade 2 (ages 6 & 7)	Child learns relation between letters and sounds and between printed and spoken words; child is able to read simple text containing high frequency words and phonically regular words; uses skill and insight to "sound out" new one-syllable words.	Direct instruction in letter-sound relations (phonics) and practice in their use. Reading of simple stories using words with phonic elements taught and words of high frequency. Being read to on a level above what child can read independently to develop more advanced language patterns, knowledge of new words, and ideas.	The level of difficulty of language read by the child is much below the language understood when heard. At the end of Stage 1, most children can understand up to 4,000 or more words when heard but can read only about 600.

Table 10-1 (Continued)

1 Stage Designation	2 Grade Range (Age)	3 Major Qualitative Characteristics and Masteries by End of Stage	4 How Acquired	5 Relationship of Reading to Listening
Stage 2: Confirmation and fluency	Grades 2 & 3 (ages 7 & 8)	Child reads simple, familiar stories and selections with increasing fluency. This is done by consolidating the basic decoding elements, sight vocabulary, and meaning context in the reading of familiar stories and selections.	Direct instruction in advanced decoding skills; wide reading (with instruction and independently) of familiar, interesting materials which help promote fluent reading. Being read to at levels above their own independent reading level to develop language, vocabulary, and concepts.	At the end of Stage 2, about 3,000 words can be read and understood and about 9,000 are known when heard. Listening is still more effective than reading.
Stage 3: Reading for learning the new Phase A Phase B	Grades 4–8 (ages 9–13) Intermediate, 4–6 Junior high school, 7–9	Reading is used to learn new ideas, to gain new knowledge, to experience new feelings, to learn new attitudes; generally from one viewpoint.	Reading and study of textbooks, reference works, trade books, newspapers, and magazines that contain new ideas and values, unfamiliar vocabulary and syntax; systematic study of words and reacting to the text through discussion, answering questions, writing, etc. Reading of increasingly more complex fiction, biography, nonfiction, and the like.	At beginning of Stage 3, listening comprehension of the same material is still more effective than reading comprehension. By the end of Stage 3, reading and listening are about equal; for those who read very well, reading may be more efficient.

1 Stage Designation	2 Grade Range (Age)	3 Major Qualitative Characteristics and Masteries by End of Stage	4 How Acquired	5 Relationship of Reading to Listening
Stage 4: Multiple viewpoints	High school, grades 10–12 (ages 15–17)	Reading widely from a broad range of complex materials, both expository and narrative, with a variety of viewpoints.	Wide reading and study of the physical, biological, and social sciences and the humanities; high quality and popular literature; newspapers and magazines; systematic study of words and word parts.	Reading comprehension is better than listening comprehension of material of difficult content and readability. For poorer readers, listening comprehension may be equal to reading comprehension.
Stage 5: Construction and reconstruction	College and beyond (age 18+)	Reading is used for one's own needs and purposes (professional and personal); reading serves to integrate one's knowledge with that of others, to synthesize it and to create new knowledge. It is rapid and efficient.	Wide reading of ever more difficult materials, reading beyond one's immediate needs; writing of papers, tests, essays, and other forms that call for integration of varied knowledge and points of view.	Reading is more efficient than listening.

SOURCE: Reprinted with permission from J. S. Chall, *Stages of Reading Development* (New York: McGraw-Hill, 1983), pp. 85–87.

Treatment

Suggestions for Further Reading

Baumann, J. F., and Ballard, P. Q. "A Two Step Model for Promoting Independence in Comprehension." *Journal of Reading* 30 (April 1987).

Brown, A. L. *Teaching Students to Think as They Read: Implications for Curriculum Reform.* Urbana, Ill.: Center for the Study of Reading, 1985.

Cooper, J. D. *Improving Reading Comprehension.* Boston: Houghton Mifflin, 1986.

Gambrell, L. B.; Kapinus, B. A.; and Wilson, R. M. "Using Mental Imagery and Summarization to Achieve Independence in Comprehension." *Journal of Reading* 30 (April 1987).

Goodman, Y. M.; Burke, C.; and Sherman, B. *Reading Strategies: Focus on Comprehension.* New York: Holt, Rinehart & Winston, 1980.

Hanus, K. S., and Moore, D. W. "Reading Comprehension Questions in Secondary Literature Textbooks for Good and Poor Readers." *English Quarterly* 18 (Winter 1985).

Holmes, B. C., and Roser, N. L. "Five Ways to Assess Readers' Prior Knowledge." *Reading Teacher* 40 (March 1987).

Johnson, D. D., and Johnson, B. H. "Ten Inference Types and a Three Step Teaching Procedure for Inferential Comprehension." *Journal of Reading* 29 (April 1986).

Pearson, P. D. "Direct Explicit Teaching of Reading Comprehension." In *Comprehension Instruction: Perspectives and Suggestions,* edited by G. G. Duffy, L. R. Roehler, and J. Mason. New York: Longman, 1984.

———. "Changing the Face of Reading Comprehension Instruction." *Reading Teacher* 38 (April 1985).

Poindexter, C., and Prescott, S. "A Technique for Teaching Students to Draw Inferences from Text." Newark, Del.: International Reading Association, 1985.

Ruddell, R. B. "Vocabulary Learning: A Process Model and Criteria for Evaluating Instructional Strategies." *Journal of Reading* 29 (April 1986).

Ryder, R. J. "Teaching Vocabulary through External Context Clues." *Journal of Reading* 30 (October 1986).

Sadoski, M. "The Natural Use of Imagery in Story Comprehension and Recall: Replication and Extension." *Reading Research Quarterly* 20 (1985).

Thelen, J. N. "Vocabulary Instruction and Meaningful Learning." *Journal of Reading* 29 (April 1986).

Thompson, S. J. "Teaching Metaphoric Language: An Instructional Strategy." *Journal of Reading* 30 (November 1986).

Wenglinski, J. C. "Vocabulary Teaching: Translating Research into Classroom Practice." *Journal of Reading* 30 (March 1987).

Wong, B. Y. L. "Self-Questioning Instructional Research: A Review." *Review of Educational Research* 55 (Summer 1985).

11

Reading Expository Texts Is Different—And Harder

by Florence G. Schoenfeld*

SEVERAL YEARS AGO, the writer was invited to address the faculty of a small elementary school on the subject of reading. A small group of teachers met informally to discuss the children's reading habits and interests, the parents' requests or complaints, and the teachers' problems with reading programs, materials, and so on. Each of the writer's questions was met with another tale of pride and achievement. No one had any complaints about the school's reading programs. Then came the question, How do the children handle expository texts in such academic areas as social studies and science?

Suddenly, the floodgates opened wide. The teachers discovered that they had been silently and separately sharing a common disbelief that children who achieved so highly on reading tests could have so much difficulty reading certain texts. Different teachers said: "That's the most baffling thing! . . . These kids score well on reading tests, enjoy great works of literature, memorize long pieces of poetry, but have real trouble understanding their own Social Studies textbooks. . . . They have to go over every page so many times that we often find it's easier not to use the text at all. . . . We just teach the lesson orally. . . . We use a lot of audiovisuals."

When it came to using expository texts, these high achievers were being taught as though they had reading disabilities. Their textbooks were set aside because they had difficulty comprehending the material in them. Yet

*Supervisor of Reading Projects (retired), New York City Board of Education.

scrapping textbooks was, obviously, not a solution since the students would ultimately be expected to read that type of discourse and to read it independently. The episode shows the dichotomy that can develop between reading narrative and expository material and clearly demonstrates the need for different teaching strategies.

It was interesting to note that the teachers had not identified the children's difficulties as a reading problem at all. But it was. Expository reading was an area of instruction that needed remedial intervention. If this was true for these "good readers," it must surely be so for students known to be encountering reading difficulties.

A great deal of instructional time is devoted to teaching the "once upon a time" genre of literature. We teachers select stories that we think will be interesting and meaningful to students, which offer good literary quality and are written at an appropriate level. But these objectives may be irrelevant when we are selecting expository materials for content area teaching. The match with the curriculum—not with the student—is the guiding consideration in selecting such a text. We may even have to accept that a new topic has little or no meaning for students at the outset. Expository texts are written by content area experts: historians write history books, biologists write biology books, and so it should be. The final product is meant to inform more than entertain.

We also use expository texts differently. In teaching narrative, we encourage students to appreciate the nuances of character development, to empathize with the principals in the story, to understand the behavior of those characters, and to see how characters influence the whole course of the unfolding plot. The author helps by writing the narrative tale in language designed to intrigue and entice. The expositional text, in contrast, is written in an impersonal, didactic style, depriving the reader of opportunities to relate to or identify with individual characters.

The author of the informational or expository piece has to presume that the reader has acquired a certain store of knowledge. Obviously, learning sixth-grade science is predicated on having learned fifth-grade science; the sixth-grade literary anthology presents no such specific constraints. The two excerpts that follow are about hurricanes; the first presents an exposition of relevant information, while the second narrates the experience of two people during a hurricane.

A hurricane is a violent tropical storm. The winds blow at least 119 kilometers (74 miles) an hour. And they have sometimes reached 322 kilometers (200 miles) an hour. The storm begins over southern seas. In satellite photos it first appears as a dark, swirling cloud. Weather watchers study these pictures to see how the storm will develop. It may grow very large, often reaching a diameter of 483 kilometers (300 miles). At the center, called the eye, air pressure is low. The air around the eye rushes into the low pressure region. As the air rushes in, it curves. The hurricane is a huge mass of air speeding around the eye.[1]

Now consider this story:

> The moment he stepped into the kitchen, however, Matt blurted, "Andy, there's a hurricane called Esther headed this way. I heard it on the radio just now." Andy went to the radio and turned it up. "The eye of the hurricane is not expected to reach this area for about forty-eight hours," the announcer said. "I'm scared," admitted Matt honestly. "Let's get out of here."
> . . . Then, protecting their eyes from the driving sand that cut and stung their faces, they struggled to the top of the dune. The sea was a nightmare of towering waves, booming and boiling in angry turmoil. Trying to speak into the smothering wind, Matt swallowed great mouthfuls of air.[2]

Although both passages deal with the same subject and both appear in the same fifth-grade basal reader, it is obvious that the expository piece presents greater demands for the reader's attention, processing, and recall. The narrative can be read for a more general understanding of plot and characterization with little need for precise recall of data. The reader of the narrative can hear the story and even imagine similar conversations from personal experience. In contrast, the expository text has no characters with whom to empathize, and there is no dialogue to evoke the recall of comparable language. This brief passage is laden with bits of information each of which requires attention because of its interrelationships with the others.

Teachers typically focus more on identifying the content of an expository text than on developing the strategies needed for understanding that content. Rather than devoting time to developing students' interest in the subject before they read—as they do routinely for narratives—teachers are likely to present subject texts as assignments: "Read chapter 3 and answer the questions at the end." Expository texts are more often read silently, and discussion usually takes the form of teacher-directed questioning.[3] Since there is usually a limited time to cover the curriculum, teachers may

1. Economy Reading Series, *Uncharted Waters* (Oklahoma City: Economy, 1986), p. 383.
2. Ibid., pp. 390–91.
3. D. Durkin, *Comprehension Instruction—Where Are You?* Reading Education Report No. 1, Center for the Study of Reading, University of Illinois, Urbana, 1977.

focus discussion on the recall of literal information, allotting less time to higher order comprehension processes such as drawing inferences and making critical judgments.

Activation of Prior Knowledge

Reading research has consistently demonstrated the power of prior knowledge to spark an interactive process between the reader and the text, the net effect of which is comprehension.[4] Awareness of what one already knows about a new topic creates an "ideational scaffolding" which, in turn, provides a slot or niche for a piece of new information.[5] Therefore, helping students with reading difficulty to access, share, and apply their knowledge of a new topic must be a foremost concern.

In fact, teachers usually open lessons with a question, statement, or picture intended to elicit students' recall of relevant experiences or information, a process known as *schema activation.*[6] But one of the most difficult challenges in teaching students with reading or learning problems is overcoming the pervasive feelings of failure that have convinced them they have learned "nothing" and probably expect to learn nothing more.

The teacher says: "Today we will begin to read about the life of lumberjacks in Canada. What do you know about lumberjacks in Canada?" Most students will be able to recall some previous experience with the words *Canada* or *lumber* or *lumberjacks.* But the students who perceive themselves as unsuccessful learners are quick to answer "nothing." The persevering teacher will dig deeper, trying to evoke some relevant bit of recall. But the most disheartened students not only have stopped expecting to learn but have stopped listening to instruction. Their answer is ready before they hear the question. If the teacher doesn't do something to break this cycle, the students will effectively exclude themselves from the teaching-learning process, and any instruction that follows will be lost.

Authors presume that their readers come to the text with a particular experience and understanding. For those readers who are not knowledgeable the text may well seem incomprehensible nonsense. Whether some-

4. P. H. Johnston, "Prior Knowledge and Reading Comprehension Test Bias," *Reading Research Quarterly* 19 (Winter 1984); R. J. Tierney and J. Mosenthal, "Discourse Comprehension and Production: Analyzing Text Structure and Cohesion," in *Reader Meets Author: Bridging the Gap,* ed. J. A. Langer and M. T. Smith-Burke (Newark, Del.: International Reading Association, 1982).

5. J. H. Osborn, B. F. Jones, and M. Stein, "The Case for Improving Textbooks," *Educational Leadership* 42 (April 1985).

6. P. H. Johnston, *Reading Comprehension Assessment: A Cognitive Basis* (Newark, Del.: International Reading Association, 1983).

thing is nonsense depends to a large extent on what the reader already knows.[7] Prior knowledge is the nonvisual information the reader brings to the text and which interacts with the visual information the text is presenting—the printed language, illustrations, charts, graphic cues, punctuation marks, and so on. Through this interaction between the reader's store of information and the information provided by the text, a synthesis of prior and new knowledge will emerge.

Try reading the following passage:

A newspaper is better than a magazine, and a seashore is a better place than a street. At first it is better to run than to walk. Also you may have to try it several times. It takes some skill but it's easy to learn. Even young children can enjoy it. Once successful, complications are minimal. Birds seldom get too close. One needs lots of room. Rain soaks in very fast. Too many people doing the same things can also cause problems. If there are no complications, it can be very peaceful. A rock will serve as an anchor. If things break loose from it, however, you will not get a second chance.

Nonsense? Now reread it with kites in mind. Knowledge and experience make up a powerful force that not only directs comprehension but also prompts the decoding of individual words. Try reading the next passage to see the confusion that ensues when words that are spelled exactly alike have totally different meanings.

The boys' arrows were nearly gone so they sat down on the grass and stopped hunting. Over at the edge of the wood they saw Henry making a bow to a small girl who was coming down the road. She had tears in her dress and tears in her eyes. She gave Henry a note which he brought over to the group of young hunters. Read to the boys, it caused great excitement. After a minute but rapid examination of their weapons they ran down to the valley. Does were standing at the edge of the lake, making an excellent target.

Word recognition and simple decoding were equally influenced by your familiarity with elements of the situation being described (nonvisual information) and the actual letters printed on the page (visual information).

The task for teachers is to structure the preparatory, or *prereading,* lesson so that all students have the opportunity to explore their own stores of prior knowledge. This conveys the explicit message to the students that

7. F. Smith, *Reading without Nonsense,* 2d ed. (New York: Teachers College Press, 1985).

"everyone may know something about everything." This is why prereading is always done in the whole class or large group setting. As the teacher guides and probes individual memories, students spark each other's thinking, reminding themselves of information they may have forgotten, didn't know, or hadn't thought important or relevant. They clarify and even correct each other's facts and opinions. (Teachers should make sure that clarifications are done in a constructive and helpful way.)

Semantic Mapping

Semantic mapping, also known as *semantic webbing* or *networking,* provides a graphic display of words and concepts that students associate with a central topic or theme. The diagram that follows illustrates the almost limitless associations that may evolve on each subtopic. During this type of brainstorming, the teacher actively encourages students' associations and contributions without judgment or exclusion. All contributions are accepted and recorded on a chalkboard or large chart paper.

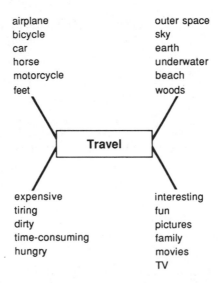

airplane	outer space
bicycle	sky
car	earth
horse	underwater
motorcycle	beach
feet	woods

Travel

expensive	interesting
tiring	fun
dirty	pictures
time-consuming	family
hungry	movies
	TV

1. The teacher points out that certain words or phrases share common semantic or syntactic characteristics and may be grouped into categories.
2. The teacher interjects into the discussion specific words, phrases, or concepts that he or she expects the students to encounter.
3. The teacher gently separates or groups together associations that are incorrect or misleading to the semantic context. These items should be reconsidered at a later time, perhaps during a summary session.

The display provides the base to which students will add new information and the structure upon which students can build their new understanding. The map presents graphic evidence that they know something, that they have been learning all along and that they should expect to continue learning. The semantic map should be preserved for later review. This is how students will see their new learning and have the opportunity to expand and correct their previous misconceptions.

Semantic Feature Analysis

As the term implies, *semantic feature analysis* examines the meaningful features of a topic. It is a more concrete approach to exploration than the semantic map, more focused on the specifics of function and information than on abstract concepts. It enables students to understand relationships among pieces of information and to expand vocabulary. The diagram that follows is a grid in which the topic of animal homes was analyzed. In the left column are listed items within the category *animal homes;* the column headings name the particular animal. Through group discussion it is decided which of the features of homes is characteristic of each animal.

This grid is also preserved for additional discussion, clarification, and correction during medial and final summaries of the reading assignment.

Animal Homes	Dog	Cat	Bird	Mouse	Horse	Whale
Forest						
Jungle						
Ocean						
Zoo						
Farm						
People's Home						

(Students write a plus in each box if the animal lives in that home; a minus if it doesn't.)

The Time Line

The time line is a brainstorming technique that is particularly useful when integrated into the teaching of material that follows some sequence of time. Although historical texts and scientific developments come first to mind, the reading of biographies in the English class would surely be enhanced by a graphic display of the sequence of events. Like the semantic map and semantic feature analysis, the time line provides an opportunity for the whole group to share the knowledge and experience they bring to the assignment.

William Shakespeare

| Born 1564 | Married 1582 | Actor 1592 | Playwright 1595 | Retired 1612 |

The primary purpose of these and other prereading strategies is assessment. The teacher can gauge the students' readiness and awareness of the topic. It may well become clear through extensive brainstorming that the students do not really have the knowledge base needed for a particular assignment. It may be that the teacher will have to postpone the assignment and provide some intermediary learning experiences to bring students back to the original plan. This is a temporary delay. How much better to discover the students' lack of readiness before the reading lesson begins than after they forge ahead into mutual frustration and failure.

There is no need to create a special curriculum or additional study materials to introduce students to expository texts. Using required materials, a teacher can prepare students with specific directions so that they will know what is expected of them.[8]

The Stages of Expository Reading Development

Immature students will be slow to achieve independence in expository reading. The teacher should explain that informational reading is more difficult than narrative reading and that the students will be given the necessary direction, support, and time.

When students reach the intermediate grades and a more mature stage of reading development, they need to develop more objectivity in their approaches to reading assignments. At about the fourth-grade level the language of textbooks becomes more abstract and more removed from the here and now (see table 10-1).[9] Because intermediate level students may be self-referential in their thinking, their first experiences in analyzing text

8. H. L. Herber, *Teaching Reading in the Content Areas,* 2d ed. (Englewood Cliffs, N.J.: Prentice-Hall, 1978).

9. J. S. Chall, "Research in Linguistics and Reading Instruction: Implications for Further Research and Practice" (Paper delivered at the Thirteenth Annual Meeting of the International Reading Association, Boston, 1968).

should be in terms of their own strengths and difficulties. They need to look at a text objectively and ask questions that will compare their own abilities to the demands of the text: What is this about? What do I already know about this topic? Is the language technical or otherwise unfamiliar to me? Is the organization of the chapter unclear? Is the author's style so complex that it confuses me? What can I do to deal with these problems? Who and what can help me? The answers to these questions may come from the text itself when the student learns to use guides such as glossaries, indexes, charts, graphs, and headings.

During the junior high school years, students who are lacking in social maturity may be resistant to the style of a text. Students who are not accustomed to dealing with unfamiliar ideas, whose personal experiences have not encouraged interest and curiosity in the world, are likely to have difficulty relating to and comprehending the concepts and information presented in their textbooks.[10]

In one large junior high school, a social studies teacher was frustrated by just such a problem teaching his ninth-grade classes. Although the students complained that their textbook was too hard, they were actually able to recognize the words and their meanings. But they were unable to assimilate the information because of their limited background knowledge. In spite of their age, their social perspective was immature, more characteristic of the here-and-now view of the primary years.

After reading about customs of aboriginal people on Pacific islands, for example, the students reacted with comments like "weird" or "disgusting," viewing the behavior of these people as not only different but unacceptable. The students still operated through a self-referential orientation in which ideas were judged—accepted or rejected—based on their familiarity. If these students were ever to learn about life in the Pacific islands, ancient Greece, or any other time and place, they would need to move beyond their self-centered views. They would have to accept a reality unrelated to their personal actions, thoughts, or experience and to begin to understand customs of a contrasting society.[11]

The remedy in this instance was found not in offering conventional remedial reading but in recognizing the cognitive base on which the poor reading had been built. A ten-week program of sociodramatic treatment of attitude formation was instituted, using two of the five social studies periods each week. Following traditional protocols of sociodrama the students were led through role-playing sessions in which they volunteered to

10. G. L. Bond and S. B. Kegler, "Reading in the Senior High School"; C. M. McCullough, "Reading in the Intermediate Grades"; M. G. McKinn, "Reading in the Primary Grades"; and W. D. Sheldon, "Reading Instruction in Junior High School," in National Society for the Study of Education, Sixtieth Yearbook (Chicago: University of Chicago Press, 1961).
11. H. G. Furth, *Piaget for Teachers* (Englewood Cliffs, N.J.: Prentice-Hall, 1970).

act not as an individual but as a representative of a social group or class.[12] The students, after some instruction and rehearsal, chose their own topics and roles. For example, they chose the topic of curfews imposed by parents and assumed roles of mother, father, siblings, friends, and neighbors; they chose to role play a conflict around a school regulation and represented the views of the principal, teachers, students, and parents.

As they became comfortable with assuming the perspective of other individuals, they began to choose broader, more socially distant and less personal situations, such as that of a job applicant facing racial discrimination. They eventually role played a session of a congressional investigating committee.

Sociodrama proved to be a powerful experience in accelerating the social maturation and perspective of these immature ninth graders. They were able to approach their texts with an objectivity gained through walking in someone else's shoes, even if only in a classroom simulation.[13]

With the demand for independent silent reading at the senior high level comes the responsibility for the reader to initiate all the strategies that should have been developed through the earlier grades. Teachers emphasize students' actual roles and responsibilities in completing an assignment. What will they contribute to the reading process? How will they interact with the text? What will be the end product or purpose of their reading? Students need a clear idea of what they might gain from reading. Directions to read chapter 2 or complete the unit do not offer the reader (especially one who is having difficulty) a sufficient purpose for making a substantial effort. "Discover how the water gets to your kitchen sink," or "Can you find out what led to Scandinavians' living in Minnesota?" could lead to a meaningful interaction with the text and would focus the reader's attention. The result is new knowledge that may have some purpose in the reader's life.

Just as students learn several ways to analyze individual words, they should be prepared to apply alternative approaches to the analysis of the text itself. Knowing the organizational pattern of the text will provide a framework for purposeful, systematic reading, especially for students who are experiencing difficulties.[14] Reading within an identifiable pattern provides a structure that will help the student process the information, integrate it with prior knowledge, and internalize it for future recall.

12. R. B. Haas, ed., *Psychodrama and Sociodrama in American Education* (New York: Beacon House, 1949), pp. 177–79.
13. F. G. Schoenfeld, "A Sociodramatic Treatment of Attitude Formation with a Sociometric Analysis" (Unpublished Masters Thesis, Teachers College, Columbia University, 1950).
14. R. Farr and R. F. Carey, *Reading: What Can Be Measured?* 2d ed. (Newark, Del.: International Reading Association, 1986).

Suggestions for Further Reading

Armbruster, B. B.; Osborn, J. H.; and Davison, A. L. "Readability Formulas May Be Dangerous to Your Textbooks." *Educational Leadership* 42 (April 1985).

Farr, R., and Carey, R. F. *Reading: What Can Be Measured?* 2d ed. Newark, Del.: International Reading Association, 1986.

Goodman, K. "Reading: A Psycholinguistic Guessing Game." Paper presented at the annual meeting of the American Educational Research Association, New York, 1967.

Johnston, P. *Reading Comprehension Assessment: A Cognitive Basis.* Newark, Del.: International Reading Association, 1983.

Meyer, G. J. F. *The Organization of Prose and Its Effects on Memory.* Amsterdam: North Holland, 1975.

Osborn, J. H.; Jones, B. F.; and Stein, M. "The Case for Improving Textbooks." *Educational Leadership* 42 (April 1985).

Roller, C. M., and Schreiner, R. "The Effects of Narrative and Expository Organizational Patterns on Sixth Grade Children's Comprehension of Expository and Narrative Prose." *Reading Psychology* 6 (1985): 27–42.

Smith, F. *Reading without Nonsense,* 2d ed. New York: Teachers College Press, 1985.

12

Older Students with Severe Reading Difficulty

THE SEVEREST CASES of reading difficulty occur among older students—those in junior or senior high school and adults—who are nonreaders or who read significantly below grade level. These pupils present special problems. The older the pupils and the lower the achievement, the more defeated, frustrated, angry, or fearful they become; finally they are unwilling to try, or they pretend not to care whether they learn to read or not. They often become the hard-core discipline problems of the school and are a tribulation to all those who deal with them. Not only are they a blight on the school's record, but no one is certain how to cope with them in a school setting. Even when a teacher tries to work with them, these pupils usually proceed so slowly that the teacher's patience is sorely tried and he or she may feel like giving up, too. Although working with them one at a time is beset with problems, the teacher needs to find suitable methods and materials so that they can benefit from schoolwork.

This chapter will discuss ways to improve these pupils' attitudes toward reading and teach them through adapted methods and special materials.

Improving Attitudes toward Reading

Teachers who try to help such pupils need not despair even when they gaze upon distraught, belligerent youngsters. Despite their utter misery, their lack of surface appeal, they can be transformed. They desperately need a forceful, inspiring influence on their lives. Such an influence can cause them to drop their armor and start afresh.

Such pupils need someone to believe in them enough to help them help themselves. When the pupils see that there are all kinds of useful and meaningful things to learn and that they can actually master them, they begin to feel competent. Through the teacher's respect, through connecting schoolwork with their personal lives and feelings, these pupils may finally emerge as earnest and resolute.

Ways to Handle Students with Serious Reading Problems

Besides overcoming entrenched resistance and finding qualified teachers, the major considerations in handling severely retarded readers center on setting realistic goals and finding ways to reach pupils in a learning situation. It is not that these pupils need anything so different from other young people. They have the same strivings for self-exploration and knowledge of the practical and esthetic world as others. It is just that their poor academic skills have alienated them from school. To bring them back, we need to have a realistic view of their problem and adapt the program to their present situation. They may then absorb the essentials that will carry over into their life after they leave school; at the same time they may at last experience the joy of a job well done in the classroom. Each school and each teacher improvises according to the pupils' stage of development, the subject matter to be taught, and the materials available. Some overall suggestions concerning goals, adaptation of the program, and the finding of suitable materials follow.

As in all cases of reading disability, diagnosis determines individual expectations and suggests realistic goals. (Diagnosis has been discussed in chapters 5 and 6.) However, for pupils with severe difficulty, individual assessments are of utmost importance. Trial sessions as described in chapter 5 are particularly suitable in evaluating pupils' needs. Prognosis remains tentative because these pupils have failed for so many years that they are likely to have developed antipathy toward formal examinations of any kind. Therefore, test scores tend to underestimate their ability.

Improvement—even though very slow—is the realistic goal. Even those pupils who are far behind *can* improve. Perhaps their extreme disability will prevent their ever reaching their potential, but they can move ahead; their poor foundation and years of failure may cause severe handicaps, but they can be surmounted to some extent.[1] It is hoped that most pupils can be brought up to at least sixth- or seventh-grade reading level before they leave school. This is probably the minimum for getting along in our world. Every effort must be made to prepare them to fit into society, to help them better their vocational chances, and to see that they get as much out of school as they can.

The cases of Karl and Dirk that follow describe two boys of about the same age and reading level who needed very different kinds of teaching. Karl could follow accepted procedures for remedial instruction, and Dirk needed a special program.

Karl and Dirk—Both Twelve Years of Age, Reading at Third-Grade Level: A Contrast in Treatment

KARL

Karl, aged twelve years, five months, had a long history of school problems. He had particular difficulty in absorbing reading instruction. Karl had sustained so many failures during his schooling that a psychologist was called in to diagnose his problem. During the testing, he was pleasant and friendly but unable to give consistent or sustained effort to any task. Questions and instructions had to be repeated over and over. Karl's responses were incomplete, poorly expressed, and accompanied by the almost constant refrain, "I don't know that one." He seemed to anticipate failure and had so little faith in his abilities that he felt that there was no use trying. He needed an inordinate amount of encouragement to keep functioning.

In the diagnostic sessions, his intelligence was found to be within normal range, with deficiencies in his background of general information and ability to define words. His reading test scores were as follows:

1. R. Gottesman; I. Belmont; and R. Kaminer, "Admission and Follow-up Status of Reading Disabled Children Referred to a Medical Clinic," *Journal of Learning Disabilities* 8 (1973): 642–50.

	Grade Score
Oral Reading Test	3.6
Silent Reading Achievement Test for Grades Three and Four	
Word Knowledge	3.2
Reading	2.2
Wide Range Achievement Test	
Word Pronunciation	3.8
Spelling	3.2
Arithmetic	4.7

A test of basic decoding skills showed a grasp of phonics skills but difficulty in handling polysyllabic words.

It was found that when the author sat next to Karl, he could work reasonably well. However, when independent effort was required, his concentration span was extremely short and little was accomplished. Furthermore, as soon as he encountered challenging tasks, he gave up.

It was clear that on his own Karl read everything in a vague, unfocused way, which probably accounted for his very low silent reading score. He stated that in order to answer questions about a passage he would have to read it many times. Thus, when a new selection was introduced, Karl and the author discussed the content of the passages together. Difficult concepts and unfamiliar words were explained, and poor questions in the workbook were eliminated. For example, for an article entitled "Wetlands, Wildlife, and Wells,"[2] the author explained the meanings of *swamp, reservoir,* and *wildlife.* Then Karl was asked to read the article to find out why it is important to preserve swamps. With this type of preparation, his comprehension of the selection was quite good. Students whose backgrounds are meager cannot understand such an article without prior preparation.

For oral reading, materials at fourth-grade level seemed suitable. It was not difficult to find books that interested this boy because he was quite immature for his age and reacted well to stories that generally appealed to younger children. During trial learning sessions he chose several books that he would like to read (these were subsequently suggested to his tutor).

At the completion of the examination, Karl seemed interested in the author's detailed explanation of what he needed in reading, spelling, and expressive writing, and he appeared willing to receive individualized instruction in these areas. Accordingly, arrangements were made with a reading specialist outside the school to work with him twice a week. Regular conferences were to be held with his classroom teacher so as to coordinate their efforts.

2. W. Liddle, *Reading for Concepts,* Book C (New York: McGraw-Hill, 1970).

Karl's tutor created a two-stage plan. The first was to try to help the boy overcome his deficiencies, especially in comprehension; the second was to assist him with his schoolwork. The tutor communicated with Karl's classroom teacher, either by telephone or through messages delivered by Karl, whenever clarification of assignments or remedial instruction was indicated. Thus Karl became aware of collaborative efforts on his behalf. Previously he had had a feeling of being on the fringe of his class; now he had a sense of being cared for. Gradually he became willing to enter into group activities. He was also encouraged to take full responsibility for his homework and could receive the tutor's help when necessary, thereby freeing his parents from constantly having to check. In time, his parents' anxiety diminished as they recognized that Karl's instructional needs were being met. Therefore, they could focus on more pleasant ways of spending time with their son. For example, it was suggested that they take Karl to special exhibits and talk over what they were viewing, and when they took trips they could talk about cities and states they were in. His tutor felt this would strengthen Karl's geographical knowledge and lessen his vagueness.

In the beginning of remedial work, materials at fourth-grade level were used. When reading aloud, Karl and his tutor read alternate paragraphs so that he was helped with phrasing, expression, and learning new words. For silent reading, he was given a good deal of preparation so that he could understand vocabulary and content. For recreational reading, only short stories were used at the outset. Then longer stories divided into short chapters were introduced, and finally, toward the end of the year, Karl completed several full-length books at about fifth- and sixth-grade reading levels. There was also emphasis on developing spelling and writing skills, starting with simple sentences and progressing to simple paragraphs. Words taught in spelling were regularly reviewed through dictation in sentences. Karl needed a great deal of reinforcement because of his poor ability to recall what he seemingly learned.

Karl developed an excellent relationship with his tutor, who observed that along with progress in school, there were discernible changes for the better in his posture and stance and degree of independence in many areas. Even his tendency to shrug his shoulders and say "I don't know" decreased markedly. Improvement was steady but uneven, with occasional lapses in one area or another that required patient reteaching and review. Yet overall gains were apparent both at school and at home. Nevertheless, it seems likely that Karl will need supportive help until a higher level of competence and independence is achieved. Furthermore, consideration might eventually be given to supplementing his curriculum with nonreading materials, as discussed in the case of Dirk which follows.

Dirk

Dirk, aged twelve years, eight months, reading at third-grade level, was referred to one of the authors by his school. He needed guidance in connection with educational planning, as he was becoming increasingly resistant to reading instruction.

For several years, Dirk had been placed in special classes for children with learning disabilities, where he had accepting, specially trained, competent teachers. Yet he was a frustrated boy who said that he was "completely turned off" by reading and remedial reading materials. His mother described him as a child who asked bright questions at a very early age but could not remember the names of anything for many years and could not even remember the names of colors at five years of age. Examination revealed some indication of neurophysiological dysfunction.

On the Wechsler Intelligence Scale for Children (appendix A) Dirk's verbal scale IQ was high average, performance scale very superior, and full scale IQ in the bright normal range. The subtest scores revealed wide variability in his intellectual functioning, with extremely high abilities on most performance tests and striking deficits on tests involving short-term memory and learning of new symbols. Tests of similarities and vocabulary were average because of his difficulties with abstract thinking. Dirk's reading test scores were as follows:

	Grade Score
Oral Reading Test	3.2
Silent Reading Achievement Tests for Grades Three and Four	
Word Knowledge	3.3
Reading	3.0
Wide Range Achievement Test	
Word Pronunciation	4.2
Spelling	2.0
Arithmetic	4.5

In evaluating decoding skills he revealed a lack of basic phonics ability.

Informal procedures indicated that Dirk could handle materials at about third-grade level. Even though he could give a fairly good oral report of what he had read, he had enormous difficulty writing. He used a solely phonics approach. For example, he wrote *ej* for *edge* and *citchn* for *kitchen*. Furthermore, even though he could succeed with some of the spelling approaches used during the trial learning session, he indicated that he found them too tedious to apply.

179

Treatment

Dirk was charming, pleasant, and cooperative during the testing, but he was totally frank about the fact that he disliked heartily the books customarily used for pupils like him. It appeared that we were dealing with the type of child who needed a supplementary curriculum that would not rely on reading as the only means of gathering information. Other media would need to be used to develop background information, such as cassettes, recorded books, tape recordings, television, films, filmstrips, and slides. For example, in the areas of science and ecology, rich sources of materials are now widely available. Such experiences for Dirk would need to be expanded to meet his needs.

Accordingly, the school was advised to encourage any activities that would use this boy's unusually good manual skills and creativity. Fortunately, the school was equipped with facilities for woodworking, and this was an area in which Dirk excelled. The school was advised to present reading incidentally in connection with his shop work. Technical vocabulary could be selected from directions for assembling units or whatever type of work he was engaged in. Spelling and writing might be introduced gradually wherever actually needed.

Thus, for Dirk, alternative ways to educate him had to be explored until he reached the point where he would willingly participate in some form of remedial program. The authors have encountered many such students who have become more amenable to help in later adolescence, when plans for their future became realistic and the need for learning became more compelling.

In a follow-up study one year later it was found that through family counseling Dirk and his mother had discovered that his dyslexia was being used as a means of maintaining a close, dependent relationship. Dirk learned further that he had been perpetuating many immature patterns of adjustment by clinging to his dyslexia, including using dyslexia as an excuse for not having to cope with academic demands.

Dirk eventually decided to enter into a program for improving his school performance. The medium that provided the greatest motivation proved to be recorded books. He found these talking books, which were at a mature level, fascinating and, according to his mother, "gobbled them up." The recorded books had introduced Dirk to literature as it was originally written. They had also aroused his curiosity to learn more about a wide variety of subjects, and his outlook broadened in innumerable ways. As he began to recognize that he did not always have to succeed and that failure was part of the learning process, the possibility of failure became less threatening. Gradually his rationalizations about his inability to learn lessened and he was willing to engage in reading and related activities again.

Additional follow-up after fifteen years revealed that during Dirk's high school years remediation was again instituted—this time successfully. After completing one year of college Dirk decided on a career related to interior design and was able to use his good visual-spatial skills.

The Teacher's Role

Karl and Dirk are typical of the large number of older pupils with severe reading problems. In helping these pupils understand various subjects, the teacher first presents material orally, visually, and concretely. Reading fits into the total framework, but the teacher cannot count on independent use of books the way he or she can with better prepared pupils. Thus the teacher depends heavily on films, recorded books, television, videotapes, dramatic productions, oral discussion, and the like for elaboration of the subject and tries in every way to humanize the material before books are used. This usually gets the pupils thinking and responding actively and helps them surmount listlessness and resistance. Although they need to develop a broader background and to extend their skills just like other pupils, this cannot be done in the usual ways.

Formal practice on techniques, such as finding the main idea and important details and so on, must be delayed until the pupils learn to apply their thoughts and efforts to the subject matter under discussion, regain sufficient confidence and discipline to undertake study-type reading, and develop enough competence to proceed independently. When they reach this point they can benefit from instruction similar to that described in chapter 10. In the meantime, the teacher assumes an active role and wherever possible evokes interest in the topics, relates factual material to their personal lives, and shows them that discovery of the information can have real value.

Those who work with such pupils are well aware that most of them have little desire to learn academic subjects. They are usually not willing to work toward higher education goals or improvement of their status. So they need presentations that come alive and emphasize those aspects that make sense to them; their attitude at the beginning is usually "What does this mean to me?"

The teacher can introduce the text by providing necessary background information, vocabulary, and questions about the student's prior knowledge of the subject. Then the individual or class is guided to find the answers through the discussion and oral reading that follow. For minimal readers the teacher postpones expectations of independent work.

181

These pupils can engage in a certain amount of simple supplementary reading. Books of historical and informational interest with low vocabulary are readily available (see publishers in appendix B). These books are less difficult than regular texts. Naturally, the pupils cannot be expected to do extensive research, particularly in the beginning. But they can be encouraged to do more than they have ever done before. When assignments are clear cut and properly circumscribed, they can experience the satisfaction of finding answers without fruitless effort and discover that they actually can obtain the information they wish from reading material.

After the preparatory discussion, collaborative textbook work, and supplementary reading, the teacher helps the pupils organize information into a logical and useful order. The teacher and class consider what is important for the students. The information can be compiled into notebooks for future reference. Notebooks help students remember what they have learned and can also be used for review tests.

The Place of Test Taking

The taking of tests by pupils with severe reading disability deserves special comment. Their general attitudes of extreme indifference or acute anxiety come forward here. Some of the students have failed for so many years that another failure rolls off their backs; others have a great deal of apprehension about attaining the required reading level for promotion. Or, as graduation looms near, still others may have a great stake in passing tests because getting a certificate or diploma has intrinsic meaning or because it is crucial for future job placement. Whatever the ramifications, passing tests creditably can play a specialized role with such pupils: renewed effort, and best of all, achieving satisfactory scores can engender personal pride and satisfaction.

Therefore, it is important that the teacher explain the purpose and place of classroom tests. If the pupils perceive a test as something punitive or devastating, the teacher tries to relieve their fears. He or she explains that the test will be used only as a measure for assessing understanding of the subject matter and to help clarify ambiguous points. The teacher makes certain that the pupils know that tests will be based directly on their classwork. They should be familiar with the content because of their previous class discussions and notes. *The tests in such sessions are never used for report cards or recorded for school use.*

Short quizzes, oral or written, with two or three simple questions can serve as a start. Tests may be objective or essay, closed or open book, depending on the teacher's preference. The important point is that they be related directly to the material covered in class and formulated in such a way that the pupils have every fair chance of doing well. As short a time as possible should intervene between taking tests and learning the results. Tests can be corrected in class by the pupils themselves and marks deemphasized. Questions that have been answered incorrectly may be discussed in class, or pupils can be directed to sources with the necessary information. Ultimate knowledge of the material, not right and wrong answers, is stressed, so that the pupils come to care about what they are learning and how they are improving. When the pupils realize a measure of success through competency on tests and increased understanding of the subject matter, they may feel an entirely new sensation—a sharp sense of accomplishment.

As students have concrete evidence that they are learning and becoming better informed, they have a chance to develop some dignity. Their self-esteem often diminishes their outbursts and their antipathy toward school. When they consider, in addition, that they are no longer second-class citizens and that they are improving beyond their wildest expectations, they react with untold pride. Too often in the past, they had been relegated to the jobs of messenger, chalkboard washer, or bulletin board monitor. In a situation designed to compensate for their difficulties and promote competence, this need no longer be. Instead of standing on the periphery or failing abysmally, these pupils become an integral part of their group.

Unfortunately, there are many people who finish school and still have very poor reading skills. The case that follows shows how Theresa suffered in her daily life.

Theresa—Twenty-one Years Old, Reading at Fourth-Grade Level

Theresa, an attractive twenty-one-year-old woman, had graduated from high school after having struggled with every subject because of her severe learning difficulties.

Theresa was working as a receptionist in a small office. She greeted people easily and did the filing, but could not take phone messages if she had to write down any information. Her employer recognized that her general ability surpassed her spelling and writing skills, and referred her for help.

An intelligence test showed Theresa's ability to be above average. Word recognition and oral reading test scores showed that she was functioning at low fourth grade level. Spelling was at low third grade level. Theresa knew the sounds of the initial consonants, and most of the consonant combinations, but did not know any of the other basic word analysis skills. She had difficulty distinguishing between the short vowel sounds.

Although Theresa was motivated to improve, she felt shame and embarrassment because of the extent of her problem. Although she was hopeful about improving her reading ability, the prospect of writing anything on paper was frightening. Because Theresa's spelling was so poor, she had avoided writing whenever possible during her school years. As a result, she had virtually no practice in formulating her thoughts and committing them to paper.

The remedial program, which was carried out through once-weekly sessions,* was focused on helping Theresa develop an image of herself as a person who *could* learn by developing her reading, writing, spelling, and thinking skills.

Reading improvement was approached through a variety of methods. Theresa loved to read romance novels, but she skipped many of the words because of their unfamiliarity. She said she enjoyed dialogue the most. She was encouraged to read the romance novels as much as possible, although she and her tutor rarely discussed the content of the books. She continued to read them at the rate of two a month.

Theresa wanted to get her driver's license, but the driver's manual was well beyond her reading level. However, her motivation to drive a car helped her to stick with the complicated structure and difficult technical vocabulary. To review and understand the material better, between sessions Theresa constructed three or four new sentences, using the material from the manual, such as, "Colors and shapes help motorists to recognize the various types of road signs." By the end of a year, Theresa was able to pass the written part of the driver's test.

In order to increase fluency in reading, Theresa and the writer both collected written versions of songs Theresa liked. She was encouraged either to read along while listening to the songs on her tape cassette, or just to read the written songs without listening to the cassette. Since she was

*By Susan Blumenthal, a psychologist in private practice.

already familiar with the songs, she got a sense of what it was like to read with fluency.

At work, one of Theresa's responsibilities was to call in the lunch order for employees staying in during the noon break. Theresa dreaded the lunch hours because reading the menu to check off orders was virtually impossible for her. Theresa brought to her sessions the take-out menus for the two restaurants favored by her co-workers. Since there is generally a great deal of predictability about what people eat for lunch, she learned the most frequently ordered items first. Then she and the tutor went through the rest of the menu systematically, from appetizers to desserts. As a result, Theresa was not only able to carry out her responsibility at work, but was much more independent when she went out to restaurants with her friends.

Expressive writing was most difficult for Theresa, because of her limited spelling ability, her weak sense of grammar, and her apprehension at putting words on paper. In order to facilitate the process, the tutor assigned her a paper to write each week. Theresa was asked to pick a person she knew well, such as a member of her family, and to tell the tutor that person's most outstanding characteristics. While Theresa was talking about the person, the tutor printed eight or nine of the descriptions across the top of the page. For example:

My father: very quiet; bad temper; restless; fixes things; works on the docks; 190 pounds; strict but not a nag; not as old-fashioned as my mother.

Asking Theresa to tell the outstanding characteristics helped her to formulate her impressions with greater clarity. These written words and phrases on top of the page provided a model of correct spelling for Theresa as well as a structure with which to build her own composition at home. When she returned for the following session, the tutor would read her production aloud.

These were the first connected writings she had ever done, and it was clear that she felt pride as the compositions began to increase in length and complexity. By the end of the year, her story generally took up an entire page. The compositions were not corrected or marked in any way as they were read. Instead, specific short lessons were devised and taught separately (tense agreement, use of quotes, spelling, and so on). Because she did not have to correct the many errors at the time of reading, she remained willing to write, and in fact, eventually became enthusiastic about writing. Focusing on one thing at a time (such as the use of *ed* to indicate past tense) helped Theresa begin to make improvements that she could monitor as she read the composition aloud to herself.

As mentioned earlier, taking telephone messages at work was very difficult for Theresa, partly because of her poor spelling ability. In addition, the speed with which people gave their name, telephone number, and message created a feeling of pressure. The tutor made a cassette tape with fifteen model telephone messages (for example, "This is Fred calling Jack Brown. I have an appointment with him tomorrow at two o'clock. My number is 969-9290 if he needs to call me today"). At home, Theresa listened to the model messages on her tape cassette and practiced writing them down in a relaxed setting. In this way, she learned some of the words that occurred frequently when people called her office, such as *appointment* and *o'clock.*

Theresa's sight vocabulary was at approximately fourth-grade level, and she knew the initial consonant sounds and most of the consonant combinations. However, she had little knowledge of other basic word analysis skills. Because it was difficult for her to distinguish separate sounds in words and then blend them together, a foundation was built for word analysis skills by using a word family approach.

The tutor began by finding a word that Theresa recognized to use it as a key word for a list of rhyming words. For example, Theresa knew the word *rock* from her interest in pop music. So, *rock* became the key word. Under *rock* were listed *lock, dock, clock, flock,* and so on. In this way Theresa increased her sight vocabulary, and by practicing the rhyming words, she began to distinguish among sounds. With considerable support and encouragement, Theresa also tried to blend separate sounds in multisyllable words, but improvement was slow, probably because of her specific type of learning difficulties.

After one year of remediation, Theresa read orally at mid fifth grade level, and was able to obtain a position with better opportunities and benefits. She also had less apprehension when she went to restaurants with her friends, since she no longer needed help in reading the menu. Theresa started to read about show business personalities in her newspaper, and she continued to enjoy romance novels. For the first time, she began to talk about going to a community college to study fashion design. Remedial work will continue until Theresa reads at about seventh-grade level and writes with sufficient fluency.

General Suggestions for Materials

Interesting materials for older pupils with very low reading ability are necessarily limited. The lower the reading level, the narrower the choice and the less appealing the subject. For authors to write interesting, let alone mature, prose using very few words repeated constantly is very difficult. Therefore, the teacher has to choose reading matter that is as acceptable as possible and depend on skillful presentation. Thus, when a teacher starts working with sixteen-year-olds who are practically nonreaders, it would be advisable to begin with materials directly related to the students' immediate needs. Can they read the signs on the street, road, bus, or train on the way to school or after-school activities? Can they identify the names of different foods and their prices in the school cafeteria, at the supermarket, or in other stores?

The teacher next presents a few of the signs, labels, directions, and other words or phrases that appear to be of critical importance to the student and teaches them by methods described in chapter 8. Some of these common words and phrases follow:

Help Wanted	Men	Employees
Boy Wanted	Women	No Smoking
Danger	Boys	Fire Escape
Poison	Girls	Doctor
Keep Off	Fire Extinguisher	First Aid
Keep Out	Live Wires	Employment Agency
Stop	Bus Stop	Wet Paint
Go	Beware of Dogs	Hands Off
Walk	Out of Order	Elevator
Don't Walk	Glass	Telephone
Wait	In	Box Office
Entrance	Out	Thin Ice
Exit	Hospital	
Up		

In addition, headlines from newspapers or listings of the students' favorite television or radio programs can be presented; even ads for help wanted might be relevant if they are looking for an after-school or summer job. Students are also responsive to lyrics from popular songs; many have repetitive phrases that are familiar, so that students can follow the print without much difficulty while they enjoy the experience.

Still another procedure that older students have found appealing is reading simple quotations, proverbs, and poetry. The following illustra-

187

tions are at low reading levels, yet mature in concept. The teacher can find additional examples.[3]

- Laugh and the world laughs with you
  Weep and you weep alone.

- He who laughs last laughs best.

- When the cat's away, the mice will play.

- She let the cat out of the bag.

- The only thing we have to fear is fear itself.

- Where there's smoke there's fire.

- Here's to you as big as you are
  And here's to me as small as I am
  But as big as you are, and as small as I am
  I am as good as you are, as small as I am.

For students who have previously failed to learn to read, the successful handling of some material, even with help, can be a powerful motivating force. It can spur them on to accepting the first step—learning decoding skills. As the teacher continues to provide simple reading matter, he or she gradually introduces various procedures for developing basic word analysis abilities. The teacher then orients students to the unique contribution of each method in developing independence in word recognition, perhaps explaining that these approaches are called *decoding skills* because they refer to learning the reading code. This code may be compared with other codes that they have probably tried to figure out or have followed on television. The broader objectives of the reading program are to assist the students in developing knowledge, reading a variety of interesting materials, and functioning more effectively in school or at a job.

To coordinate the teaching of the skills with the students' reading, the teacher selects directly from the reading material words that lend themselves to the visual, word family, phonics, or other methods that will be taught. He or she proceeds along the lines described in chapter 8. For additional practice, materials published for adult literacy programs might be helpful (see appendix B). However, exercises need to be carefully selected to avoid those with immature format and content, reminiscent of those the students have rejected at earlier levels. In addition, computers can have a special place in the teaching of decoding skills. Several programs are available, but teachers need to be careful in choosing suitable ones.

3. J. Bartlett, *Bartlett's Quotations* (Boston: Little, Brown, 1882 to present).

By the time the student reaches third-grade reading level, there are available short books pertaining to biographies, short stories, adventure, and coping skills. Most of the major publishers are listed in appendix B and have separate divisions for handling materials at all reading levels for high school and adult literacy programs. Subject matter includes a wide range—all forms of literature, history, geography, science, government and civics, life coping skills, job information, world news, and other subjects needed by this population.

Older pupils generally react favorably to reading matter suited to their stages of maturity as well as at a reading level they can handle.

Thus in choosing suitable books for older pupils with severe disability, the main goal is to whet their appetites, to pick subject matter that is of general significance as well as related to topics being studied in school, and to find material that is not too overwhelming. Some teachers may frown upon rewritten material that does not convey the richness of style and ideas of the originals; some of the reading may be considered inconsequential. However, anything that can help pupils who have a serious reading difficulty serves an important function. Just as a convalescent may need to be coaxed to eat by means of attractive trays and special tidbits, so children with reading disability must be lured to read by providing them with exciting but uncomplicated reading matter. Books that are inherently too complex quickly discourage students whose reading power is weak, and they end up reading nothing.

The ways in which two teachers handled group situations with severely retarded readers in junior and senior high school follow. The programs can be adapted to similar school situations. Their accounts show graphically how, even under the most trying circumstances, difficult pupils can be salvaged.

An Individualized Program for Junior High School Students with a Wide Range of Reading Ability

A teacher in a New York City junior high school was confronted with a group of twenty-three boys in eighth grade.* Not only were most of them extremely behind in reading, but they were resistant to learning and had disciplinary problems besides. The following account was supplied by Dr. Simon.

*Louis Simon, formerly associate professor, City College of the City University of New York.

Treatment

My most immediate need was to establish a classroom atmosphere in which discipline could be maintained without resorting to the dire threats and punishments to which the boys had long become inured. I attempted to establish rapport by getting across the feeling that I was keenly interested in each member of the class. Various devices that had a noticeable effect in a relatively short time included visits to homes when pupils were ill, monthly birthday parties, and my participation in games in which the boys could demonstrate their proficiency. My position was made secure when I performed rock and roll music for them at our parties. Day by day there was an improvement in class morale and deportment.

The pupils' record cards revealed a reading range of second to fourth grades. An informal textbook test, however, indicated that one boy was on a pre-primer level, four were at first-grade level, and eighteen ranged from second- to fourth-grade reading levels. Results of the Diagnostic Reading Test revealed severe lacks in almost all word recognition skills. The IQ range was from 66 to 104, and ages from thirteen to sixteen.

I set up three reading groups, using the *Reader's Digest* Reading Skill Builders, but I soon realized that this plan would not work. I had no suitable material for the slowest group, nor had I the knowledge of how to devise my own. The two other groups had both been exposed to the Skill Builders in years past, and resented the grade levels on the covers. Furthermore, discipline problems arose because the groups could not work independently. Out of this confusion and frustration came the idea of an individualized reading program.

I broached the plan to my principal and found a willing and sympathetic ear. Unfortunately, the purchase of books for this class was not possible since funds for the current year had already been spent. Asking the boys to bring books from home was out of the question. Most of them had never owned a book.

Finally I arranged a trip to the public library. My class returned to school with twenty-three library cards and a collection of books. With their shop teacher the students constructed two mobile carts for the books.

The next four months were spent in reading library books during the English periods. Pupils were encouraged to recommend books that they found interesting, and these were freely exchanged. Volunteers for the privilege of reading a third-grade level book, *Curious George,* or a book on magic to the five slowest readers were plentiful. The boys in this group would then read to each other, with assistance from me or another pupil.

My time was spent in individual conferences during which I assisted with vocabulary, comprehension, and word recognition skills. The chief benefit lay in the opportunity for giving encouragement and individual attention. Almost magically, reading had become a "good" period. Pupils were called for conferences in alphabetical order. We sat together at a desk in the rear of the room. A conference usually included some oral reading, a brief discussion of what the story was about, and some direct teaching or review on a needed skill.

If John was laboriously reading word by word, our conference time might be devoted in part to taking turns in reading so that his interest in the story might be maintained. At the same time, I provided a model for more fluent reading. I also made a note to assign a page in a workbook to help him in phrase reading.

If Dominick was deeply absorbed in a book that was on his independent reading level, our conference might be merely a brief discussion of what had happened so far, a conjecture as to how the book would end, and an admonition to be sure to let me know how the story turned out. But I made a note to steer Dominick to something more challenging for the next book.

Each conference was an opportunity for diagnosis, skill teaching, vocabulary enrichment, and oral communication in a relaxed one-to-one relationship.

I found that a touch of humor each day was of inestimable value in getting activities started or keeping them moving. One of the most effective devices was the daily chuckle. A two- or three-line joke taken from a magazine or jokebook was displayed in the front of the room before the class arrived. The class looked forward to the little treat and vied for the privilege of reading or acting out the joke. Of course, this could not take place until everyone was seated and ready for work.

With a little practice, I developed a feeling for the type of humor that the children enjoyed the most. The following are typical:

NED: What are you doing with a pencil and paper?
ED: I'm writing a letter to my brother.
NED: Who're you kidding, you don't know how to write.
ED: Sure, but my brother doesn't know how to read.

VISITOR: Why is your dog watching me while I eat?
HOST: Maybe it's because you're eating out of his plate.

After a while pupils brought in jokes, and I appointed a rotating committee to select those to be posted. I learned that asking what was funny about a joke was not the unpardonable sin that it would be with a more sophisticated audience. The discussions that followed provided an ideal opportunity for oral communication, comprehension development, vocabulary enrichment, and exchanges of experiences in an atmosphere that was light and comfortable.

Since there were many stages of learning going on at the same time, I found that a record of each pupil's progress was advisable. An anecdotal account of each conference, results of diagnosis, assignments, and subjective evaluation of progress in skills and attitudes were kept in a notebook; a page or two was devoted to each pupil. The method was invaluable in my planning.

Two records were maintained by the pupils. One was a mimeographed form on which the student indicated the title and author of the book being read, the number of pages read each day, the kind of reporting activity planned, new vocabulary, and a brief sentence or two on his reactions to the book. This form was helpful in eliminating squabbles about who was reading a particular book and also enabled me to maintain a check on the amount of reading being done.

The other record was a large wall chart which listed the names of all the pupils and the titles of books they had read. Separate colored slips were available to paste next to each pupil's name. On the slip, pupils wrote the title of the book that they had completed and its author. Each color signified their opinion of the book. For example, a blue slip meant the book was excellent, green indicated good, yellow meant fair, and so forth. This device served as a record of accomplishment for each student and also guided other members of the class in their choice of a book.

In January, after four months of individualized reading, standardized tests revealed some satisfying results. The average gain for the class was one year. Individual gains ranged from 2 months to 2.6 years. Fourteen pupils had scores over the 5.0 mark necessary for promotion to the next grade, as opposed to twenty-three pupils who began the term reading between pre-primer and fourth-grade level.

Other evidence of progress was equally heartening. The number of books each student had read ranged from four to fourteen. There was a decided improvement in fluency in written and oral communication. Most encouraging was the evidence of positive attitudes toward reading. It is heartwarming to see a child linger in the room after the bell has rung, regretfully return his book to the cart, and say as he leaves, "Gee, that's a good story!"

Dr. Simon's report shows what a devoted teacher can accomplish. It shows how a serious condition, which is prevalent in many urban areas, can be successfully handled. When confronted with such an unfortunate situation, the teacher must rise to the occasion or collapse in despair. We can all find a way to teach our pupils after our own fashion.

A Group of Resistant High School Students

The pupils in the next instance were sixteen to eighteen years of age in an ungraded class at a special urban school for dropouts. They had been given up on by almost everyone in the area. Their parents insisted that they get a high school diploma, so they were forced to remain in school beyond the usual age limit. The pupils all read at about fifth-grade level. Their IQs fell within normal range, 90–110. They were uninterested in school, surly, and unmanageable. The first day was spent amidst frequent explosions from firecrackers—"hot foots" and "cherry bombs." That night the teacher contemplated not lesson plans but a scheme that might capture the hearts and feelings of these youths.

The next morning they were told that they would all be given a "diagnosis" to help them and their teacher find out what they could do well and where they needed help. The pupils were told that the test would not count for their school marks or an official record of any kind. In fact, they could throw away the test booklet as soon as it had served its usefulness. They were told that the test consisted of items that increased in difficulty; therefore they might find it harder to answer questions as they went along. In any case they would not be expected to get all the answers correct. The important thing was to assess the kinds of errors they made so that they could be taught to avoid such mistakes in the future. The process was compared to a physician's examination in which the patient might be told that his weight and height were proportionate and his general health good, but he was somewhat anemic. Just as a doctor would prescribe a regimen for physical improvement, so would they be taught how to increase their achievement.

A reading test designed for grades four, five, and six was chosen. After the students completed the test, they took turns coming to the desk for their "diagnostic interpretation." The test was scored immediately with pupils, so that they could be shown exactly where their strengths and weaknesses lay. This took the mystery out of the test taking and engendered a feeling of collaboration and self-respect in the student. Of course this had to be handled most skillfully to avoid undue anxiety regarding failure. Each one came away with as much concrete, constructive informa-

193

tion as possible. For example, one child did very well on answers requiring factual information but could not read between the lines for implied data. Another was excellent at understanding the main idea but poor on recall of details; another showed misunderstanding of directions but strong vocabulary; two boys were highly accurate but were penalized by time; and so on. Students were given some immediate suggestions for overcoming their difficulty and shown some of the materials they might be working with for practice.

The effect of this procedure was electric. First, the students felt that someone might really be trying to help them, and second, the selections indicated that there might be something of true interest for them. It was not "the same old hard, boring stuff," as one student commented later.

From that day forward, discipline problems diminished, although they never disappeared completely. It was clear that a spirit had been captured. These dispirited, disruptive young people had become willing to try again. In order to keep up their morale, the author continued to foster feelings of competence. Periods in social studies, English, science, and math were conducted in a group, and the particular skills were practiced individually for a half-hour three times a week. At that time the teacher helped with and checked their work. Besides using some fourth- and fifth-grade comprehension workbooks, they worked with materials such as crossword puzzles specially prepared for those with reading disability, card tricks, fortune-telling cards, magic books, simple science experiments, and magazines at appropriate levels. Simple books with high appeal—such as *Alec Majors, The Trojan War,* and *The Spanish Cave*—helped develop fluency and speed in reading. Such material proved dramatic, compelling, and sufficiently different to stimulate their curiosity. In addition, they were encouraged to bring in anything with which they wished help, such as driver's manuals, menus, and the like.

In each subject area, lively discussions and explanations preceded every reading lesson. In this way, demands never became overwhelming. The pupils used textbooks to fill in their knowledge. Often subject matter was related to personal experience in order to evoke attentiveness. For example, when learning about the Food and Drug Administration, the students were asked, "Have you ever seen the purple stamp on meat? Have you ever, to your knowledge, eaten meat without this stamp?" Sometimes discussions combined general student attitudes and subject matter. In discussing the Constitution of the United States, the students thought that perhaps a class constitution would maintain better order, and they decided to draw one up. It is reproduced here in its original form, including errors:

Constitution of Class

ARTICLE 1

Sec. 1   There shall be no throing of books, erasers,
chalks, pensils, can openors, paper airplanes and spit balls
and other thing that go in that category.

Sec. 2   There shall be no giving hot foots handeling of other
persons while class is being conducted and you can do as
you wish as long as it doesn't affect any one else. There
shal be respect for the person in charge and Prophanity
shall be kept to respected minimum. This constitution
shall be respected by the person kuo sines this, and if not
respect chall leave the class.

Through communicating to the students her desire to help them and by
making available actual means for improvement, the author helped them
make slow but steady progress during the term. Although they never
turned into model pupils, they became a cohesive unit willing to listen,
reasonably well behaved, and less antagonistic toward learning.

The foregoing accounts of students with serious learning problems
treated individually and in groups show that extremely poor readers who
have already given up are able to gain a fair degree of skill and confidence.
Even though achievement may not always be spectacular in terms of
potential, the startling fact is that some of these pupils became sufficiently
interested to improve and keep on trying. Their teachers were able to
succeed despite the obstacles and unfavorable conditions prevalent in so
many of our crowded urban schools. With ingenuity, dedication, and hard
work, they were able to change attitudes of doom and degradation to those
of anticipation and animation.

When such pupils are ready to leave school, they can be told that
education need never stop. Once they are out in the world they can always
seek admission to adult programs. Some may eventually reach their intellectual capabilities even though it takes them many years to do so. Some
may yet enter college when they are willing to work hard enough; some
may enter careers which require exacting academic preparation. If they
have learned the rudiments of academic skills, they no longer need to scoff
at educational pursuits. But if they lack the barest essentials they may
indeed be absorbed into the morass of delinquent, antisocial, and wretched
people with whom urban societies are becoming more and more familiar.

Suggestions for Further Reading

Bender, W. N. "Secondary Personality and Behavioral Problems in Adolescents with Learning Disabilities." *Journal of Learning Disabilities* 20 (May 1987).

Bruner, J. "Education as Social Intervention." *Journal of Social Issues* 39 (1983).

Carter, B., and Abrahamson, R. F. "The Best of the Hi-Lo Books for Young Adults: A Critical Evaluation." *Journal of Reading* 30 (December 1986).

Derby, T. "Reading Instruction and Course Related Materials for Vocational High School Students." *Journal of Reading* 30 (January 1987).

Deshler, D., and Schumaker, J. "Learning Strategies: An Instructional Alternative for Low Achieving Adolescents." *Exceptional Children* 52 (April 1986).

Mastropieri, M. A.; Scruggs, T. E.; and Levin, J. R. "Mnemonic Strategy Instruction with Learning Disabled Adolescents." *Journal of Learning Disabilities* 18 (January 1985).

McConaughty, S., and Ritter, D. R. "Social Competence and Behavioral Problems of Learning Disabled Boys Aged 12–16." *Journal of Learning Disabilities* 19 (February 1986).

Meltzer, L. J.; Roditi, B. N.; and Fenton, T. "Cognitive and Learning Profiles of Delinquent and Learning Disabled Adolescents." *Adolescence* 21 (Fall 1986).

Sabornie, E. J., and Kauffman, J. M. "Social Acceptance of Learning Disabled Adolescents." *Learning Disability Quarterly* 9 (Winter 1986).

Silver, A. A., and Hagin, R. A. "Outcomes of Learning Disabilities in Adolescence." Paper presented at the Twenty-second International Conference of the Association for Children and Adults with Learning Disabilities, San Francisco, February 20–23, 1985.

Stevens, R., and Pihl, R. O. "Seventh Grade Students at Risk for School Failure." *Adolescence* 22 (Summer 1987).

Test, D. W., and Heward, W. L. "Teaching Road Signs and Traffic Laws to Learning Disabled Students." *Learning Disability Quarterly* 6 (Winter 1983).

Waldron, K. "The Learning Disabled Adolescent: A Curriculum for Written Expression." *The Pointer* 31 (Winter 1987).

13

Bright High School Students Achieving below Capacity

SOME high school students of above average intelligence continue to have difficulty reading as well as expected. These students also need special attention and present a different set of challenges to the teacher or reading specialist.

Evaluation

A standardized test at a level appropriate to the students' age and grade level is administered to assess reading comprehension and vocabulary. Students who read slowly and who cannot complete enough items to provide a valid measure of their comprehension or understanding of word meanings are allowed to continue until they complete the test or until they appear to be experiencing too much difficulty to continue; the examiner marks where each pupil was at the end of the time limit. This permits the examiner to analyze the results in comparison with the students' age and grade level as well as for accuracy.

Rate of reading is estimated through the use of informal measures introduced during the trial learning sessions. For example, several articles at the students' reading level, including both narrative and expository material, are presented. The examiner keeps a record of each student's rate and degree of comprehension. In this way, reading efficiency and flexibility according to the nature and difficulty of the material can be evaluated. The use of both standardized tests and informal measures is illustrated in the cases of Jack and Carol later in this chapter.

Wherever possible, test results are interpreted to students in a constructive manner. The teacher might find that a student answers questions accurately but is penalized by time limits or has misread words that look alike, and so on. The pupils learn where their approach to reading is weak, find out what to do about it, and often become more interested in receiving help. In this way, diagnosis lays the groundwork for future cooperation and sustained effort.

Bright underachievers are likely to have as much difficulty with written work as with reading. They generally report that this is an area of deep concern to them. One of their greatest problems is answering essay questions on tests without prior preparation. When confronted with complex questions—such as "Discuss Hamlet's relationship with his mother" or "What issues did the framers of the Constitution face?"—they are at a loss to get their thoughts on paper in a way that is well organized and expresses what they really know about the subject. Term papers and summaries present additional problems. (Informal appraisal of students' written work is discussed in the section on trial sessions in chapter 5 and instruction in written expression is fully treated in chapter 15.)

Dealing with Adolescent Underachievers

The teacher or specialist who works with adolescent underachievers has to find ways to help students overcome their basic distrust, locate reading matter and workbook exercises, and assist with any other aspect of schoolwork that interferes with functioning—handling assignments, improving rate of reading, and the like.

Underachievers do not suddenly obtain the grades or test scores predicted for them. In fact, too much emphasis on these measures may produce even lower scores because of increased tension or resistance. Instead of repeatedly admonishing them to improve and reminding them of their untapped possibilities, the authors discuss with students the various alternatives available. We point out that their lives will not be ruined if they fall short of the high standards set for them. We may mention that famous scientists, presidents of colleges, and other outstanding people did not receive high grades in high school or attend well-known universities.[1]

Furthermore, we have observed that although many with whom we have worked eventually ranked high in their classes, achieved outstanding scores on their college entrance examinations, and even attained degrees from graduate schools, these incentives rarely were effective at the outset. Rather, students are helped to gain insight into their strengths and deficiencies. They are shown how they can improve their skills and cope with their problems.

To begin with, the teacher chooses stories that touch upon universal human experiences. The most important objective is to find something that will induce students to read further on their own. A story that directly relates to a personal need or problem can have a powerful influence. Not only can it heighten their interest but sometimes it can be forceful enough to help them relate better to other individuals and to their schoolwork.

Sometimes the teacher must search long and diligently through anthologies, comprehension exercises, and workbooks to find material that will move the students. But the impact of good material will be unmistakable: their inherent interest will carry them along. Yet often the students read grudgingly or merely to improve grades. This is an acceptable start. Reading to obtain higher marks can improve students' functioning in school and can open the door to future academic plans that are more in line with their ability. Rather than deplore such an attitude, the teacher accepts it for the time being and realizes that as the students mature, they may develop sounder goals. In the meantime every effort is made to find appealing short stories and articles that will serve as a springboard to other books.

Sometimes one brief, dramatic story will have a lasting effect and inspire the student to read more. For example, one adolescent boy who rarely read for pleasure or enjoyment completed a short story by Steinbeck in an anthology. He became fascinated with Steinbeck's style of revealing a character's secret thoughts. Before this experience he had believed that he alone had "bad thoughts." He felt that he was the only one who said one thing and thought another. He began reading everything by Steinbeck that he could find. He finally became an avid reader of a variety of authors.

The case of Carol, which follows, shows how the careful choice of subject matter was significant in changing her discouragement with school.

1. L. Thompson, "Language Disabilities in Men of Eminence," *Journal of Learning Disabilities* 4 (1971): 34–45.

Carol—In Eleventh Grade, Discouraged, and Unable to Cope with Advanced Reading Skills

Carol, an eleventh grader with superior intellectual potential, felt very discouraged about her prospects. She had had reading instruction from time to time but nevertheless obtained fairly low scores on her Scholastic Aptitude Tests (SATs). She was not at all certain that she wished to enter a reading program again, and she also wavered about attending college. The one area in which she showed some talent was painting.

Carol made a few tentative appointments for instruction with one of the authors. They agreed that she would be free to cancel them should she decide against receiving help. Her only reason for coming was that she felt she read extremely slowly, but she seemed skeptical that any instruction could help her.

Carol presented a challenge to the author to search painstakingly for subject matter that might be meaningful and relevant to her present situation. Accordingly, along with many general selections, Carol was given articles on subjects that might be of special interest. Her responsiveness was indeed striking.

For example, an excerpt on the modes of operation of the two hemispheres of the brain was particularly intriguing to her.[2] Being artistic, she was fascinated with the explanation that the right hemisphere is responsible for spatial orientation, artistic endeavor, and probably intuitive thinking, among other things. This kind of information was new and stimulating and was an area that she stated she would like to learn more about.

She also liked an article by John Holt in which he discussed the unrealistic standards of admission to colleges in contrast to the policies of public libraries.[3] He pointed out that librarians do not quiz people on books to ascertain whether they can understand their contents, nor do they refuse to lend records of serious music to individuals who they believe are not educated well enough to appreciate them. He regretted the fact that young people start living under the shadow of universities almost as soon as they are born. Holt's article led to a very serious discussion of the many college programs now available that do not rely heavily on SAT scores, but that meet special needs.

Another article that had particular meaning was one by John Fisher, who made several points: (1) A person could drop out, as did some Hindus, mystics, Buddhists, monks, and those who took hallucinogens. (2) One

2. R. Ornstein, *The Psychology of Consciousness* (New York: Viking, 1974).
3. J. Holt, "Admission to College," in *Developing Reading Proficiency*, ed. B. Schmidt et al. (Columbus, Ohio: Charles E. Merrill, 1971).

could run away, as people have always done. (3) One could plot a revolution. (4) One could try to change the world gradually.[4] This article brought forth the response from Carol, "I guess I have only one choice—to go to college."

A large number of carefully chosen articles kept Carol involved and interested. In time, she became motivated enough to ask for help in vocabulary development and spelling, in addition to working on rate of reading. One area in which she functioned well was comprehension. However, as in the case of Jack (later in this chapter), flexibility in handling different types of materials had to be stressed.

Probably even more significant than her progress in reading was that Carol was able to think in terms of constructive educational plans and that she had developed sufficient confidence in herself to pursue her goals.

Dramatic changes had occurred in this student, who at first had claimed that she was so fed up with the demands of school that she planned to stop her education at the end of twelfth grade. Yet, before instruction was terminated, she asked, "Do you think that some day I could work with children with problems, because I really know how they feel?" Even the thought of graduate studies did not faze her.

The Benefits of Workbooks

In addition to compelling narrative material, it is important to use a variety of comprehension exercises in different fields. Through them students gain a wealth of background information and new vocabulary in a short time. These selections also develop flexibility in reading. Articles from social studies, science, current affairs, and other fields are similar to students' textbooks and hence develop study skills as well.

Articles must be selected with care so that time is not wasted on irrelevant or poorly constructed ones. The main criteria for selection include the intrinsic interest of the subject matter, a wide choice of content and style, clear exposition of paragraphs, and properly constructed questions. If the teacher makes it a practice to review the articles and answer the questions he or she will soon discover which are most suitable and which are too difficult, ambiguous, or inappropriate.

The instructor shows students how different articles will be used. Some selections are very short; others are a thousand words or longer. They include newspaper articles, technical reports, informational material, and

4. J. Fisher, "Four Choices for Young People," in *Design for Good Reading*, ed. M. Schumacher (New York: Harcourt Brace, 1969).

so forth. In handling these materials, students practice shifting their pace from one article to another, learning when to read carefully and when to skim. The goal is efficiency in reading rather than increased rate per se.

Some selections are followed by one or two questions that seek the main idea; others have about ten questions that search out details. Some questions are reflective, others inferential, and so on. Students will answer questions and correct their own work. It is enlightening for the students to discuss the nature of their errors after completing the comprehension exercises. For example, did one misunderstand a question because it was ambiguous or because he or she was not familiar with the subject? This student might be told to leave confusing questions aside and answer the rest. (Perhaps there will be time at some point to use an encyclopedia or other source to obtain the information.) If a student makes wild guesses, he or she must learn to read more accurately. If another confuses personal reactions or past knowledge with the information specifically stated in the paragraph, it will be important to learn to make the distinction between individual experience and material presented in a book. Someone who tends to read every word can be encouraged to read for ideas; someone who skims too rapidly and loses the details should be shown the value of becoming more precise.

Some students may find that keeping a record of accuracy or rate of reading is an incentive for improvement. But others may find the written record too threatening, since there is apt to be wide fluctuation in performance. Some benefit from working under the pressure of a stopwatch; others find that this detracts from their concentration. Under the instructor's guidance each student experiments to find the best method.

The student continues workbook practice for as long as necessary. For many students, ten to twenty sessions are sufficient to show them what they need and how to proceed independently. After completing instruction, a student can always return for occasional practice when necessary. But the more responsibility the individual assumes for incorporating the new skills into general reading and school assignments, the more he or she should be able to improve his reading efficiency.

Vocabulary Development

Many high school students with limited vocabulary find themselves at a disadvantage with their more articulate peers. Frequently they wish, for the first time, to improve their vocabulary either because they have reached the point where they recognized the value of expressing themselves effectively or because of the weight given to vocabulary subtests on the SAT for college entrance.

A multifaceted approach is needed to help such students enlarge their vocabulary. At the simplest level, an alphabetized notebook in which new words are written with their definitions and use in simple sentences has proved helpful. And exposure to new words may be accelerated through the reading of articles on a wide variety of subjects, especially articles that introduce specialized vocabulary and new concepts. These may be found in many of the excellent workbooks available for high school and college students. Most of the books include vocabulary exercises.

The systematic study of the most common Latin and Greek roots, prefixes, and suffixes can increase vocabulary considerably. The older student needs greater emphasis on this aspect than the younger ones described in chapter 8.

Dictionary practice, with specific reference to choosing appropriate definitions, is another way to increase vocabulary. However, even capable students need specific instruction in order to decipher diacritical marks and use the pronunciation key at the bottom of most dictionary pages. Thesauruses and dictionaries of synonyms are also very effective for increasing and broadening vocabulary. Students should be encouraged to consult these sources to learn to use more varied and colorful language.

The least effective way to teach vocabulary is to assign lists of words to be memorized. Students learn the lists for specific sessions or tests, and unless the words are incorporated into their speech or written expression they are promptly forgotten.

Rate of Reading

Today more than ever before, a great deal is heard about rate. Some reading centers claim that they can increase an individual's rate of reading to the upper hundreds and even thousands of words per minute. To achieve or maintain such astronomical speed is in the authors' experience most unusual. There is no normal or average rate of reading. For general reading, some authorities have considered 300 words per minute fairly adequate. Very good readers read 500 to 600 words per minute, and very rarely there is one who reads at the phenomenal rate of 1,000 words per minute or faster.

How do we determine rate, and how do we decide who should have training in it? Rate is measured on some subtests of the regular reading tests. It is but one portion of a diagnosis that includes evaluation of advanced word recognition techniques, vocabulary, comprehension, and so on. Rate scores must always be evaluated in connection with comprehension. For instance, students who score in the 90th percentile in rate and the 20th percentile in comprehension are bound to run into trouble in high school and college, obviously not because of rate, but because they get so little from their reading. It is also important to investigate the student's own thoughts on the matter. Is he or she spending an inordinate amount of time on homework? Is he or she disturbed by an excessively slow rate? If the test results or informal measures confirm the impression that rate improvement is indicated, then the instructor works out an appropriate program with the student.

Students who need to speed up their reading and are able to work on their own may profit from a workbook that explains the theory of efficient reading while it measures the student's rate and comprehension. A few students find that this is all the work that they need. However, most individuals wish for some direction and guidance. This is where the teacher can provide the necessary stimulus and the systematic checking that keep the student going. The well-motivated student can make good progress.

The program consists of practice with appropriate material. All the reading matter suitable for practice in comprehension is also appropriate for rate. However, for correcting answers and measuring words per minute, it is convenient to have material that indicates the number of words in each selection, conversion tables for measuring rate, individual answer keys, and the like.

In addition to such practice, the student must agree to undertake regular independent reading at home for approximately half an hour per session. The student should choose reading matter that does not make excessive demands on concentration, such as magazine articles, short stories, or light novels. The student tries to read these as fast as possible, making certain that he or she understands the reading reasonably well. Eventually such practice usually results in facile reading.

There are always some students who do not increase their rate satisfactorily. They may worry so much about the number of words they read per minute that their progress is impeded. The instructor may help such students by discussing some of the ways to compensate for slow reading. For example, they might set aside a little more time for daily studying. Or they might take four courses rather than five a year, with additional credits in summer school. Adopting these alternatives would provide enough time to study so that slow readers could complete assignments without working under undue pressure. Apprising the students of such choices decreases their anxiety about reading rate. As they gain a more realistic attitude toward their problem, they are usually able to function more effectively. Denckla's observation is especially fitting: a "local train reaches the same destination as an express train, but only takes a longer time to get there"—a very comforting point of view.[5]

The case of Jack shows how a high school student who was plagued by slow reading was able to cope with his problem.

Jack—A Slow Reader

Jack, aged seventeen years, in eleventh grade, sought help from one of the authors because he was dismayed by the results of his Preliminary Scholastic Aptitude Test. Throughout his school years he had had a good academic record. However, in recent years he had spent more time on his homework than his peers. He attributed this to his reading at a snail's pace. He noted that he never had trouble understanding what he read, or in expressing his ideas in writing.

It was necessary to estimate Jack's reading abilities through formal and informal measures in order to get a clearer picture of his problem. A test designed for high school students was administered. Jack scored at the 92nd and 90th percentiles in vocabulary and comprehension, respectively, as compared with other eleventh grade students. However, his reading rate was at the 40th percentile, which confirmed Jack's own impression.

To further assess Jack's reading, the author conducted a trial learning session. Part of the session was devoted to the interpretation of findings and suggestions for an appropriate reading program. During the trial learning session Jack was given narrative and expository selections to read. He employed a uniformly slow rate for both types of materials, but he showed consistently superior comprehension of content.

Together Jack and the author analyzed Jack's reading performance with regard to areas of strengths and weaknesses. They discussed ways of coping, with a view toward developing more efficient and effective reading abilities.

- Since Jack employed an unvaried rate of reading regardless of the characteristics of the reading matter, he needed to develop flexibility in his approach. He needed to adjust his reading rate according to the nature and complexity of the material, taking into account his purpose

5. Quoted in J. Chall and A. Mirsky, eds., *Education and the Brain*, 77th Yearbook of the National Society for the Study of Education, Part II (Chicago: University of Chicago Press, 1978), p. 258.

for reading. For example, if he were reading mainly for recreational purposes, he might read more quickly and perhaps more superficially than if he were reading for a literature course. He certainly would not read science fiction in the same manner or at the same rate as a science textbook. Furthermore, when subject matter required profound thinking and reflection he learned that his background knowledge would influence his approach; rate of reading would be secondary or of minor concern.

- To improve his rate of reading he would set aside twenty to thirty minutes daily, if possible, to read simple materials. He should force himself to read faster than usual. School reading assignments must be strictly *excluded* from such practice because as he focused on reading rapidly there would undoubtedly be some loss of comprehension. However, he was told not to worry about this aspect in his daily practice in rate as there would be regular checks at his weekly sessions.
- The roles of the student and the teacher were defined. Jack's active involvement in the program was of critical importance in producing success. The author would explain his instructional needs, provide appropriate reading matter, and suggest other materials and procedures. In general, she would guide him all along the way.

Jack was very responsive to the discussion and arranged to see the author for one-hour sessions on a weekly basis. Within about three months (thirteen sessions) Jack showed sufficient progress and grasp of the procedures relevant to his goals, enabling him to discontinue the weekly sessions. However, it was recommended that in order to maintain his gains, he should practice reading a wide range of books and materials. In addition, to ensure that comprehension would be maintained at a high level it was suggested that he read exercises in high school– and college-level comprehension workbooks provided by the author and check his comprehension through questions at the end of each selection. He was reminded that a high reading rate without a high level of comprehension was counterproductive. It also seemed advisable for him to see the author at regular intervals in the course of the next year in order to maintain his progress. These suggestions were carried out, and Jack's achievement was reflected in very satisfactory SAT scores in twelfth grade.

Jack was encouraged to try to speed up his reading because he showed superior comprehension and vocabulary skills. However, if this had not been the case, emphasis would have been on developing these abilities before any attempt at increasing speed could be considered. When word recognition, vocabulary, and comprehension were ignored and greater speed of reading encouraged, students showed a marked decline in comprehension that greatly impaired reading ability.

Individuals differ to a great degree in tempo, so that students who wish to speed up their reading are not always successful. If progress is slow, students are cautioned not to give up (which happens so often) but, instead, to continue with a wide range of reading. In this way, their power of reading, which is of utmost importance, can be kept at a high level. They can learn ways to compensate for slow reading, as noted earlier in this chapter.

Reading and Studying

High school requirements become more stringent as students advance. Students who are reading less well than they are able may find their assignments becoming more and more arduous. The students' foundations may remain inadequate, their vocabulary insufficient, their rate slow, and their confidence low. Besides working on reading, it is sometimes profitable to give students a little extra direction in assignments. For example, helping them to look for suitable references or guiding them in organizing the salient features for an outline can be beneficial. The instructor can also give concrete explanations on the format and scope required in a term paper, for instance.

In organizing their studies, some students find the SQ3R method helpful.[6] This formula stands for "survey, question, read, recite, review." In essence, this technique suggests (1) glancing over chapter headings for major points; (2) turning paragraph headings into questions; (3) reading to answer the questions; (4) looking away from the book, briefly reciting to oneself, then writing down the information; and (5) reviewing the lesson for major points.

Whatever the method used, the student needs continued encouragement. One cannot always live up to a theoretical potential nor work at peak efficiency. But students can be helped to sharpen their techniques, increase their effectiveness, and improve their functioning.

6. F. Robinson, *Effective Study* (New York: Harper & Brothers, 1961).

Coping with Examinations

Pupils often become overconcerned and panicky during examinations. Particularly in the last years of high school, tests such as the SAT heighten fear and anxiety. Students who have minimal achievement become particularly unnerved. They may react similarly to class tests, too.

Although there is no cure for test anxiety, certain techniques have proved alleviating. The teacher and pupils can discuss the pupils' approach to taking tests. Do they freeze? Do they make careless errors through mistaking directions? Many people go blank when faced with an important test; in fact, it is almost universal to have anxiety before, during, and even after taking tests.

The students can take actual examinations for practice. This makes the ordeal more commonplace and lessens some of its overpowering tension. They are advised to exert reasonable effort on each test item, but not to puzzle too long over any one of them. There may be time to return to an omitted question. The students learn to be careful in marking the answer sheet—too often a skipped question throws off subsequent markings. On an essay examination, students are encouraged to read all the questions first; this sometimes yields valuable hints for answering several of them. Learning to gauge time correctly is also essential. After practice tests are taken, the teacher and students can score them jointly. Incorrect responses can be accounted for on the spot. Reviewing errors can help the students gain insight into the nature of their mistakes. Finally, the teacher can assure students that some colleges accept students without examinations; this knowledge takes away the unrealistic fear that their whole life depends on a test.

The Limitations of Predictive Measures

Teachers and specialists use various predictive measures in evaluating students' ability and suggesting choices for their academic future. But foretelling human outcomes is at best a risky undertaking. The largest factor, motivation, still remains a mystery. Furthermore, the growth spurt from late adolescence to maturity makes prophecy hazardous. Demosthenes, the severe stutterer, became an accomplished orator. Winston Churchill reportedly failed English composition three times; yet his prose is impeccable. Those voted "most likely to succeed" in high school may turn out to be miserable failures.

Therefore, let us not in this overtesting age be influenced by quantitative scores and other mechanical measures alone or misled by the assessment of a student who at present shows less academic aptitude than is considered desirable. Some mediocre students whose test scores suggested that they were not college material have become sufficiently interested at a later date to seek college admission and have made creditable and even brilliant college records. Others have taken advantage of junior colleges or special programs geared for those with unconventional needs. Students whose verbal scores were significantly higher than their math scores on aptitude tests have sometimes been advised against pursuing the science, mathematics, and physics studies that attracted them; yet many who ignored this counsel have turned out to be successful in scientific fields. There are some students who have suffered from reading difficulty throughout their first twelve years of schooling and are still miserable spellers; yet through sheer determination they have become doctors, lawyers, engineers, or whatever else they wished. We have known pupils who were told to give up the idea of college completely but persevered to attend college and even graduate school.

The opposite situations have also occurred. Students who were scholarship material in high school have failed in college; those who were told that they would make excellent Ph.D. material were unable to withstand the academic strain.

Although a student's failure may look unconquerable, the door must be left open. The situation should be assessed as fairly as possible, but decisions must remain tentative. Tremendous change can occur outside the confines of formal education. Life circumstances, inspiration, and growth processes after the age of eighteen have yet to be investigated. No one knows when maturation reaches its zenith, and people continue to learn throughout their lives. Teachers' most important contribution to those who have academic difficulty is to lessen their sense of failure so that they have an opportunity to make use of whatever abilities they may have.

Suggestions for Further Reading

Amman, R., and Mittelsteadt, S. "Turning on Turned Off Students: Using Newspapers with Senior High Remedial Readers." *Journal of Reading* 30 (May 1987).

Anderson, R. D. "Role of the Reader's Schema in Comprehension, Learning and Memory." In *Theoretical Models and Processes of Reading,* 3d ed., edited by H. Singer and R. Ruddell. Newark, Del.: International Reading Association, 1985.

Baechtold, S., and Algier, A. "Teaching College Students Vocabulary with Rhyme, Rhythm and Ritzy Characters." *Journal of Reading* 30 (December 1986).

Borfitz, D. "The Challenge of Sports English." *Curriculum Review* 25 (May-June 1986).

Treatment

Brueggeman, M. A. "React First, Analyze Second: Using Editorials to Teach the Writing Process." *Journal of Reading* 30 (December 1986).

Fox, L. H.; Brady, L.; and Tobin, D., eds. *Learning Disabled/Gifted Children: Identification and Programming.* Baltimore: Park Press, 1983.

Gray, M. J. "Reading in the High School." *Illinois Schools Journal* 64 (1984).

Montague, M., and Tanner, M. L. "Reading Strategy Groups for Content Area Instruction." *Journal of Reading* 30 (May 1987).

Ohlhausen, M. M., and Roller, C. M. "Teaching Students to Use a Nation Schema to Learn about Countries." *Journal of Reading* 30 (December 1986).

14

Teaching Reading
to Underprepared
College Students

by Lila Soll*

READING as a separate discipline in college is relatively new and is primarily a response to the admission of large numbers of academically underprepared students. Minimal college reading readiness might be defined as the ability to complete reading assignments and to comprehend most introductory college texts with the aid of the instructor.

Students in college reading programs who are assigned to reading classes have usually come from nonacademic secondary schools and are ill prepared to accomplish higher level subject matter. However, since they choose to be in college they are usually highly motivated for success, even if they have unrealistic ideas about college course work.

Other students who require help in college reading programs are those who learn English as a second language (ESL). This group includes students who have had adequate precollege instruction in their native language but lack proficiency in spoken or written English. It also includes students who are insufficiently literate both in their own language and in English and who may not be able to deal successfully with the challenges of college reading without an extensive ESL program. These students' reading levels

*Lecturer, Department of Compensatory Programs, Baruch College, City University of New York.

vary according to their background knowledge, skill, and vocabulary development.

College students with reading problems are a diverse population. Many are able to decode and successfully read popular adult fiction and simple expository materials but lack the repertoire of skills and background knowledge to translate, analyze, synthesize, and judge the complex materials they meet in college. They are hindered by limited reading experience and inefficient reading habits.

Many college instructors currently define reading in terms of stages that describe the relationship between the level of complexity of a passage and the task assigned. According to Chall's theory of stages of reading development (table 10-1), underprepared students at Stage 3 can read a wide variety of popular magazines, narrative material, and the like, but their scope of comprehension is not yet adequate for handling college texts. In transition from Stage 3 to Stage 4 it is necessary to develop mastery of the textbooks of introductory college courses. To come up to this level of competence students need to engage in a program designed to cover a broad range of reading matter that is complex in nature and varied in points of view. Successful completion of this type of program prepares students for Stage 5. This is the most mature reading level and entails in-depth analysis of textbooks and other reading materials. Chall characterizes this stage of reading as essentially constructive and creative. From reading what others write, students can use knowledge for themselves. (See also "Levels of Proficiency," appendix D.)

This type of qualitative assessment of a student's approach to reading is especially valuable in planning an appropriate program. Nonetheless, quantitative evaluation and other diagnostic methods also provide essential information regarding a student's functioning.

Identifying Students Who Need Reading Instruction

Assessment issues are often different on the college level. Diagnostic procedures need to be adjusted to relate to college demands and to emphasize the students' understanding of their own reading process.

Many colleges use a twelfth-grade cut-off score on a standardized reading test as an initial screening device for assigning students to a college reading program. Reading specialists always need to augment standardized reading test scores with information from other diagnostic procedures. This is especially true on the college level because college reading assignments differ significantly from the short, isolated paragraphs found on most standardized reading tests. However, when one test score determines assignment to or exit from an intensive reading program in college, reading teachers may need to include test-taking skills in their curriculum.

Some colleges rely completely on student or teacher referrals for assignment to reading programs. Classroom teachers can assess students' abilities during the first week of class by administering a teacher-constructed test based upon a selection from an introductory college-level text. Three or four open-ended questions about the text, focusing on literal meaning, analysis, synthesis, and evaluation will alert the teacher to the students' individual strengths and weaknesses as they are confronted with regular reading assignments. This exercise also provides the teacher with an overview of the group's needs. The following are sample questions from a diagnostic test based on a selection about the famous Hawthorne studies.

1. Describe the procedure of the Hawthorne experiments.
2. What is meant by the "Hawthorne Effect"?
3. Explain how the "Hawthorne Effect" affected the Hawthorne experiments.
4. Do you agree or disagree that *improved work performance will result from an improved psychological attitude*? Use the article and your own experience to support your answer.[1]

The questions progressively tap the levels of competency of translation, analysis, synthesis, and evaluation, and the scoring system can be weighted to give a higher score to the higher levels of competency.

Involving Students in the Learning Process

Some students resent placement in remedial reading programs; others are aware that they have problems but are vague about the nature of those problems. In addition, most underprepared students have unrealistic ideas about the academic demands of college work. Reading teachers can help students to assess their own needs and to become aware of the different demands of college reading by asking them to describe and analyze some of their reading habits.

The following questions might be included in such a survey:

1. J. Reitano, ed., *Work and Society*, 2d ed. (Dubuque, Ia.: Kendall/Hunt, 1982).

1. What is the most recent book or article you have read?
   What was it about?
2. How many hours a week do you spend reading
   for pleasure?
   for school?
3. What kind of reading materials do you enjoy most?
   a. novels
   b. short stories
   c. newspapers
   d. magazines
4. What do you consider the most serious problem you have when reading?
   a. keeping your mind on what you read
   b. remembering what you have read
   c. writing about what you have read
   d. understanding new words
   e. discussing what you have read
   f. other
5. What would you most like to improve about your reading?
6. Have you ever had any special help in reading?

Individual conferences or group lessons based on the initial classroom assessments help students understand the kind of tasks they will need to perform. Examples from introductory courses of actual essay questions with sample answers can also highlight college reading demands.

Underprepared students can be made aware of their strengths and helped to relate to the academic demands of college. For example, they need to use their life experiences as students, workers, and family members. While respecting each student's response to written material, teachers can encourage them to consider a variety of responses; otherwise students tend to rely on their preconceived ideas or search for what they believe the teacher wants. By acknowledging their prior knowledge and sharing it with a group, students gain confidence with their peers and the academic community.

Methods and Materials in College Reading Classes

The teacher chooses methods and materials that will build background knowledge while enabling students to function successfully in academic courses. College reading teachers need to be aware of the academic requirements of their college. Materials and skills instruction thematically linked to academic courses take priority over isolated workbook exercises or analysis of unrelated short passages and texts. The isolated skills taught in many precollege remedial programs are often inappropriate in a college setting. Moreover, slow, skill-by-skill remedial efforts are rarely tolerated by budget-conscious college administrators.

Whereas students' inadequate background knowledge and skill deficiencies are frequently apparent from the beginning, their strengths also need to be considered in the curriculum. Native speakers of English, for example, often have a strong oral facility with language, while they have limited experience with academic discourse and great difficulty expressing their ideas in writing. Discussion in both large and small groups provides a way for the more articulate students to gain confidence in the reading class. Students can write a short summary or a prediction about a selection before oral discussion begins. The teacher circulates around the room and asks a few students to put their responses on the board. The focus of these activities is not to produce polished prose but simply to get ideas into writing and to discuss them.

Small peer groups encourage the less articulate students to discuss material orally. Students who rarely offer answers in a large group participate in the smaller group. Although all students benefit from discussing their ideas, group responsibility often forces reluctant or passive learners to contribute to their own learning. This method works particularly well in ESL reading classes.

The following is an outline of steps in the process developed for classes at the writer's college in New York City. The readings used may be thematically related and adapted to the needs of the class.

Step 1
- Whole class reads one article that they respond to, take notes on, or summarize.
- Notes are put on board.
- Notes are organized under headings.
- Questions: What would you want to know more about? What didn't you understand?

Step 2
- Class is divided into at least four peer groups.
- Each group reads a different article.
- Each student takes notes on his or her assigned article.
- Peer groups meet to merge notes and prepare group set of notes.
- Teacher meets with each group.
- One member of group presents oral report of important points to class.

- Each student writes a factual summary of his or her group's article.

Step 2a
- Procedure as in Step 2, but students summarize another group's article.

Step 3
- Each peer group reads two different articles.
- Two groups read one article, while the other two groups read the other article.
- Two groups prepare to report on article to class, while other two groups prepare questions on the same article.
- Peer groups meet to prepare presentations and questions.
- Teacher meets with each group.
- Two groups report to class.
- After each presentation, questions are presented by the group that prepared them; then the whole class is encouraged to ask questions.
- Students need to know the answers to their own questions.
- Students write comparison summaries of two of the articles.

Step 4
- Each peer group reads two different articles.
- Each student takes notes on both articles.
- Peer groups meet to share notes.
- Each group prepares one article for presentation and the other for questioning.
- Teacher meets with each group.
- One member of group reports on one article; questions follow as in Step 3.
- Students write a summary that is a synthesis of at least two different articles.

Although it is important to build on students' background knowledge and experience, it is also vital to move quickly to academic materials. Frequently, this requires a transition from narrative to expository prose. The book *Working,* by Studs Terkel, is popular in both remedial and non-remedial college courses.[2] The book's personal interviews can be used to bridge the gap between the use of natural language and academic discourse. The workers interviewed in *Working* discuss serious political, psychological, sociological, and economic themes which can be related to similar themes from college texts. Students' own work experience helps them to understand the broader context of such experience in today's society. Since the book consists of interviews, the students can begin by interviewing a fellow student or friend about his or her work experience.

2. S. Terkel, *Working* (New York: Ballantine, 1974).

Students may also write and talk about their own experiences. While students are reading selected interviews in *Working* they receive written assignments based on group needs. In addition, the reading teacher introduces formal essays and questions related to *Working,* which become more abstract as the term progresses. Finally students can synthesize their class readings, work observations, and interviews with relevant articles for a research project.[3] Such thematically related materials and extended expository texts expand the background knowledge of students and are essential for success in college courses.

Students need practice with writing as a means of demonstrating proficiency in college; they will have to show their understanding by their research reports and answers to essay questions. Constructing texts can enhance the skills of interpreting texts by revealing structure and organization as well as meaning. Reproductions of students' papers make ideal reading texts to enable the class to examine reading and writing relationships.

Assessing Readiness to Enter College-Level Courses

Students' readiness for college coursework cannot be determined by a simple cut-off score on a standardized test. While these tests are somewhat predictive for large groups of students, individual students' performance in reading and writing is frequently the best guide to their readiness for entrance into academic courses. However, some institutions require students to obtain a specific score on a standardized test before being admitted into the regular college-level courses.

Although it might be necessary for reading teachers to include some practice exercises, especially for those students who have difficulty with timed test taking, teachers can devise their own assessment tools to augment standardized tests. An end of term assessment might require students to read an extended text and relate it to other materials covered during the term. Questions requiring analysis, synthesis, and evaluation can stimulate students to reflect on previous readings. For example, in the course on the *Working* theme, the students read Arthur Miller's *Death of a Salesman.* One of the questions on their final exam was to contrast Biff Loman's work attitude to that of a man interviewed in the book *Working.* Students were also asked to comment upon the following quotation from *Death of a Salesman*: "It's not what you say, it's how you say it—because personality wins

3. L. Soll, "Writing a Research Paper: A Vital Survival Skill in College" (ERIC 940331-1976).

the day. . . . . It's who you know and the smile on your face! It's contacts Ben, contacts!"[4] Their assignment was to agree or disagree with Willy and to back up their point of view using examples from *Death of a Salesman, Working,* and their own experience.

Research projects that encourage analysis of several sources to support a thesis may also serve as an assessment device in college reading courses.

The Role of the Reading Teacher in Academic Coursework

College reading teachers need to be aware of students' transition from a limited remedial program to an academic one. The reading teacher can contribute to successful transition by analyzing the reading demands of academic courses, evaluating the students' ability to meet these demands, and advising students to take appropriate courses. Linking study skills to coursework also enhances students' achievement.

It is important to guide students to the most appropriate courses and to offer help during the transition period from remedial to full participation in the college's program. Introductory programs vary considerably from one institution to another. The reading demands of the introductory courses can be described and analyzed according to standardized criteria. One method is to prepare a Reading Competency Profile, which is a simple outline of the reading requirements of an introductory academic course.

Briefly, the steps in preparing a profile are:

1. Gather as much of the material utilized in the course as possible (texts, course outline, reading handouts, test questions).
2. Describe structural features of the text (chapter headings, summaries, glossary, other study guides).
3. Evaluate at least three chapters in the text (beginning, middle, end) and outside readings according to a standardized readability formula and Chall's reading stages (table 10-1).
4. Evaluate test questions according to a scale and examine the relationship between tests and text by selecting a sampling of the questions to determine if answers to the questions can be found directly in the text, require application skills or a synthesis of several sources, or require evaluation.

4. A. Miller, *Death of a Salesman* (New York: Viking, 1977).

5. Gather sample notes from at least three lectures or class sessions. Analyze their relationship to test questions to determine the relative amount of information obtained from the lectures with or without the text. If necessary, the teacher can attend class sessions to take the notes.[5]

Underprepared college students should experience the realistic demands of college-level courses early in their program. This can be achieved by adding a study skills component to an introductory college-level course. The *study lab* is one method of teaching study skills through real course content.[6] This type of class is often referred to as an adjunct class. The student enrolls in an introductory course such as psychology for three to four hours a week and coregisters in a study lab in psychology for two hours. In the study lab the reading teacher uses the content course materials and requirements to teach the specific skills required for mastering the course. Furthermore, students are expected to use these skills in subsequent courses. Study labs foster metacognition or active control of learning. Essentially, not only does the linking of skills to content encourage the student to connect reading comprehension with retention and retrieval of information, but also it ensures that students become aware of the carry over of skills to academic tasks. More important, the reading occurs in meaningful contexts.

The reading requirements of a typical introductory college course includes a college textbook and popular or technical journal articles or excerpts from original sources. Literature courses usually include a list of readings and assignments in critical analysis. Although underprepared students often read narrative materials with better comprehension than expository materials, they often need experience with the more complex texts and analytical expectations of college literature classes.

A textbook has a very specific organization, and an introductory text is usually loaded with devices to aid the student. For example, in a business course the text, *Business Today*,[7] used the following aids:

- Learning objectives at the beginning of each chapter
- Technical vocabulary in the margin
- Vocabulary in boldface print
- Summary for each chapter

5. L. Soll, "Developing a Model Reading Competency Profile," *Journal of Developmental Education* (in press).

6. L. Soll, "Learning by Doing," *Reading Teacher* (April 1972): 496–98.

7. D. J. Rachman and M. H. Mescon, *Business Today*, 5th ed. (New York: Random House, 1987).

- List of key terms at the end of each chapter
- Review questions for each chapter
- Headings in various colors

In addition to the text, a study guide was available which included an additional vocabulary list and short-answer review questions. With all these aids, the need for a study lab might be questioned. However, students need more than good materials; they must learn how to use them.

Students review a chapter before lectures and prepare an outline and vocabulary list. These tasks may be done individually or shared by small groups. A worksheet filled out and discussed in the study lab helps students extract key concepts and clarify those they do not understand. The following tasks might be indicated in a worksheet:

- Read over your notes. State in one sentence what you think was the most important idea the lecturer wanted you to know.

- Organize your notes under the following headings: *Idea, Theory, Explanation, Example, Vocabulary,* and *Definition.*

- List any questions you have about any idea, definition, or example you do not understand.

Some students maintain that they understand a chapter better after hearing a lecture. This may be true, depending on the lecturer's style and the student's background. Ultimately, the students have the right to make a choice; however, they should try both methods.

Note-taking and underlining from a text are skills frequently practiced in a study lab. Again, the aim is to encourage students to explore different methods and ultimately come up with one that works. Turning headings into questions and writing short answers to these questions is a method of notetaking many students find useful.

Technical vocabulary in the text is often a stumbling block for underprepared students. There are so many new words that students find it particularly difficult to decide which words are important and which are not. Underlining may be successful in sorting out new words. Students love to underline in texts. Their methods are not always rational, but somehow all those yellow and green lines assure them that they have been doing more than turning the pages of the book. One study lab class evolved the following system for underlining the text:

1. Read introduction and summary and skim the headings of the text. Write a one-line sentence telling what you expect the chapter to be about. (This is the traditional survey or preview.)
2. Read chapter for new vocabulary. Put two lines under a word and a single line under its definition.
3. After chapter is complete choose about ten of the most important words.
4. Write your own definition of each word.

Word lists were compared and corrected in class. Students felt that they understood the class sessions better when they were familiar with the vocabulary, and they found reading the text easier when they knew what they were looking for.

Underprepared students often have difficulty understanding, remembering, and reporting on expository articles, which do not offer the study guides and aids of introductory texts. Unskilled readers tend to choose a particular detail that they relate to, and focus on it as the central theme of their reading. Background knowledge often becomes a key factor in understanding expository materials which are not necessarily written for the college freshman audience. Students need to learn to focus on the author's message, the facts relevant to the course, and ways of organizing the materials for later recall. Summary writing and note-taking skills are crucial. Predictions and guided discussions also help students develop effective methods of dealing with expository materials.

Teaching listening and note-taking skills is essential in the first sessions of a study lab, especially if the content teacher uses a lecture method. Notes from the class need to be discussed and summarized in the study lab. It is helpful to collect the first lecture notes, comment on them, and distribute duplicated examples of good notes using samples of different note-taking styles. Unless the class displays very good skills, it is generally desirable to teach a specific note-taking method.

Preparing for examinations becomes a significant activity in study lab because success in the content course is essential for student motivation. Initially, students must know as much about the kind of test they are going to take as possible. The study lab is an ideal place to discuss the kinds of questions and methods anticipated. If the course is evaluated by short-answer tests, practice with typical questions is needed. Past tests or questions in a study guide should be answered, corrected, and analyzed in the study lab. If no such questions exist, the study lab teacher can devise sample ones. Students benefit from comparing answers in small groups and providing their own justifications for discrepancies. Essay questions are

221

best approached by having students predict possible questions and then answer them. This exercise works well in small groups.

Finally, students learn effective test preparation methods from a self-evaluation exercise after a test. This encourages them to examine their method of study and revise it if necessary. A self-evaluation sheet might include the following questions:

- What grade do you predict you will receive?
- Approximately how much time did you devote to studying for the test?
- Do you feel you studied too much, not enough, or approximately the right amount of time?
- Do you feel that you studied the right information? If not, what should you have studied?
- Did anything on the test surprise you? Explain.
- How did you study for the test?
- Do you plan to change your method for the next test? Explain.
- Grade:*

Research assignments in the content area dictate the amount of time and kind of skills assistance provided in the study lab. Underprepared students frequently have vague or misguided notions about what is expected in a research assignment. Having students write out their assignment and compare it to their fellow students' is an important step in clarifying the teachers' expectations. Research skills should be taught for the specific subject class assignment.

The Goals of College Reading

A reading curriculum model prepared by a group of reading teachers in the City University of New York college system listed the general goals for students in its program as follows:

- To become independent learners
- To recognize the lifetime value of reading
- To succeed in a course of study leading to a degree
- To succeed in reading-based content course
- To succeed in the basic skills reading program

*Actual grade—to be inserted later, after self-evaluation is completed.

- To succeed and demonstrate competency on reading assessment tools
- To become aware of the demands of the reading process[8]

Comprehending introductory college textbooks and related expository essays is not the most important goal of a college curriculum, but it is the initial hurdle for underprepared students to experience the stimulation and pleasure of a varied college curriculum. A successful program can enable students to achieve their survival in a demanding collegiate environment and prepare them for the pleasures and rewards of confident participation in the world of ideas.

Suggestions for Further Reading

Bartholomae, D., and Petrosky, A. R. *Facts, Artifacts and Counterfacts.* Upper Montclair, N. J.: Boynton/Cook, 1986.

Bell, M. J.; Soll, L.; and Staker, D. Y. "College Reading: Responses to the CUNY Reading Seminars." New York: Instructional Resource Center, City University of New York, 1983.

Coles, N., and Wall, S. V. "Conflict and Power in the Reader-Responses of Adult Basic Writers." *College English* 49 (1987): 298–314.

Davis, A., and Clark, E. G. *T-Notes and Other Study Skills.* Metamor, Ill.: Davis and Clark, 1986.

Henderson, I. "Reading beyond the Story." *Kaleidoscope* 2 (Spring 1986).

Katz, I. C. "Adjunct Classes: Teaching College Students Strategies for Learning from Texts." *Journal of College Reading and Learning* 17 (1983).

O'Toole, J. D. *Working Changes and Choices.* New York: Human Sciences Press, 1981.

Sternglass, M. S. *Reading, Writing and Reasoning.* New York: Macmillan, 1983.

8. Chancellor's Task Force on Reading, City University of New York, "A College Reading Curriculum Model" (New York: Instructional Resource Center, City University of New York, 1983).

15

Writing as a Tool
for Learning

by Steven Tribus*

IT is universally accepted that students need to develop good writing skills. It is also critical, though less accepted in practice, that writing be used as an effective tool for learning every subject. Teachers need to recognize that writing is not a skill to be relegated only to periods of communication arts or English. Writing, as one of the major vehicles for communicating and thinking, needs to be integrated throughout the curriculum in order to facilitate and enhance students' learning of science, social studies, mathematics, and other subjects. Yet the National Assessment of Educational Progress Report (1981) revealed that only 4 percent of science and social studies teachers in grades seven through twelve provide students with opportunities to compose their own thoughts in writing.

In planning their instructional programs, teachers need to consider how writing can be used effectively to help students learn. Writing, like reading, speaking, and listening, facilitates and extends learning, not in some esoteric, theoretical model, but in practical ways every day in every subject.

"Only linguists have language as their subject matter," writes Courtney Cazden. "For the rest of us, especially children, language is learned (and used) not because we want to talk or read or write about language but because we want to talk and read and write about the world."[1] For chil-

*Director of English, New York City Public Schools.
1. C. Cazden, "Environments for Language Learning," *Language Arts* 60 (January 1983): 121–22.

dren, that world is the world of sports, friends, science, mathematics, love, fear, and confidence.

Ask most kindergartners and first graders if they can write and they will tell you, "Yes, I can." Ask most high school students if they are confident about their ability to compose their thoughts, feelings, opinions, and observations and you will probably not get a positive response. This change in attitude should be of utmost concern to teachers. Fortunately, thousands of teachers have discovered that it is possible to develop in their students the confidence needed to write well.

The challenge to teachers particularly and to all of us collectively is to be open, flexible, interested, and dedicated enough to evaluate recent research and to share our experiences of trying to find solutions to the problems. Teachers need to try out new approaches and techniques to discover how to help their students write well and think well.

Developing Positive Attitudes toward Writing

Why teach writing at all—especially in today's world of television, telephones, and video games? Because writing is thinking on paper. James Britton suggests, "For most children, language read or language written is the major vehicle through which thinking occurs."[2] Writing comprises both the cognitive and affective: it is a record of what a person thinks and feels. Students who think clearly and critically will be better writers because their writing will reflect ideas and experiences that are important to them.

To write well a person must think and reason; categorize, classify, and organize; select appropriate details and use correct vocabulary; be familiar with grammar; and make connections among what has been, what is, and what might be. To develop such skills in their students, teachers must begin by establishing a classroom environment that will support such development. The classroom needs an area that houses all sorts of writing tools: markers, pencils, paper, dictionaries, thesauruses, folders in which to keep work, and scissors and tape for revisions. When students are writing, they should be able to move about the room to talk to others about their work or to sit where they feel comfortable. Beyond the physical environment, the teacher promotes a feeling of community where everyone is participating in writing activities and where everyone is available to support and assist the others.

2. J. Britton, *Language and Learning* (New York: Penguin, 1970).

Students frequently think that their ideas and feelings are not important enough to be written down, and they are intimidated by the prose of published authors. It is therefore crucial that teachers help their students to develop a sense of authorship—a feeling that what they have to say is worthwhile and that they have the ability to communicate these ideas to others. One popular way to accomplish this is to encourage students to read their writing to the class. In the lower grades the class may sit together on the floor while the writer sits on an "author's chair." After the "author" reads his or her work the others can respond with support, constructive criticism, and questions.

Another important way to promote writing skills is for the teacher to participate in the composing process. Most students have had opportunities to see adults read in public or at home. It is unlikely, however, that they have watched adults write, seen them struggle with putting their ideas down on paper. When a teacher assigns an essay, he or she should write one also. This will provide a palpable way for the teacher to understand what the students are going through. Thus, the teacher will become more empathetic with the students and gain insight into how to help them. For their part, the students will have a helpful role model.

Sharing their experiences and supporting each other will promote students' positive feelings about their work and help them gain confidence. But we know that sharing one's writing is taking a risk. Most of us are unwilling to take such a risk unless we trust those with whom we share our thoughts and feelings. The teacher who shares his or her writing with the class will do much to establish a classroom environment that supports and promotes the advantages of writing.

What Is the Writing Process?

After establishing a classroom environment that is conducive to writing, the teacher should focus on developing effective writers. The National Council of Teachers of English makes the following statement about the composing process: "Although teachers' assignments and expectations for student writing are usually expressed in terms of a product—that is, a whole piece of writing—instruction must necessarily focus on the process of arriving at the finished piece. A whole piece of writing results from the selection, combination, arrangement, and development of ideas in effective sentences, paragraphs, and, often, longer units of discourse."[3]

3. *Standards for Basic Skills in Writing Programs* (Urbana, Ill.: National Council of Teachers of English, 1979).

The writing process, therefore, is comprised of prewriting, drafting, revising, editing/proofreading, and publishing. Teachers need to teach the skills and concepts that students will need, but not everything that students write needs to go through the entire process. The writer decides whether a particular piece is important enough to work on further. Frequently, a piece may be put aside in the student's writing folder until the writer decides that it is time to go back to it. Finally, it is important to understand that writers do not all work at the same pace. Just as different people read at different rates, so do they write at different rates. Thus, some students might be drafting while others are revising and still others are preparing to publish. Students progress through the various stages in a recursive rather than a linear way. The clear implication for the teacher is that writing lessons designed to have all students write at the same pace and at the same time will inhibit more students than it will help, and they will assuredly become frustrated and eventually stop caring about their written work.

Prewriting

Just as teachers prepare students for the act of reading, so must they prepare them for writing. Students need to focus on the subject about which they will be writing and have some idea of its scope and its audience. There are many different prewriting activities that can be used to accomplish this:

- Class discussions about a general topic
- Storytelling to help clarify an experience
- Role playing and other dramatic activities
- Reading about a subject
- Conducting interviews
- Watching a film or live performance
- Listening to a speech

These activities can be used with the whole class. Sometimes the teacher may divide the class into small groups, which enables more students to interact within a short period of time. The teacher may appoint a spokesperson from each group to share its experiences and ideas with the whole class before they begin composing. Some of the groups may be ready to write before others and should have the opportunity to begin before everyone is ready. Whatever prewriting activities are used, the teacher does not lose sight of their purpose: to help students decide why they are writing, what they are writing about, and for whom they are writing.

DRAFTING

Writing a draft means setting ideas down on paper free of concern for spelling, punctuation, transitions, sequence, and the like. There is time enough for such concern during the editing/proofreading stage. As students write their drafts, they should focus on the content of the writing. Too often, students edit prematurely, never giving themselves an opportunity to find out what they think, to share their thoughts with others, or to evaluate the usefulness of their ideas.

Teachers can assist students in drafting by reminding them that what they're drafting will not be graded, that they will be able to change and consult with others about it and make many revisions before it is ready to be polished and published. In addition, it is helpful if teachers give students yellow paper on which to make their draft copies and white paper when they are ready to write the final version. This has the benefit of convincing the students that when they are writing on the yellow paper, they are just getting their ideas down and need not be concerned with making mistakes. Suggesting to them that they skip lines and leave spaces when they can't think of what to say will also increase the benefits of writing a draft.

A useful technique to help students write drafts without premature concern for precision is *freewriting.* In freewriting, students are instructed to write without stopping. They write for ten to fifteen minutes about anything that comes to mind, without censoring. They are instructed not to correct misspellings or to stop to consider what is the best word to come next. The purpose of the exercise is for them to get their ideas down on paper first. Then, when they have completed this activity, they can go back over what they have written, underlining the ideas on which they would like to focus. An alternative is to let the students freewrite about a general topic of their choice.

Regardless of the activity used for a first draft, the purpose is to allow students to think on paper so that they can consider their ideas, share them with others, and extend them. Later they can revise and polish.

REVISING

There is a strong argument to be made that the heart of the composing process is revising. Many of our students believe that the stories that they read emerged full-blown from authors' heads. They are unaware of the number of drafts and many months, if not years, that it takes for writers to finish a published piece. One of the results is that students do not see the process part of composing. Writing is hard work for anyone, not just students but experienced authors as well. Understanding this may not make writing any easier, but it will certainly help students recognize that they, like all writers, need to look over what they have written and improve it. Teachers need to encourage students to revise their work again and again. This entails helping them learn how to revise as well as providing the time for them to do it.

To assist students in understanding the benefits of revision, teachers need to respond to the content of their written work. They can respond as an interested reader or listener, ask questions to seek clarification, and suggest ways to improve the writing. The teacher remains sensitive to the ideas and feelings of the student so that students become convinced that what they are saying is important and that the teacher recognizes the worth not only of the written work but of the writer as well.

Teachers as well as peers can be trained to listen to the writing of others for the purpose of providing feedback. In this regard, it is useful for the teacher to devise questions that can be used by the students to assist them in responding to a written piece. Such a set of questions might include the following:

- Is my message clear?
- Have I included enough information?
- Does my writing speak to the intended audience?
- Does my writing accomplish the purpose?[4]

The questions will vary according to the age of the class, but the purpose remains the same: to assist the writers in looking at their pieces anew in order to make necessary changes. Teachers have found it helpful to hang these questions on charts around the room as a reminder to students.

Most changes in writing are made during the revision process. It is logical, therefore, for teachers to spend a great deal of time conferring with students as they revise. To manage a classroom where there are many conferences, teachers can organize the students in groups to make it easier for them to help each other. Small writing groups help the students learn to trust each other, and they also become more willing to share their work. It is impossible, and unnecessary, for a teacher to confer with each student during a class period. Students need to learn that the small groups can help them immeasurably and that the teacher is not the only person who can assist them. Students in small groups can ask questions about a writer's first draft using the same model as the whole class uses. Some small groups

4. New York State Education Department, *Manual for Composition K–12* (Albany: State University of New York, 1986).

will quickly become proficient in helping each other; other small groups may need more time before they are able to work independently and productively.

EDITING/PROOFREADING

In this stage students need to focus on the "how" of writing rather than on the "what." The purpose of editing/proofreading is to be sure that paragraphing, sentence structure, spelling, punctuation, and the like are as accurate as possible.

There are several ways to help students edit and proofread. One way is to use an editing checklist that contains questions about what to look for. While the students can use these lists independently, it is more effective for them to work in peer editing groups: three or four students take turns looking at the writing of other members, while recording comments and suggested changes for the writer. Another way to teach editing is to assign a different task to each group member. For example, one student reads the group's writing and checks for spelling errors, another looks for usage or punctuation mistakes. By rotating the responsibilities over a period of time, each student will develop better editing and proofreading skills.

When the editing and proofreading are completed, and all needed changes have been made, students can write their final copies (perhaps on the white paper referred to earlier) in preparation for handing them in to the teacher or publishing them.

PUBLISHING

There is probably no greater satisfaction for writers than having their work published. It is both a wonderful reward and a motivation to continue writing. Publishing students' work can be as simple as hanging a composition on a bulletin board under a heading such as "Writing of the Authors of Class 301" or as complex as producing a school literary magazine.

Regardless of the method, the purpose is the same: to give student writers an audience. If we as teachers want our students to develop the concept of writing for an audience, then publishing their writing will go a long way toward motivation and confidence.

The increasing access to computers in most schools is a boon to publishing students' writing (see chapter 16). Certainly, computers make the act of revising less painful and easier, thus motivating students to do more revising. In addition, the computer enables students to print their work in a neat, clear way that increases publishability. As their schools purchase computers, teachers can use these machines to promote class newspapers, literary articles, and other writings.

Connecting Writing and Reading

Every recent analysis of writing instruction in American classrooms has reached the same conclusion: students do not get many opportunities to write. According to one recent study, in grades one, three, and five, only 15 percent of the school day was spent in any kind of writing activity. Two-thirds of the writing that did occur was word-for-word copying in workbooks.[5]

Opportunities to write contribute to knowledge of the relationship between written and oral language, as well as to growth in phonics, spelling, vocabulary development, reading comprehension, and critical thinking. Students who write frequently and discuss their writing with others approach reading with what has been termed the "eye of the writer."

The teaching of writing need not be isolated from the other communication arts of reading, listening, and speaking. Further, teachers can see the acts of reading (decoding) and writing (encoding) as a continuum and can seek ways to integrate the two into their instructional programs. The chart below highlights some of the similarities between writing and reading.

Before Writing	Securing ideas
	Organizing ideas
	Determining point of view
	Considering audience
Before Reading	Preparing to comprehend
	Relating to prior experience
	Establishing purpose
	Looking for the author's stance
During Reading or Writing	Composing or comprehending
	Being actively engaged emotionally and intellectually
After Writing	Evaluating
	Editing and revising
	Applying outside standards of correction

5. R. Anderson et al., *Becoming a Nation of Readers* (Washington, D.C.: Center for the Study of Reading, 1985).

After Reading Evaluating
          Studying parts in relation to whole
          Analyzing how effects are achieved
          Applying independent judgment

The chart clearly indicates that as students participate in the act of writing they are also improving their skills for reading. In similar ways, increased experiences in reading will have concomitant benefits for writing.

As a result of their research, Robert Tierney and Margie Leys concluded that what students read influences what they write in both a positive and negative way. Students should read the best literature to affect their writing positively. "Students will compare their own writing with the plot or character development present in what they are reading [and] the quality of writing produced is related to the quality of reading during writing." Tierney and Leys also indicate that

- Selected reading experiences definitely contribute to writing performances; likewise, selected writing experiences contribute to reading performance.
- Writers acquire certain values and behaviors from reading and readers acquire certain values and behaviors from writing.
- Successful writers integrate reading into their writing experience.[6]

In order to enhance these complementary benefits, teachers should create literate environments in their classrooms by surrounding their students with books. If we want to create a community of writers then we must also create a community of readers who experience the writing of others in as many different genres, styles, and subjects as possible. The more the writer reads, the more he or she is able to draw on in writing. Just as teachers can encourage students to write whole pieces of literature, they can encourage them to read whole pieces of literature.

There are a number of effective ways in which to connect reading and writing activities. One of the best is to read student literature in the class alongside professional literature and then to write about the topic. Of course, the professional piece will be more precise and polished, but the student's piece can still be enjoyed and discussed. An added benefit of using student writing is that the "author" can respond to questions and share insights about the work. Student writing can be used at story time

6. R. Tierney and M. Leys, "What is the Value of Connecting Reading and Writing?" in *Convergences: Transactions in Reading and Writing,* ed. B. Peterson (Urbana, Ill.: National Council of Teachers of English, 1986), pp. 15–29.

in the lower grades, with older students visiting the younger ones to share their stories.

For reading lessons teachers can plan to incorporate writing before, during, and after the reading. Students need to process ideas again and again, retelling stories and re-creating prose through speaking, reading, and writing. For example, a teacher might read the title of a story that the students are about to read and ask the class to write what they think the story will be about. Their predictions can be discussed both before they read or hear the story and after it is read. Follow-up discussions might focus on the relationship between titles and stories, with students seeing how a title is a generalization that is directly related to the specific details of the story—certainly useful in reading other works.

Students can write in response to literature in a number of ways. They can write personal reactions to a plot twist, a character's behavior, the ending of the story, or the writer's opinion. Both reading and writing skills improve if students re-create a work read by changing male and female roles (using the reading skill of character analysis), by writing a different ending (using the reading skills of predicting outcomes and re-lating them to specific details), by writing a new beginning (again by understanding details), by writing from a minor character's point of view (using character analysis and point of view), by changing locations (un-derstanding the importance of setting), and by reordering events (using sequencing skills).

Clearly, students will not understand the benefits of writing if they share their writing only during a forty- or fifty-minute period. In learning different subjects, students need to be given opportunities to speak, read, and write about their ideas. By so doing, they are helped to reemphasize what they have read, heard, and written. Content area teachers help to improve students' communication skills and subject area knowledge when they include some specific activities in their lessons:

- Allow students to speak and write about a subject before they study it. Thus the activity becomes an assessment, helps students to focus on the subject, and taps their prior knowledge to aid their learning.
- Teach specialized vocabulary before students encounter it in their textbooks; ask them to use such vocabulary when speaking and writing.
- Give practice in putting together, in writing, sequences of events—for example, in social studies write a chronology; in science write the steps in an experiment; in language arts describe the plot of a story.
- Ask students to write as a part of every homework assignment as well as on every major examination.

Treatment

One of the easiest and most effective ways to include writing in content area lessons is to use the learning log. Logs can vary in both purpose and design. Their essential purpose is to allow students to reflect on what they have learned in a particular subject that day. They help students to think about what they did in class, what they understood about the lesson, what they are confused about, and, perhaps more important, what they think about as a result of their learning.

In the New York City school system, a program to improve students' reasoning skills is being conducted in selected junior and senior high schools for students who are taking the ninth-grade sequential mathematics course and the regular English class. A major part of this project is to use a learning log in both subjects as part of the students' daily homework assignment. The theory is based on the idea that in order for students to make what they learn a part of their long-term memory, they need to sit down to think about what they did in class each day—to develop the habit of reflection as part of their daily routine. In this particular project, the log has five parts, introduced over a period of several months.

1. Today I learned about (or how to):
2. The most important idea I learned today is:
3. A question I have about what I learned today is:
4. Something I learned today about thinking is:
5. A way that I will use these ideas is:[7]

Processing new learning helps students clarify their understanding of new concepts and helps the teacher identify areas in need of review and reinforcement. It also helps the students to focus on the task rather than on their own anxiety, and will help them appreciate their progress. The teacher can provide positive feedback and show how each student has improved or learned something new.

There is an added benefit in using logs for students who have language difficulties or who learn at a slower pace than most of the class. Their logs provide the teacher with specific information that can be used to discuss their difficulties. Since the log is a personal record and should not be graded, these students can use it as a way to ask for help while they practice writing to communicate their thoughts.

As writing becomes a common activity in content area lessons, students will become less likely to see writing as a skill to be used only during their communication arts lessons. They will find that writing is an effective way of communicating not only with others but also with themselves. Teachers

7. New York City Board of Education, *Reasoning Skills Project: Teachers' Manual,* 1986.

who use writing as a learning tool are helping their students to develop their use of language as readers, writers, and speakers.

The benefits that accrue to students who develop effective writing skills are many. They feel confident that what they have to say is important and that they are capable of communicating their ideas to others. They are able to think more logically and critically. They recognize the power language gives them in their roles as students, as citizens, and as workers. Accomplishing this requires a great deal of planning and classroom management, but the rewards for students will more than make up for the time and effort that teachers give on their behalf.

Suggestions for Further Reading

Calkins, L. *The Art of Teaching Writing.* Portsmouth, N.H.: Heinemann Educational Books, 1986.

Elbow, P. *Writing with Power: Techniques for Mastering the Writing Process.* New York: Oxford University Press, 1981.

Graves, D. *Writing: Teachers and Children at Work.* Portsmouth, N.H.: Heinemann Educational Books, 1983.

Moffett, J. *Coming on Center: English Education in Evolution.* Upper Montclair, N.J.: Boynton/Cook, 1981.

Petersen, B., ed. *Convergences: Transactions in Reading and Writing.* Urbana, Ill.: National Council of Teachers of English, 1986.

Zinsser, W. *On Writing Well.* 3d ed. New York: Harper & Row, 1985.

16

Integrating Word
Processing into
Writing Instruction

by Barbara Sherr Roswell*

$\mathbf{S}$EVERAL YEARS AGO, Peter McWilliams, author of *The Word Processing Book,*[1] popularized a word processing system he called the McWilliams II. This word processor allowed the user to erase and replace chunks of text effortlessly and to print graphics and characters from every known language. Best of all, it was easy to use, portable, and extremely inexpensive. This word processor was a number 2 pencil.

The McWilliams II word processor provides teachers of writing with a useful warning. Just as we would never ask, "What is the effect of the pencil on students' composing processes?" we would be naive to ask, "What is the effect of the computer on students' writing?" The impact of students' computer use will depend largely on the instructional context—the atmosphere the teacher creates, the ways in which word processing is connected to the rest of the writing curriculum, and the degree to which students are empowered to use word processing to achieve individual and group writing goals.

Rather than taking the computer as a given and asking how teachers can accommodate themselves to the technology, a teacher might ask instead, "How can I adapt word processing to enhance the ways my students learn

*Director, Goucher College Writing Program, Towson, Maryland.
1. P. A. McWilliams, *The Word Processing Book* (Los Angeles: Prelude Press, 1982).

to write?" When viewed as an enhancement to instruction rather than a substitute for it, word processing can provide a valuable opportunity to improve the teaching of writing.

Writers and Word Processors

Considerable research has been conducted recently on writers composing at the word processor. Unfortunately, much of the preliminary research on student writers' use of word processors suffered from serious flaws in design, often ignoring the instructional context of word processing use. In some cases, for example, students received insufficient instruction in word processing or were never explicitly shown how to use the word processor to solve particular writing problems. Equally problematic were the studies that were based on primitive word processing software or that placed artificial constraints on writers by denying them access to pen, paper, or printed copies of their drafts.

Despite these caveats, nearly every researcher—whether interested in the writing of elementary school children or professional adults—has found several important patterns to writers' use of word processors. The most important is that the computer provides writers with a changed context and fresh approach to writing. Student writers using word processors consistently report an improved attitude toward writing, and with it a newfound sense of freedom and experimentation.

Writing with a word processor offers several other advantages. Because word processing eases the physical strain usually associated with writing, writers tend to work on given tasks for longer periods of time. This is especially true for writers who experience fine motor or eye–hand coordination problems. Many writers, and especially those who are poor readers and might otherwise become discouraged by the messiness of multiple corrections on drafts, enjoy the instant availability of clean copy that the computer affords. Writers composing at the computer report almost universally that, because they can change the text at any point without the drudgery of recopying, they are less fearful of error and make many more revisions than they would if working with pen and paper.

Students' improved attitudes and fluency, increased willingness to revise, and reduced fear of making mistakes all contribute to teachers' interest in using word processing in the classroom. Teachers should also be aware, however, that even those studies reporting improved attitudes toward writing can report no improvement in students' final written products. Similarly, although writers composing at a computer make a greater number of local revisions in which they change a word or phrase, they make fewer global revisions in which they "re-vise" or "re-see" their entire texts. This pattern has been attributed to the finished appearance even early drafts may have and to writers' tendencies to see the text screenful by screenful, losing sight of the text as a whole. Perhaps most important, researchers find that writers come to the computer with already established composing processes. Depending on their previous writing instruction and already established learning styles, individual writers will make very different uses of the same word processor.

While most research has focused on individual writers' use of word processing, many of the most exciting possibilities for teachers come from using word processing within a classroom context. Working with computers can inspire new ways of teaching writing and help us to form communities of collaborative learners in which writers' work—not only the product but also the process—is shared. A class that meets regularly in a computer center makes both the products and the processes of writing public and available for discussion and evaluation. Thanks to the ease with which several people can together invent or respond to a single text on the screen, computers provide an extremely effective way for students to confer about texts. Students can watch other students compose, can cluster around a single machine to compose together, and can seek help from a teacher or peer at any point during the composing process. The computer, then, takes writing "out of the closet," demystifying writing and facilitating more comprehensive, process-oriented instruction.

A computer classroom provides new opportunities both for individualization of instruction and for peer collaboration. Thus the teacher can create a workshop atmosphere in which student writers with different needs can each draw on the resources that will best help them learn.

Students' Difficulties in a Writing Classroom

Teachers of writing have long operated with a canon of students' writing problems. Students need, teachers say, to organize their ideas more clearly, to elaborate, to link specific examples to more general claims, and to support general claims with specific examples. Students need to anticipate questions, to correct mechanical errors, to polish their prose for their readers. Underprepared student writers encounter a host of difficulties in trying to meet these demands.

In her seminal work on Basic Writing, Mina Shaughnessy identifies three major sources of difficulty for ill-prepared writers in academic settings. She explains that students (1) may not have internalized the language patterns of academic writing; (2) may be unfamiliar with composing processes; or (3) may lack confidence, fearing that writing will not only expose but magnify their inadequacies.[2] Each of these factors may be viewed as a complex network of concerns.

LACK OF FAMILIARITY WITH ACADEMIC WRITING

Student writers may be unfamiliar with the conventions of academic discourse or may have difficulty anticipating readers' questions and reactions. They will not yet have the experience to judge when readers will demand elaboration and explanation, and they may have difficulty identifying the requirements of different genres. Alternatively, these students may lack the vocabulary necessary to write about academic subjects and may not yet have adequately internalized the rules and conventions governing spelling, punctuation, and syntax.

Teachers of Basic Writing will recognize the language patterns of Sharon, a high school junior struggling with academic discourse. In the opening of one essay, she wrote, "Shakespeare was a writer who wrote plays and he was really an incredible writer." We can feel both Sharon's inability to determine accurately what an audience can be relied upon to know (that Shakespeare was a great writer) and her inability to use the more sophisticated vocabulary (the word *playwright*) that would enable her to streamline her prose. The lack of appropriate vocabulary is frequently manifested in vague and syntactically strained sentences ("In college there are too many things required to take" for want of the word *requirements*) and in students' failed attempts to write words they have heard and spoken but never seen, resulting in spellings like *forfilling* in place of *fulfilling*.

LACK OF FAMILIARITY WITH COMPOSING PROCESSES

Many students are unfamiliar with the range of interrelated processes writing involves. Students frequently believe that writing "flows" effortlessly for successful writers; consequently they become rapidly frustrated and discouraged by the obstacles they confront in their own composing. These students may believe writing to be a single activity and may never have developed a composing repertoire that includes distinct planning, drafting, revising, and editing strategies.

Students who do not see revision as part of writing, for example, may retreat from any inconsistencies or dissonances they perceive in their writ-

2. M. Shaughnessy, *Errors and Expectations* (New York: Oxford University Press, 1977).

ing. Rather than taking the opportunity to develop and refine ideas as more experienced writers might, they see questions or inconsistencies as dangerous obstacles to be avoided. Alternatively, poor revisers may write prodigiously but lack a set of strategies with which to evaluate, structure, and improve their texts.

Some students assume that their writing must be perfect from the beginning and consequently labor intensively on each word, sabotaging their own attempts to build fluency and create meaning. These writers cannot turn off the monitors or editors in their heads and become so concerned with mechanical correctness that they find themselves unable to sustain writing or develop ideas.

Still others assume that they must know exactly what they want to say before they begin composing. Rather than seeing writing as an opportunity to discover new ideas, they plan their writing extensively and become frustrated and disoriented when they lose track of these plans or encounter snags in a plan's execution.

Lack of Confidence

Confounding the difficulties caused by a lack of flexibility in and control over composing processes is the anxiety many students experience when asked to write. These students may have suffered failure and wish to avoid a repetition of that humiliation. They may find that, in the words of Sally, a college freshman, "Even after I finally start, I have trouble starting." These students may be unwilling to take the risks writing so often demands. They may have trouble beginning a piece of writing or may not trust that their ideas are valuable. Once they begin writing, they may finish quickly, resisting new ideas and the chaos that often accompanies the shifting of perspectives.

For some underprepared students, lack of confidence combines with other problems to block almost completely the development and communication of ideas. John, for example, is a college freshman who is very anxious about correctness and is prematurely concerned with editing his writing. Asked to write an essay about how his life differs from his parents' lives, John seemed to engage in no planning and immediately wrote down his first sentence. This is the essay he produced over the next fifteen minutes:

~~My father was boarn in New York.~~
~~My father was born in New York.~~
My father was borne in New York ~~and he and then he and~~ my mother is not from here. ~~She was She was~~ She is from Puerto Rico.

One can sense John's fear of making a mistake, his almost paralyzing concern with spelling, and his difficulties both envisioning an extended text and developing strategies for completing the assigned task.

Difficulties are further compounded for student writers who speak English as a second language, who suffer from either diagnosed or undiagnosed learning disabilities, or whose school background has left them ill prepared for the academic demands of their current writing situations.

The writing teacher faces numerous challenges in addressing these writing difficulties. One way to begin to meet those challenges is to integrate the use of word processing into the writing curriculum. Creative use of word processing in the classroom should enable a teacher both to customize activities to individual students' particular needs and to arrange for effective and genuine collaboration among peers.

Adapting Word Processing to Students' Needs*

A teacher can incorporate word processing in any or all of the stages of the writing process: planning, drafting, revising, editing, and publishing. It is important to remember, though, that the notion of stages is more a useful way for us to organize our discussion of writing than an accurate description of writers' behaviors. Successful writers, especially when composing at the computer, frequently shift back and forth between planning, drafting, revising, and editing, with editing possibly initiating a cycle of revisions, or revision requiring a new set of lists or plans.

INVENTION, PLANNING, AND PREWRITING

Teachers can make use of word processing in numerous ways for teaching invention. Students might be asked to freewrite at the computer for fifteen minutes or to engage in a series of five-minute focused freewrites. In these exercises designed to increase fluency, students are encouraged to accept whatever ideas come to mind without judging or editing. When this kind of exercise is performed at the word processor, unlike with pen and paper, the teacher can reassure students that they will later be able to revise the writing or incorporate it into a more formal paper.

Even more important and liberating for a compulsive editor like John is *invisible writing.* In this activity, students use the computer but not the monitor so that they are temporarily unable to see the text they are

*See appendix E for a case history that describes how computers were used specifically to help students with learning disabilities.

creating. By literally turning off the monitors, students also turn off the editors in their heads, which say, "It's no good, that's dumb," or which insist on editing each word. A teacher might ask the class to freewrite or list ideas invisibly for five or ten minutes. Students can then turn the monitors back on to review their texts, looking for main ideas or *looping* back into a second and third freewrite. Invisible writing can greatly increase fluency, and with the increased fluency often comes increased confidence as well.

Students might also brainstorm or list their ideas for a piece of writing at the computer. Again, although programs that prompt students to create lists are available, the teacher can create files with suggestions for invention—for example, for character analysis ask, "What does your friend look like? What kinds of shoes does he wear? How does he spend his free time?" The students can also generate questions to which everyone responds according to the characters or topics they have chosen.

An advantage to creating lists on the computer is that they are easy to expand. If a student describes a character as "selfish, unfriendly, and conceited," he or she can turn each adjective into a paragraph or outline heading and insert a series of details to support the characterization.

Depending on their cognitive types and learning styles, other students may begin with a jumbled list of details and require instruction in order to organize the elements into categories. These students may be asked to propose topic sentences and then to rearrange the list under those sentences.

The on-line thesaurus that is included with almost every word processing program today can also serve as a powerful invention tool. Students may identify the key words in their lists or freewrites and then consult the thesaurus (usually just by placing the cursor on the key word and then pressing one function key) for related terms and ideas. With most systems, students can easily transfer the words from the thesaurus into their own files as ready-made "brainstorm lists" for generating new ideas.

DRAFTING

Although some students may need additional training in typing, the ease of correction frees most students to draft more fluently, focusing initially on the ideas and content of the writing.[3] Students are less likely to tire

3. Among younger students or inexperienced writers, even poor typists can usually type as quickly as they can write. A sixth grader, for example, usually handwrites at about ten words per minute, a speed most students writing at a keyboard soon surpass. Additionally, several good programs are available for teaching students to type at the computer.

writing at the computer, and many writers report that the screen acts as a kind of audience, prompting them to continue drafting.

One of the difficulties of writing is the number of demands on the writer's attention. Teachers may offer students different means of using the computer to facilitate shifts in attention from one activity to the next (for example, from drafting new ideas to reviewing plans). Students may split the computer screen or take advantage of multiple windows in order to work from planning notes, outlines, or on-screen prompts. With multiple windows, a student may refer to an outline or consult a list of questions to help guide a draft. Students who would otherwise lose track of their ideas may find it helpful to insert a series of *icons* (visual reminders ranging from question marks to sophisticated individual symbol systems) that can later be erased to remind themselves to return to an idea, check on a fact, and so on.

Once again, the on-line thesaurus can help students (like Sharon, mentioned earlier) to identify vocabulary words inaccessible to them from memory, helping them past a particular snag in their composing or enabling them to change the tone or register of their writing. For example, if I wish to reconsider the word *change* in the preceding sentence, I can with a single keystroke obtain the following alternatives from the thesaurus. The menu at the bottom of the screen makes replacing the word very easy.

change-(v)

1	A	• alter	5	• rotate		• transformation
	B	• convert		• shift		transmutation
	C	• correct		• vary		
	D	• modify			10	• diversion
			change-(n)			• novelty
2	E	mutate	6	• difference		• variety
	F	transfigure		• fluctuation		
	G	• transform		• variation	11	• anomaly
						• deviation
3	H	• invert	7	remodeling		• exception
	I	• reverse		reorganization		
	J	transpose		restyling	12	• coins
						• money
4	K	• exchange	8	• innovation		silver
	L	• replace		• modification		
	M	• substitute		reformation	change-(ant)	
	N	• swap			13	• retain
	O	• switch	9	• metamorphosis		remain

1 Replace Word; 2 View Doc; 3 Look Up Word; 4 Clear Column: 0

source: SSI Corporation, *WordPerfect,* version 4.1 (Salt Lake City, 1980).

REVISION

Revision, often considered the most essential element in successful writing, is greatly facilitated by the word processor. Even professional writers emphasize the importance of distancing themselves from their work; for students with poor handwriting or little experience in revision, seeing their words in printed form can be essential to evaluating and improving their writing. At the word processor, a student can easily reread the text, incorporate changes immediately on the screen, and print a draft if desired.

Students can be taught to exploit the many formatting commands of the word processor to build additional strategies for revision. These strategies employ visual clues to help students who may read poorly to see what they have written more clearly. Students can triple space their texts to insert new ideas more easily. Alternatively, they can print out a paper in a single column, leaving half of the page for their own, a peer's, or a teacher's responses. In this version of the double entry notebook introduced by Ann Berthoff, the student creates a visual format for "thinking about her thinking."[4]

Blockbusting, separating out each sentence so that it can become the beginning of a distinct paragraph, is a powerful technique for increasing students' fluency and enabling them to expand on ideas in a manageable way. Teachers can easily use the word processor to create a *macro,* or small collection of commands, to search for the end of each sentence and after each sentence insert several blank lines. Students are then free to expand on the new topic sentence or perhaps to create better transitions between the sentences already written. This technique can also be useful for highlighting the structure both of individual sentences and of texts as a whole.

In another exercise, students might use the "search" command on the word processor to find each occurrence of a particular word. This technique might help students track a single idea in order to improve organization, or, with the thesaurus, it might help them find ways of varying their language and expanding their ideas.

Teachers can also create macros to highlight certain elements of structure. The student might be asked, for example, to highlight the topic sentence of each paragraph, checking the flow of the argument, eliminating repetition, or bringing together related ideas.

Students can routinely make use of the "move" command to experiment with different organizational patterns or rhetorical strategies. They might

4. A. Berthoff, *The Making of Meaning* (Upper Montclair, N.J.: Boynton/Cook Publishers, 1981).

move a final paragraph to the beginning of the essay to consider as an introduction, or they might move a topic sentence to the end of a paragraph to create greater variety in paragraph structure.

EDITING

Many revision strategies can also be used to help students improve their editing abilities. Students can make use of the macro that separates sentences to see each clause in isolation more clearly and then to check for sentence completeness or variety.

Many students who experience writing difficulties have a set of trouble spots that they can learn to identify and then to search for with the "search" command. Students who confuse certain homonyms, for example, can search for troublesome words, such as *it's* or *their,* and insert corrections wherever necessary.

Teachers or students can also create editing checklists, customized to the assignment or the student, to organize students' editing. Scrolling backward through the text, perhaps using a macro in which the cursor jumps to the beginning of successive sentences, can be a powerful proofreading technique for writers at any level.

Nearly every word processor currently on the market comes with an on-line dictionary and spell check program. The spell checker can ease the editing and proofreading process for any writer, sometimes simultaneously helping students to recognize patterns in their errors. One cannot overestimate the liberating effect a spell checker can have for students with severe spelling problems.

PUBLISHING

The word processor can be used to publish students' work in any number of forms. The production of class newspapers and school magazines is greatly simplified by the computer. But teachers can also help students publish their work for audiences outside the school. Students can reasonably create texts that look professional, thus facilitating functional or real-world writing, increasing students' motivation to write and to communicate effectively with an audience, and increasing the likelihood of a serious response.

The word processor may also provide new ways for students to publish their writing for each other. One possibility is for the teacher to create an anthology of students' writing on a given topic and then to make that anthology the text for a synthesis assignment.

Using Word Processing to Create Collaborative Exercises

Many of the most interesting adaptations of word processing expand on individual writing strategies to give students opportunities to work cooperatively on writing tasks. Collaborative activities encourage students to work together, ideally drawing on each other's strengths and capitalizing on the importance of response to students' growth as writers.

In their materials on how to use cooperative learning in computer classrooms, Mary Male and her colleagues stress the advantages of increased motivation and involvement; the opportunity to integrate writing with conversation, often resulting in higher levels of conceptual understanding; immediate response to writing; and an increased ability to solve writing problems.[5] The possible arrangements of cooperative activities in computer classrooms are virtually unlimited; this section will offer several preliminary suggestions.

STUDENTS WORKING COOPERATIVELY IN PAIRS

Students can work in pairs at the computer at almost any stage of the writing process: inventing, drafting, revising, or editing. Some activities will draw on the importance of supportive response to help struggling writers sustain their writing and develop ideas. In one freewriting exercise, for example, the teacher might cross-cable the computers so that what student A types will appear on student B's screen, and vice versa. Student A is then asked to freewrite on a topic of her choice. Her text will be invisible to her but visible to her partner. Student B can type back responses or questions to prompt Student A to continue writing and to aid her in the exploration and development of her ideas.

Several other arrangements are possible: students might (1) work in pairs to create lists of possible topics for each partner to explore individually; (2) jointly draft an entire paper (or the first paragraph of each student's paper); (3) together view each student's paper on the computer screen, jointly planning revision strategies; or (4) together edit each student's draft, identifying for each other sentences that are unclear or incorrect and collaborating to solve the problems.

Students can also profitably work together on computer-assisted drill and practice programs. Students working in pairs should be encouraged to come to agreement before any answer is entered and to explain their reasoning to each other.

5. M. Male, R. Johnson, D. Johnson, and M. Anderson, *Cooperative Learning and Computers: An Activity Guide for Teachers* (Los Gatos, Calif.: Educational Apple-cations, 1986).

STUDENTS WORKING COOPERATIVELY IN GROUPS

Teachers of writing in computer classrooms consistently report that the computer facilitates group work and makes collaborative exercises more engaging and productive. The teacher can draw on several different models to structure the group activities effectively.

Male and her colleagues identify positive interdependence among group members as crucial to the success of cooperative learning. Most relevant for writing instruction are the interdependence based on task, with individual students responsible, say, for different aspects of a story (characterization, plot, setting), the interdependence based on resources, with the information necessary to complete the task "jigsawed" or divided among the group members, making each individual's contribution necessary for the group's success; and the interdependence based on roles, with the teacher identifying the different roles writers might assume (planning, gathering information, drafting, reviewing the draft, and monitoring progress toward the goal) and assigning a distinct role to each member of the group. Although the teacher may initially want to structure the group work according to one of these models, students themselves will usually arrange to rotate the position of scribe or "keyboarder" and will develop effective strategies for negotiating roles and integrating each participant's ideas.

STUDENTS WORKING COOPERATIVELY AS A CLASS

Students can benefit not only from the spontaneous sharing that often arises in a computer classroom but also from whole-class writing exercises. The teacher might arrange, for example, for students to begin drafting an interior monologue, and then, in round-robin fashion, to change computers to continue the next writer's essay. Students could similarly be asked to create alternative introductions or conclusions for other students' essays. If the word processing program allows for hidden comments, students might also insert comments and questions directly into another writer's draft.

Perhaps most valuable is to have a projection screen cabled to one of the classroom computers. The projection screen allows the teacher to project anything that has been entered into a computer: drafts of student essays, responses to questions or exercises, alternative texts for analysis. With the projection screen, the class can together compose, revise, or edit a text, discussing options and strategies. Unlike an overhead projector, the computer projection screen offers the advantages of continuously

247

readable text and the capacity to compare different versions of a draft with ease.

An equally useful alternative is to have the computers in the classroom connected by a common memory. The network allows for simultaneous access by the entire class to any teacher- or student-generated text. It facilitates frequent sharing and intervention by teacher and peers at multiple points in the evolution of student texts.

General Guidelines for Teachers

Before integrating word processing into classroom instruction, a teacher may want to consider several general issues. From the outset, the teacher embarking on the creation of a computer writing classroom must assume that this environment will be different from a traditional classroom. The computer is not simply a better tool for the same old task, it acts as a distinct medium with consequences for the ways students interact and learn to write. Teachers committed to a workshop approach, for example, will welcome the opportunity to relinquish some authority to students, to acknowledge the occasional messiness the writing process involves, and to engage in brief, spontaneous, and informal on-line conferences with students.

The teacher should be comfortable with the word processing system used in the school. To teach writing with a word processor effectively, a teacher should write regularly with it, too, in part because students will most likely detect any hesitancy in the teacher and become more anxious themselves. Moreover, teachers may want to develop their own techniques for incorporating word processing into the classroom. Simply put, teachers should try as much as possible—with word processing as with any other pedagogy—to practice what they teach.

Students also require careful training on the word processor. This training may be spread out over several weeks, with new commands introduced as they are needed. Whether the training is provided by an academic computing resource person or by the classroom teacher, it should be structured to minimize students' frustration, to increase students' confidence, and to reassure students that the computer is a tool designed for their use, and not a machine to be feared. Students initially need only to learn how to create, save, and print a file and how to insert, delete, and replace text. Once they have mastered these maneuvers they can be encouraged to experiment with other possibilities. Here, too, the teacher can draw on pedagogical principles from the writing classroom. Just as a lesson on the colon is most effective after a student asks how to introduce a list of several elements, so may advanced word processing commands best be taught serendipitously as students find the need to make certain changes.

Virtually all writers at all levels report that they first use the word processor as a "fancy typewriter" and only gradually begin to compose directly at the computer. Given this seemingly natural progression, a useful first lesson in word processing would be to invite students to type into the computer a paragraph they have prepared before class. This enables students to become comfortable with entering and saving text without fear of losing their ideas or erasing the only copy of an assignment. A second lesson might have students first edit a problematic or error-filled paragraph the teacher has generated (to familiarize the class with inserting, deleting, and replacing text) and then edit their own or a partner's paragraph from the previous lesson. Having students work cooperatively in pairs for this second class should dispel fear and encourage students to troubleshoot for and cooperate with each other. The third lesson might introduce students to composing at the computer with a freewriting or brainstorming exercise that could later be followed by a related, extended piece of writing.

Students need to be trained not in word processing alone, but in word processing as a tool for writing. Teachers will want to discuss with students the connections between particular word processing commands and related writing activities. For example, if students are not accustomed to a cut-and-paste writing method, they will be unlikely to appreciate how they can make use of the commands to move paragraphs or sentences.

Teachers of word processing must be acutely aware of the possibility of creating a kind of double bind in which the complexities of computer use serve only to increase students' frustrations with writing. The double bind issue is especially important when teaching students with learning disabilities. Some of the techniques writing teachers have used successfully in the past include teaching computer commands in logically consistent ways, providing extremely clear documentation and instructions (often color-coded) for students' use, and eliminating visual distractions both from the room and from the software (elaborate menus, and so on) whenever possible.

Teachers should also be sensitive to the more subtle double bind they potentially create when they introduce technology to a group of students of mixed backgrounds. Often the students who are the least successful writers have also had the least exposure to computers. Their lack of facility with the technology may reinforce a negative self-image and make it even more difficult for these students as writers.

Frequent meetings in the computer room are of far greater importance than the ratio of machines to students. In fact, working on drills, drafts, or revisions, students can profitably double up at the computers to work cooperatively. Ideally, a computer writing center would allow for a series of arrangements: individual composing, writing in pairs, work in groups, and work as a full class. The room might be arranged as a horseshoe so that students can face inward toward the chalkboard (or demonstration screen) or outward to the terminals.

Teachers should certainly take advantage of the many publications on educational computing to familiarize themselves with what other educators are doing in this field. For example, many schools have already adopted procedures to maximize use of the computer centers while troubleshooting for technical and administrative problems. Some of these procedures include sign-up sheets, problem logs, and signs that students can place nearby that say "Collaborate with me" or "Do not disturb, composing." Teachers may also want to consider different varieties of computer-assisted grading. Instead of littering students' papers with cryptic marginalia like "awk," they can offer typed responses or a collection of minifiles that, in handbook fashion, address mechanical problems with definitions, suggested corrections, and examples.

Finally, teachers should keep in mind that computers are, at their best, supplements and enhancements to instruction. Just as computers cannot replace teachers, they need not replace pen and paper, doodles, or drawings. Writers should be encouraged to view the computer as only one tool among many. Students will need to experiment to learn which tools best suit their needs; students with learning difficulties, especially, may find that they establish effective rituals that employ different tools at different times. A writer may make notes on paper, outline on paper and draft at the computer, or print out a draft on which to make editorial changes by hand.

When the computer is viewed as an adjunct to writing instruction, it can provide student writers with new resources, increased flexibility, and expanded options. To the degree that the word processor can give students more awareness and control of their composing processes, it can be an invaluable tool in writing instruction.

Suggestions for Further Reading

Bridwell-Bowles, L. "Writing with Computers: Implications from Research for the Learning Impaired." *Topics in Language Disorders* 7 (1987).

Collins, J., and Sommers, E. *Writing On-Line.* Upper Montclair, N.J.: Boynton/Cook, 1985.

Daiute, C. *Writing and Computers.* Reading, Mass.: Addison Wesley, 1985.

Halpern, J., and Liggett, S. *Computers and Composing: How the New Technologies are Changing Writing.* Carbondale, Ill.: Southern Illinois University Press, 1987.

Hawisher, G. "The Effects of Word Processing on the Revision Strategies of College Freshmen." *Research in the Teaching of English* 21 (May 1987).

Hult, C., and Harris, J. *A Writer's Introduction to Word Processing.* Belmont, Calif.: Wadsworth, 1987.

Male, M.; Johnson, R.; Johnson, D.; and Anderson, M. *Cooperative Learning and Computers.* Los Gatos, Calif.: Educational Apple-cations, 1986.

Rodrigues, D., and Rodrigues, R. *Teaching Writing with a Word Processor, Grades 7–13.* Urbana, Ill.: National Council of Teachers of English, 1986.

Schwartz, H. *Interactive Writing: Composing with a Word Processor.* New York: Holt, Rinehart & Winston, 1985.

Schwartz, H., and Bridwell-Bowles, L. "Selected Bibliography on Computers in Composition." *College Composition and Communication* 35 (1984).

————. "Update." *College Composition and Communication* 38 (December 1987).

Sudol, K. *Textfiles: A Rhetoric for Word Processing.* New York: Harcourt Brace Jovanovich, 1987.

See also:

Research in Word Processing Newsletter (South Dakota School of Mines, Rapid City, SD 57701).

Computers and Composition (Kate Keifer and Cynthia Selfe, Department of Humanities, Michigan Tech University, Houghton, MI 49931).

Computers, Reading and Language Arts (Gerald Block, Box 13247, Oakland, CA 94602).

Special journal issues:

Writing Teacher, Summer 1983.

Focus: Teaching English Language Arts, Spring 1983.

College Composition and Communication, February 1984, October 1985.

Appendix A—Tests

Prereading and Reading Readiness

Metropolitan Readiness Tests, 5th ed.
(Psychological Corp., 1986)
Range: grades K–1
Levels I and II

Stanford Early School Achievement Test (SESAT), 2d ed.
(Psychological Corp., 1984)
Range: grades K–1.9
Two levels

Reading

Adult Basic Learning Examination (ABLE), 2d ed.
(Psychological Corp., 1986)
Group tests designed to measure adult achievement in basic learning
Range: grades 1–12
Three levels

California Achievement Tests, rev., Forms E and F
(CTB/McGraw-Hill, 1985)
Group tests consisting of seven subtests
Range: grades K–12
Eleven levels

Diagnostic Reading Scales (Spache), rev. ed.
(CTB/McGraw-Hill, 1981)
Range: grades 1–8

Durrell Analysis of Reading Difficulty, 3d ed.
(Psychological Corp., 1980)
Individually administered
Range: grades 1–6

Gates-MacGinitie Reading Tests, 3d ed.
(Riverside Publishing Co., 1988)
Group tests
Range: grades K–12
Seven levels

Gates-McKillop-Horowitz Reading Diagnostic Test
(Teachers College Press, 1979)
Detailed diagnosis of deficiencies. Fifteen individually administered tests
Range: grades 1–6

Gray Oral Reading Tests, rev.
(Psychological Corp., 1986)
Individually administered
Range: grades 1–12

Iowa Silent Reading Tests
(Psychological Corp., 1973)
Group silent reading tests that include measures of vocabulary, reading
  comprehension, and speed of reading
Range: grades 6–college
Three levels

Iowa Tests of Basic Skills, Forms G and H
(Riverside Publishing Co., 1986)
Range: grades K–9
Ten levels

Metropolitan Achievement Tests, 6th ed.: *Reading Diagnostic Tests*
(Psychological Corp., 1986)
Six batteries of group tests
Range: grades K–9

Nelson-Denny Reading Test
(Riverside Publishing Co., 1981)
Group test measuring vocabulary, comprehension, and rate
Range: grades 9–16 and adult

Peabody Individual Achievement Tests
(American Guidance Service, Inc., 1970)
Screening test to survey basic skills and knowledge
Range: grades K–adult

Roswell-Chall Diagnostic Assessment of Reading and Teaching Strategies
(Riverside Publishing Co., in press)
Individually administered
Range: grades 1–12

Screening Tests for Identifying Children with Specific Language Disability (Slingerland)
(Educators Publishing Service, Inc., 1974, 1977)
Range: grades K–6
Three levels

Sequential Tests of Educational Progress (STEP), Series III
(CTB/McGraw-Hill, 1979)
Range: grades K–12
An earlier edition (Series II) is available in large type from American
    Printing House, 1839 Frankfurt Ave., Box 6085, Louisville, KY 40206

Stanford Achievement Test, 7th ed.
(Psychological Corp., 1986)
Range: grades 1.5–9.9

Stanford Diagnostic Reading Test, 3d ed.
(Psychological Corp., 1984)
Four batteries of group tests
Range: grades 1.5–12

Stanford Test of Academic Skills (TASK), 2d ed.
(Psychological Corp., 1982)
Range: grades 8–13

Test of Written Spelling II
(Pro-Ed Publishing, 1986)
Range: grades 1–8

Wide Range Achievement Test, rev.
(Jastak Associates, Inc., 1984)
Word pronunciation, spelling, and arithmetic computation
Range: age 5–adult

Special Tests

Beery-Buktenica Developmental Test of Visual-Motor Integration
(Modern Curriculum Press, 1981)
Range: age 2–15

Bender Visual-Motor Gestalt Test
(Psychological Corp., 1946)
Test involving copying visual designs
Range: age 6–adult

Benton Revised Visual Retention Test
(Psychological Corp., 1974)
Test involving recall of visual designs
Range: age 8–adult

Einstein Assessment of School Related Skills
(Gottesman and Cerullo, Modern Curriculum Press, 1988)
Range: grades K–5

Goodenough-Harris Drawing Test
(Psychological Corp., 1963)
Range: age 3–15

Illinois Test of Psycholinguistic Abilities (ITPA)
(Slossen Educational Publishing Co., 1969)
Evaluations of linguistic strengths and weaknesses
Range: age 2–10

Kaufman Assessment Battery for Children (K-ABC)
(American Guidance Service, 1983)
Range: age 2.5–12.5

Peabody Picture Vocabulary Test, rev. ed.
(American Guidance Service, 1981)
Individually administered
Range: age 2.6–adult

Raven Progressive Matrices
(Psychological Corp., 1972)
Range: age 8–adult

Silver & Hagin [SEARCH]: A Scanning Instrument for the Identification of Potential Learning Disability, 2d ed.
(Walker, 1981)

256

Stanford-Binet Intelligence Scale, 4th ed.
(Riverside Publishing Co., 1986)
Range: age 2–adult

Wepman Auditory Discrimination Test, rev. ed.
(Western Psychological Service, 1973)
Range: age 5–8

Wechsler Adult Intelligence Scale (WAIS-R)
(Psychological Corp., 1981)
Range: age 16–adult

Wechsler Intelligence Scale for Children (WISC-R)
(Psychological Corp., 1974)
Range: age 6–16

Appendix B—
Selected Publishers

General

Academic Therapy
20 Commercial Blvd.
Novato, CA 94947

Allyn & Bacon
7 Wells Ave.
Newton, MA 02159

American Guidance Service, Inc.
Publishers Building
Circle Pines, MI 55014

Barnell Loft
958 Church St.
Baldwin, NY 11510

Barron's Educational Services
250 Wireless Blvd.
Hauppauge, NY 11788

Basic Books, Inc.
10 E. 53rd St.
New York, NY 10022

CTB/McGraw-Hill
Del Monte Research Park
Monterey, CA 93940

D.L.M. Teaching Resources
1 D.L.M. Park
Allen, TX 75002

Dell Publishing Co., Inc.
1 Dag Hammarskjold Plaza
New York, NY 10017

Doubleday & Co., Inc.
666 Fifth Ave.
New York, NY 10103

E. P. Dutton & Co.
2 Park Ave.
New York, NY 10016

Economy Co./McGraw-Hill
School Division
Box 25308
Oklahoma City, OK 73125

Educational Testing Service
Rosedale Rd.
Princeton, NJ 08541

Educators Publishing Service
75 Moulton St.
Cambridge, MA 02238

Ginn & Co.
191 Spring St.
Lexington, MA 02173

Grosset & Dunlap, Inc.
51 Madison Ave.
New York, NY 10010

Grune & Stratton, Inc.
Curtis Center
Independence Sq.
Philadelphia, PA 19106

Harcourt Brace Jovanovich, Inc.
Harcourt Brace Jovanovich
Building
Orlando, FL 32887

Harper & Row, Publishers
10 E. 53rd St.
New York, NY 10022

Harvard University Press
79 Garden St.
Cambridge, MA 02138

D.C. Heath & Co.
125 Spring St.
Lexington, MA 02173

High Noon Books
20 Commercial Blvd.
Novato, CA 94947

Henry Holt & Co.
113 W. 18th St.
New York, NY 10011

Holt, Rinehart & Winston, Inc.
111 Fifth Ave.
New York, NY 10003

Houghton Mifflin Co.
1 Beacon St.
Boston, MA 02108

International Reading Association
800 Barksdale Rd.
Box 8139
Newark, DL 19714

Jastak Associates, Inc.
Box 4460
Wilmington, DL 19807

Johns Hopkins University Press
701 W. 40th St.
Baltimore, MD 21211

Jossey-Bass, Inc., Publishers
433 California St.
San Francisco, CA 94104

Ladybird Books
49 Omni Circle
Auburn, ME 04210

Laidlaw Bros.
Thatcher and Madison Sts.
River Forest, IL 60305

J.B. Lippincott Co.
E. Washington Square
Philadelphia, PA 19105

Little, Brown & Co.
34 Beacon St.
Boston, MA 02108

MIT Press
Hayward St.
Cambridge, MA 02142

McGraw-Hill Book Co.
11 W. 19th St.
New York, NY 10011

David McKay Co., Inc.
201 E. 50th St.
New York, NY 10022

Macmillan, Inc.
866 Third Ave.
New York, NY 10022

Merriam-Webster, Inc.
47 Federal St.
Springfield, MA 01102

Charles E. Merrill Publishing Co.
936 Eastwind Dr.
Westerville, OH 43081

Modern Curriculum Press
13900 Prospect Rd.
Cleveland, OH 44136

William Morrow & Co., Inc.
105 Madison Ave.
New York, NY 10016

National Council of Teachers of
English
1111 Kenyon Rd.
Urbana, IL 61801

N.Y.C. Board of Education
110 Livingston St.
Brooklyn, NY 11201

W. W. Norton & Co., Inc.
500 Fifth Ave.
New York, NY 10110

Open Court Publishing Co.
315 Fifth St.
Peru, IL 61354

The Orton Society
724 York Rd.
Towson, MD 21204

Partners in Publishing
Box 50347
Tulsa, OK 74150

Plays, Inc.
120 Boylston St.
Boston, MA 02116

Pocket Books/Simon & Schuster
1230 Sixth Ave.
New York, NY 10020

Prentice-Hall, Inc.
Sylvan Ave.
Englewood Cliffs, NJ 07632

Pro-Ed
5341 Industrial Oak Blvd.
Austin, TX 78735

The Psychological Corp.
Harcourt Brace Jovanovich, Inc.
555 Academic Court
San Antonio, TX 78204

G. P. Putnam's Sons
51 Madison Ave.
New York, NY 10010

Rand McNally & Co.
8255 Central Park Ave.
Skokie, IL 60076

Random House, Inc.
201 E. 50th St.
New York, NY 10022

Reader's Digest Assn.
Reader's Digest Road
Pleasantville, NY 10570

Remedial Education Center
2138 Bancroft, N.W.
Washington, DC 20008

Riverside Publishing Co.
8420 West Bryn Mawr Ave.
Suite 1000
Chicago, IL 60631

Schocken Books, Inc.
201 E. 50th St.
New York, NY 10022

Scholastic Book Services
730 Broadway
New York, NY 10003

Science Research Associates (SRA)
155 N. Wacker Dr.
Chicago, IL 60605

Scott Foresman & Co.
1900 E. Lake Ave.
Glenview, IL 60025

Scott Foresman & Co./
Elementary-High School Division
99 Bauer Drive
Oakland, NJ 07436

Charles Scribner's Sons
866 Third Ave.
New York, NY 10022

Silver Burdett & Ginn Co.
250 James St.
Morristown, NJ 07960

Simon & Schuster, Inc.
1230 Sixth Ave.
New York, NY 10020

Slossen Educational Publishers
536 Buffalo Rd.
East Aurora, NY 14052

Syracuse University Press
1600 Jamesville Ave.
Syracuse, NY 13244

Teachers College Press
1234 Amsterdam Ave.
New York, NY 10027

Three Trees Press, Inc.
(Discovery Series)
85 King St. East
Toronto, Ontario
M5C 163 Canada

Troll Associates
100 Corporate Drive
Mahwah, NJ 07430

Viking Penguin, Inc.
40 W. 23rd St.
New York, NY 10010

Franklin Watts, Inc.
387 Park Ave. South
New York, NY 10016

Western Psychological Services
12031 Wilshire Blvd.
Los Angeles, CA 90025

John Wiley & Sons, Inc.
605 Third Ave.
New York, NY 10158

Publishers of Special Materials
for High School Students and Adults in
Reading, Writing, and Coping Skills

Cambridge Book Co., Inc.
888 Seventh Ave.
New York, NY 10106

Contemporary Books, Inc.
180 N. Michigan Ave.
Chicago, IL 60601

The Continental Press
520 E. Bainbridge St.
Elizabethtown, PA 17022

Dormac, Inc.
Box 1699
Beaverton, OR 97075

Educators Publishing Service
75 Moulton St.
Cambridge, MA 02238

Fearon Education
David S. Lake Publishers
19 Davis Drive
Belmont, CA 94002

Globe Book Co., Inc.
50 W. 23rd St.
New York, NY 10010

High Noon Books
20 Commercial Blvd.
Novato, CA 94947

Jamestown Publishers
Box 9168
Providence, RI 02940

Janus Books
2501 Industrial Parkway West
Hayward, CA 94545

Longman, Inc.
95 Church St.
White Plains, NY 10601

New Readers Press
Box 131
Syracuse, NY 13210

Scott Foresman & Co.
1900 E. Lake Ave.
Glenview, IL 60025

Steck-Vaughn Co.
Box 26015
Austin, TX 78755

Appendix C—Word Lists[1]

The Basic Sight Vocabulary of 220 Words

a	before	cut	found
about	best	did	four
after	better	do	from
again	big	does	full
all	black	done	funny
always	blue	don't	gave
am	both	down	get
an	bring	draw	give
and	brown	drink	go
any	but	eat	goes
are	buy	eight	going
around	by	every	good
as	call	fall	got
ask	came	far	green
at	can	fast	grow
ate	carry	find	had
away	clean	first	has
be	cold	five	have
because	come	fly	he
been	could	for	help

1. E. W. Dolch, *Teaching Primary Reading* (Champaign, Ill.: Garrard Press, 1960). Reprinted by permission. Copyright 1960 by E. W. Dolch.

her	my	say	too
here	myself	see	try
him	never	seven	two
his	new	shall	under
hold	no	she	up
hot	not	show	upon
how	now	sing	us
hurt	of	sit	use
I	off	six	very
if	old	sleep	walk
in	on	small	want
into	once	so	warm
is	one	some	was
it	only	soon	wash
its	open	start	we
jump	or	stop	well
just	our	take	went
keep	out	tell	were
kind	over	ten	what
know	own	thank	when
laugh	pick	that	where
let	play	the	which
light	please	their	white
like	pretty	them	who
little	pull	then	why
live	put	there	will
long	ran	these	wish
look	read	they	with
made	red	think	work
make	ride	this	would
many	right	those	write
may	round	three	yellow
me	run	to	yes
much	said	today	you
must	saw	together	your

The Ninety-five Most Common Nouns

apple	day	home	school
baby	dog	horse	seed
back	doll	house	sheep
ball	door	kitty	shoe
bear	duck	leg	sister
bed	egg	letter	snow
bell	eye	man	song
bird	farm	men	squirrel
birthday	farmer	milk	stick
boat	father	money	street
box	feet	morning	sun
boy	fire	mother	table
bread	fish	name	thing
brother	floor	nest	time
cake	flower	night	top
car	game	paper	toy
cat	garden	party	tree
chair	girl	picture	watch
chicken	good-bye	pig	water
children	grass	rabbit	way
Christmas	ground	rain	wind
coat	hand	ring	window
corn	head	robin	wood
cow	hill	Santa Claus	

Appendix D—Levels of Proficiency[1]

Rudimentary (150)

Readers who have acquired rudimentary reading skills and strategies can follow brief written directions. They can also select words, phrases, or sentences to describe a simple picture and can interpret simple written clues to identify a common object. *Performance at this level suggests the ability to carry out simple, discrete reading tasks.*

Basic (200)

Readers who have learned basic comprehension skills and strategies can locate and identify facts from simple informational paragraphs, stories, and news articles. In addition, they can combine ideas and make inferences based on short, uncomplicated passages. *Performance at this level suggests the ability to understand specific or sequentially related information.*

1. *National Assessment of Educational Progress: The Report Card* (Princeton: Educational Testing Service, 1985).

Intermediate (250)

Readers with the ability to use intermediate skills and strategies can search for, locate, and organize the information they find in relatively lengthy passages and can recognize paraphrases of what they have read. They can also make inferences and reach generalizations about main ideas and author's purpose from passages dealing with literature, science, and social studies. *Performance at this level suggests the ability to search for specific information, interrelate ideas, and make generalizations.*

Adept (300)

Readers with adept reading comprehension skills and strategies can understand complicated literary and informational passages, including material about topics they study at school. They can also analyze and integrate less familiar material and provide reactions to and explanations of the text as a whole. *Performance at this level suggests the ability to find, understand, summarize, and explain relatively complicated information.*

Advanced (350)

Readers who use advanced reading skills and strategies can extend and restructure the ideas presented in specialized and complex texts. Examples include scientific materials, literary essays, historical documents, and materials similar to those found in professional and technical working environments. They are also able to understand the links between ideas even when those links are not explicitly stated and to make appropriate generalizations even when the texts lack clear introductions or explanations. *Performance at this level suggests the ability to synthesize and learn from specialized reading materials.*

Appendix E—The Use of the Computer with Students Who Have Writing and Reading Problems

by Miriam Brous*

The case history in this appendix illustrates how the computer can be used in both the prewriting and writing processes specifically to help students with learning disabilities.

Don—A Fourteen-Year-Old Who Profited from Using the Computer in Writing and Reading

Don, a fourteen-year-old ninth grader, had a longstanding learning disability that manifested itself in uneven motor coordination, expressive language problems, writing difficulties, and poor memory in integrating information. An articulate child, he was described by his teacher as a persistent worker whose patient and methodical concentration sustained his learning. He had few friends, however, and was more or less a loner.

*School Psychologist, Early Childhood Learning Center, Ridgefield, New Jersey, and the Winston Preparatory School, New York City.

Don's class was taught keyboarding in preparation for computer use, and he became a relatively comfortable typist through a tutorial typing program. When introduced to the word processor, he became fascinated, getting particularly excited when he learned that he could type much faster than he had been able to write. Don's handwriting was often illegible and he wrote at a slow pace, so the computer was particularly useful to him because it bypassed his small muscle problems. Don soon began to enjoy changing words and sentences around and reshaping his work on the computer.

Don was later exposed to LOGO, a computer language whose strength is in graphics and text. He became adept at doing his own editing and was better able to understand the grammatical structure of language by creating his own sentence-generator program. These processes, once difficult, became fairly easy when the computer presented them in manageable parts.

Another help to Don was on-line data bases, which can be connected to computers in the classroom by a modem. The texts they offer, including one or several current daily newspapers and an updated encyclopedia, are all written in straightforward language and presented on the screen in small, graspable portions, so students can usually read the information with relative ease. Don found it easier to understand material in such subjects as history, science, and current events because of these uncomplicated, clear texts.

On-line data bases also made information easily accessible to Don, enabling him to avoid the difficulty most students experience when they are inhibited, overwhelmed, or intimidated by quantities of resources in traditional libraries. For instance, if a student calls up a book review or a historical article on the screen, he or she concentrates only on one short, discrete piece. If the student needs more substance he or she calls up another article, and so on.

By forming the students into groups to learn the use of data bases, the teacher also helped Don to interact with his peers. In one instance, the students in Don's class undertook to plan and organize their school trip. Researching the location, proper transportation, schedules, and fares was the major component of the project. The problem-solving activity integrated several curricular content areas. Using the data bases available, students found information, used cross-referencing, and became adept at working with the material. Noncomputer resources such as maps, travel guides, and atlases were included, and the merging of these materials gave depth to the information. Students were encouraged to work collaboratively. They learned to call up background material from the encyclopedias and other sources with relative ease. Besides encyclopedias, they screened newspapers for timely political and social information, investigated the on-line weather report for forecasts, and researched the bus and train guides for specific costs and schedules.

Several teachers saw an opportunity to use the units in another learning experiment. For example, time, distance, and rate information generated a series of math problems for which the teacher could make up word problems that entailed such calculations as the distance between train stations. The science teacher offered exercises using geographical material, weather patterns, and the like. The history teacher discussed past events as well as contemporary issues. Motivation to investigate the relevant and practical events in life generated high enthusiasm and camaraderie while at the same time teaching Don and the other students basic research methods, which are often as important to the writing process as composition and editing skills.

Index